AF824946

Christianity *and* Ethics

Dr. R. P. Jain

Mahaveer & Sons
(Publishers & Distributors)
New Delhi-110002

Christianity and Ethics

[All rights reserved. All responsibities of this book's is author. No part of this publication may be reproduced, stored in a retrieval system or transmitted, in any form or by any means, mechanical, photocopying, recording or otherwise, without prior written permission of the publisher.]

First Published 2011

© Reserved

ISBN 978-81-8377-311-9

Published by :

MAHAVEER & SONS

(Publishers & Distributors)

H-2/16, Ansari Road, Darya Ganj,

(Near Shiv Mandir) New Delhi-110002

E-mail : mahaveersonspub@rediffmail.com

Ph. 011 23242069, Mob. 09899608339

PRINTED IN INDIA

Published by Mahaveer & Sons, Publishers & Distributors, H-2/16 Ansari Road, Near Shiv Mandir, Daryaganj, New Delhi-110002, Printed at Himanshu Printers, Delhi.

Contents

Preface

From the early days of Christianity to the present, various courses have been followed with regard to the relations of Christian ethics to moral philosophies stemming from other sources. One has been the process of incorporation and amalgamation. In practice, this has often meant the accommodation of Christian principles to what was incorporated. Starting from a laudable desire to propagate Christianity by finding points of contact with the non-Christian world, it has tended to de-emphasize what is distinctive in Christianity in order to stress common ground. At its worst, this has meant the complete subsuming of Christian ethics within philosophical ethics even to the point of disclaiming that anything to be called Christian ethics exists. At its best, it has bred a form of "coalition ethics" in which natural law and the insights of Plato, Aristotle, and other great philosophers are drawn upon to supplement Christian ethics in areas where the gospel gives no specific directives. Examples of such incorporation and amalgamation, with varying levels of success, are seen in the incorporation by Clement of Alexandria of the best in Greek philosophy, the Thomistic assimilation of Aristotle, and the present-day tendency to adjust Christianity to a workable synthesis with the rationalistic, scientific, and humanitarian ideals of modern culture.

A second course follows as a reaction from the first. In alarm at the tendency to accommodate Christianity to the accepted standards of the secular world, there is a repudiation by Christian leaders of all sources of moral decision not specifically grounded in the Bible. This is seen in the familiar Barthian mood of the present. In general this movement in ethics has gone along with the rejection of philosophical theology in the attempt to base Christian theology solely on the Bible. It was illustrated in the early Church by Tertullian, who refused to give any credence to Greek philosophy, asking scornfully, "What has Athens to do with Jerusalem?" It is illustrated today by the neo-orthodox school in its suspicion of not only liberal theology but the liberal social gospel, though the tendency is not uniform throughout neo-orthodoxy.

The ethics of the Church, and individually of the churches, stands midway between the ethics of Christendom and the ethics of the gospel as it comes to us in Jesus Christ. The Church, insofar as it is faithful to its mission as the carrier of the gospel and is a fellowship of persons sincerely trying to follow Jesus, sees more clearly what is right than does the surrounding society. It is for this reason that it is called to be the "conscience of the State" and is obligated without falling into a trite and secularistic moralism to proclaim and practice the principles of Christian morality. Its official pronouncements, whether in a papal encyclical or a statement of the World Council or National Council of Churches, or an action of a General Conference, are likely to be on a plane above that of current practice. This is not to say that any human document is flawless, but when the Church through its leaders tries to speak from a Christian frame of reference, it both indicts current practices and sets higher goals. This is as it should be if the Church is to be effective in applying the principles of its eternal gospel to the changing temporal scene.

The book will prove an informative and most useful asset for students, scholars and teachers in the field of Christianity and Ethics.

—*Editor*

1

Religion and Ethics

Joachim Wach was born in 1898 in Chemnitz, Saxony, and died in 1955 while vacationing in Orselina, Switzerland. He was a descendant of Moses Mendelssohn, a lineage that affected his life and career both positively and negatively. His paternal grandfather, the noted jurisconsult Adolph Wach, married Lily, the daughter of Felix Mendelssohn, the composer. His father, Felix, married Kathe, granddaughter of the composer's brother, Paul. Young Wach was early exposed to music, literature, poetry, and both classical and modern languages.

After attending the Vitzshumsche Gymnasium in Dresden and spending two years in military service (1916-1918), Wach enrolled at the University of Leipzig, but in 1919 and early 1920 he studied with Friedrich Heiler at Munich and with Ernst Troeltsch at Berlin. He then returned to Leipzig to study Oriental languages and the history and philosophy of religion. For a time he came under the spell of the enigmatic poet Stefan George, whose writings spoke of a heightened sense of "experience," through which one perceives the multiple threads of the tapestry of life as a transparent whole. Wach received his Ph.D. degree in 1922 from Leipzig with a thesis entitled

"The Foundations of a Phenomenology of the Concept of Salvation," published as *Der Erlosungsgedanke und seine Deutung* (1922).

When Wach started teaching at Leipzig in 1924, the discipline of the history of religions (*Religionswissenschaft*), still in its infancy, faced serious dangers. On the one side, its right to exist was questioned by those who insisted that whoever knows one religion (*i.e.*, Christianity) knows all religions; on the other, its religio-scientific methodology was challenged by reductionist psychological and social-scientific approaches. Thus in his habilitation thesis, *Religionswissenschaft: Prolegomena zu ibrer wissenschaftstheoretischen Grundlegung* (1924), Wach insisted on the integrity and autonomy of the history of religions, liberated from theology and the philosophy of religion. He emphasized that both historical and systematic dimensions are necessary to its task, and he argued that the discipline's goal was "understanding" (*Verstehen):* "The task of *Religionsruissenschaft* is to study and to describe the empirical religions. It seeks descriptive understanding; it is not a normative discipline. When it has understood the historical and systematic aspects of the concrete religious configurations, it has fulfilled its task" (p. 68). His *Religionswissenschaft* is still regarded as a small classic in the field.

Wach's agenda centring on understanding led him to produce a three-volume work on the development of hermeneutics in the nineteenth century (*Das Verstehen*, 1926-1933). The first volume traced the hermeneutical theories of such major figures as Friedrich Schleiermacher, G. A. F. Ast, F. A. Wolff, August Boeckh, and Wilhelm von Humboldt. The second volume dealt with theological hermeneutics from Schleiermacher to Johannes von

Hofmann, while the third volume examined theories of historical hermeneutics from Leopold von Ranke to historical positivism. Understandably, Wach felt it absolutely necessary to establish solid hermeneutical foundations for the history of religions.

Wach was convinced that the history of religions (*Religionswissenschaft*) should not lose its empirical character. He felt C. P. Tiele and P. D. Chantepie de la Saussaye had failed to make an adequate distinction between the history of religions and the philosophy of religion. He was critical both of those who started with philosophy and developed science and of those who started with science and moved toward philosophy. In his view, the history of religions lay, rather, precisely between the two. In this respect he followed Max Scheler, who posited a "concrete phenomenology of religious objects and acts" between a historical study of religions (a positive *Religionswissenschaft*) and the essential phenomenology of religion (die *Wesensphanomenologie der Religion*). According to Scheler, this intermediate discipline aims at the fullest understanding of the intellectual contents of one or more religious forms and the consummate acts in which these intellectual contents have been given. It was Wach's conviction that an inquiry such as Scheler envisaged could be carried out only by employing the religio-scientific method of *Religionswissenschaft*.

Wach's reputation for erudition attracted many students to Leipzig. However, his productive career there came to an abrupt end in April 1935. The government of Saxony, under pressure from the Nazis, terminated Wach's university appointment on the ground of his Jewish lineage, even though his family had been Christian for four generations. Fortunately, through the intervention of American friends, Wach was invited to teach at Brown

University in Providence, Rhode Island, where he stayed until 1945. His adjustment to the new environment was by no means easy; he was especially anxious about his mother, sister, and brother, who were suffering under the Nazi tyranny. From 1945 until his death, Wach taught at the University of Chicago.

Wach always asserted that the method of the history of religions must be commensurate with its subject matter, that is, the nature and expressions of the religious experience of humankind as that experience has been unfolded in history. Following his mentor, Rudolf Otto, Wach defined religious experience as the experience of the holy. Throughout his life, he never altered his views on the basic structure of the discipline: its twin tasks (historical and theoretical); the centrality of religious experience and its threefold expressions (theoretical, practical, and sociological); and the crucial importance of hermeneutics. But Wach emphasized three different methodological accents in three successive phases of his career.

During his first phase, Wach was preoccupied with the hermeneutical basis for the descriptive-historical task of the discipline. He was greatly influenced by the philological hermeneutics of August Boeckh, who defined the hermeneutical task as "re-cognizing" that which had previously been "cognized," that is, as articulating what has been recognized in its pristine character, even to the extent of "re-constructing" in its totality that which does not appear as a whole. Accordingly, Wach insisted that the historian of religions must first try to assimilate that which had been recognized as a religious phenomenon and "re-produce" it as one's own. Then he must observe and appraise that which has become one's own as an objective something apart from oneself.

During his second phase, Wach attempted to develop the systematic dimension of the history of religions by following the model of sociology. In Wach's view, the sociological (systematic) task of *Religionswissenschaff* had two main foci: (1) the interrelation of religion and society, which requires an examination, first, of the sociological roots and functions of myths, doctrines, cults, and associations, and, second, of the sociologically significant function and effect of religion in society; and (2) the study of religious groups. In dealing with religious groups, and especially with the variety of self-interpretations advanced by these groups, Wach employed the typological method. As he stated in his Sociology of Religion (1944), he was convinced of the need to develop a closer rapport between *Religionswissenschaft* and other disciplines, especially with the social and human sciences. In this sense, his Sociology of Religion was an attempt to bridge "the gulf which still exists between the study of religion and the social sciences" (p. v). Yet the ultimate aim of his sociological (systematic) study of religion was "to gain new insights into the relations between the various forms of expression of religious experience and eventually to understand better the various aspects of religious experience itself" (p. 5).

During the third phase, Wach's concern for an integral understanding of the various aspects of religious experience and its expressions led him to reassess not only the relationship of *Religionswissenschaft* with the social sciences but also its relationship with normative disciplines such as philosophy of religion and the various theologies. After Wach's sojourn in India, where he delivered the Barrows Lectures at various universities in 1952, this concern became more pronounced. It was, in fact, one of the key motifs of his lectures on the history of religions sponsored by the American Council of Learned

Societies in 1954. Increasingly the vocabulary of "explaining" (*Deuten; Erklaren*) came to be used side by side with that of "understanding" (*Verstehen*) in his lectures. Wach shared his dream of pursuing a new grand synthesis for the, study of the human religious experience, a sequel to earlier works such as *Religionswissenschaft* and *Das Verstehen*, with friends during the Seventh Congress of the International Association for the History of Religion, held in Rome in the spring of 1955. But death came that summer and robbed him of this venture.

When A. Eustace Haydon retired as professor of comparative religion at the University of Chicago, Wach agreed to take his place. There he spent the last ten years of his life, 1946 to 1955, as professor of the history of religions in the Divinity School (then part of the Federated Theological Faculty) and with the University of Chicago's Committee on the History of Culture.

When Wach arrived in Chicago, the university was not even sixty years old. William Rainey Harper, who founded the university in 1892, had counted among his close friends Rabbi Emil G. Hirsch, the first professor of rabbinical literature and philosophy; John Henry Barrows, pastor of the First Presbyterian Church and permanent chairman of the 1893 World's Parliament of Religions; and Mrs. Caroline E. Haskell, who donated to the university the Haskell Lectureship on Comparative Religion and the Haskell Oriental Museum. A11 were keenly interested in comparative religion, however that subject was understood, and so a foundation was well laid early on at Chicago for the tradition to which Wach found himself heir.

By the mid-1940s, in fact, Chicago had seen at least three major approaches to comparative religion. The first was epitomized by George Stephen Goodspeed (d. 1905), author of *A History of the Babylonians and Assyrians.* Goodspeed established the Department of Comparative Religion in the university's Division of Humanities and was himself professor of comparative religion and ancient history. That he clearly approached religion, or religions, through the Judeo-Christian tradition can be seen in the title of a small booklet he edited after the Parliament: *The World's First Parliament of Religions: Its Christian Spirit, Historic Greatness and Manifold Results* (Chicago: Hill & Shuman, 1895). Similarly, in a presentation delivered at the Haskell Oriental Museum, Goodspeed expressed the hope that "there will go forth from these halls [of the University of Chicago] enlightenment, inspiration, and guidance in that learning which has come from the East and West, culminating in the Book of Books and in the teachings of the Son of Man, [which] will ever abide as our most precious possession."

The second approach to comparative religion at Chicago was advocated by George Burman Foster (d. 1918), who accepted a widely held three-layered scheme: (1) a narrow history of religions—conceived to be the simple historical study of "raw" religious data, often coloured by an evolutionary ideology—toward (2) "comparative religion," which aims to classify religious data and culminates in (3) a philosophy of religion (or a theology) that provides a meaning for the comparative religion enterprise as a whole. Louis Henry Jordan, too, accepted this combination of "scientific study of religion" and "philosophy of religion" as the programme of comparative religion.

The third approach, spearheaded by A. Eustace Haydon (d. 1975), was in a sense a critique of and a reaction to the first and second orientations. An erudite scholar and an eloquent speaker, Haydon had outgrown the fundamentalist faith of his childhood, as is evident in his numerous writings. For him, the loss of his childhood orthodoxy had three important outcomes. First, religious reality had given way to the ethical and the aesthetic, to use Kierkegaardian shorthand, and he found a "home" for himself in the Ethical Culture movement. Second, he was driven to a religious relativism as the alternative to affirming Christian faith as the only religion of humankind's salvation. Third, he championed comparative religion, understood by him as an umbrella term for objective studies, by specialists, of the historic religious traditions, no more and no less.

Haydon took it for granted that, originally, human needs created all the forms of religion. Throughout history, all religions had to wrestle with the problem of change or, if you will, the problem of "modernism"; yet, in the twentieth century the great historic religions were forced to come to, terms with revolutionary forces heretofore unknown, namely, the "new scientific thinking" and "applied science." The former had profound implications for all aspects of human life, especially for traditional religions and their ancient cosmologies, theologies, and supernaturalisms. And applied science—especially modern machinery, communications, and systems of transportation—was already reshaping the face of the world. By way of responding to this new situation, Haydon, qua comparative religionist, organized the World Fellowship of Faiths in 1933. The conference dealt with Islam, Judaism, Christianity, Buddhism, Confucianism, and Hinduism and tried to generate discussion on four topics: (1) World-Religions and Modern Scientific Thinking; (2) World-Religions and Modern Social-Economic Problems; (3) World-Religions and Inter-Cultural Contacts; and (4) the Task of Modern Religion. Haydon was persuaded that the six religious systems all faced the same problems.The contrast between the 1893 World's Parliament of Religions, which helped to shape the first approach to comparative religion at Chicago, and the 1933 World Fellowship of Faiths, the brainchild of its third approach, is interesting. Both divorced religious realities from human communities, so that participants could speak, for example, of Buddhism apart from Buddhist community life; and both dealt with socioeconomic problems as if they owed nothing to religious factors. In contrast, though, to the 1893 conference, which recognized the importance of the past to various religions, the 1933 conference concerned itself solely with the modern phases and movements of the living world religions.

But by far the most salient feature of the 1933 conference was the way in which it equated both religion and morality and comparative religion and science. In the words of K. Natarajan of Bombay, "The task of religion in all ages has been to assert the supremacy of the moral law over the lives of individuals and nations." And Haydon's friend, Rabbi Solomon Goldman, added: "The ancient techniques of prayer and ritual need to be retained only in so far as they are aesthetically appealing. Modern religion must become the friend and not the enemy of science." Haydon agreed: the task of comparative religion was to help people overcome the antiscientific bias and to show them the religion of tomorrow, a synthesis of science and idealism. "The whole world," he said, "wrestles with the same problems, aspires toward the same ideals, and strives to adjust inherited thought-patterns to the same scientific ideas. In such times the prophetic fire of religious aspiration flames anew and religions move into new embodiments... the religions of tomorrow are emerging surrounded by a multitude of modernizations of the old."Ironically, it was Haydon, the ex-fundamentalist, who transferred the Department of Comparative Religion from the Humanities to the Divinity School of Chicago shortly before his retirement in 1944.

When Wach arrived in Chicago, he was aware that comparative religion at the university had three successive approaches, none of which appealed to him. In order to make a fresh beginning, Wach proposed to refer to his enterprise as the History of Religions (*Religionswissenschaft*), which was the official English designation of the international association. Wach was afraid that the name might suggest a purely historical discipline, but he was more afraid that the history of religion, in the singular, the usage he had preferred in Germany, might suggest a philosophical discipline. Thus he settled on the history of religions and used the term consistently for the remainder of his career.

Wach was irenic by nature and wanted to relate himself positively to each of the earlier orientations in comparative religion. Accordingly, he paid special attention to (1) the special place of Judaism and Christianity in Western civilization, which the first approach had stressed; (2) the relationship between the history of religions and philosophy of religion (or theology), which the second approach had emphasized; and (3) the concern North Americans had shown for specific religious traditions, such as Hinduism, Buddhism, and Islam. (Wach lamented, however, the lack of interest in the so-called primitive religions in North America).

When Wach came to the campus on the Midway, the University of Chicago was an unusually exciting place under the dynamic leadership of Robert Maynard Hutchins. During the war years, the university made a point of welcoming European refugee scholars—many from Germany; some, like Enrico Fermi, from Italy—who helped to create an international atmosphere at Chicago. The

Divinity School, then under the deanship of the young theologian Bernard M. Loomer, was involved in creating the Federated Theological Faculty, which included Ernest Cadman "Pomp" Colewell, Amos Wilder, J. Coert Rylaarsdam, Allen P. Wikgren, Paul Schubert, Wilhelm Pauck, Charles Hartshorne, Bernard E. Meland, Daniel Day Williams, Sidney Mead, James H. Nichols, James Luther Adams, and Samuel Kincheloe. Wach took a modest room in the Disciples Divinity House, 1156 East 57th Street, and later moved to an apartment in the Ingleside Avenue faculty building. He was close to many scholars in the neighbourhood, notably O. J. Matthijs Jolles, one-time chairman of the Committee on the History of Culture; Peter von Blankenhagen; Ludwig Bachhofer; Robert Platt; Robert Redfield; John Nef; Wilbur Katz; Everett Hughes; and his own cousin, Otto von Simpson. Wach also received many visitors who delighted his students by appearing in his classes. Among these visitors were Martin Buber, Gershom G. Scholem (Wach's fellow student at Munich), D. T. Suzuki, Hideo Kishimoto, Gerardus van der Lecuw, Jacques Duschesne-Guillemin, A. A. Fyzee, and Swami Vivekananda.

From the beginning, it was crystal-clear to Wach that he wanted to teach the history of religions (*Allgemeine Religionswissenschaft*), which is an autonomous discipline situated between normative studies, such as philosophy of religion and theology, and descriptive studies, such as sociology, anthropology, and psychology. He was also convinced that *Religionswissenschaft* consisted of two complementary aspects, the "historical" and the "systematic" procedures of study. The "historical" task required a mutual interaction between the "general" history of religions and the historical studies of "specific" religions, while the "systematic" task aimed at disciplined generalizations and the structuring of data and depended on a collaboration of phenomenological, comparative, sociological, psychological, and other studies of religions. Historical and systematic inquiries were to be thought of as two interdependent dimensions of one and the same discipline called the history of religions (*Religionswissenschaft*).

Wach affirmed that the history of religions should start with the historic religions. Thus he shared common ground with the third approach to comparative religion at Chicago. But unlike this third approach, he never accepted the premise that what authenticated, say, Hinduism or Buddhism is simply Hindu or Buddhist religious experience. Wach was convinced that the raison d'etre of the history of religions is the hidden "religious experience" of humankind, described as the experience of the "holy" by Rudolf Otto and as the experience of "power" by G. van der Leeuw. Wach was sympathetic to the desire to find a special place in the study of religion for Judaism and Christianity, which was the emphasis of the first approach to comparative religion at Chicago. But, unlike the first approach, which viewed all religions through the window of the Jewish-Christian tradition, Wach insisted that Judaism and Christianity alike must be seen as parts of the "whole" religious experience of the human race. In the last ten years of his life, Wach was often mistakenly thought to be in the camp of the second approach to comparative religion at Chicago, which necessitated his stating repeatedly that while the philosophy of religion applies an abstract philosophical idea of what religion is to the data of empirical, historical studies, the history of religions begins with the investigation of religious phenomena, from which, it is hoped, a pattern of "meaning" will emerge. The history of religions' inquiry into the "meaning" of religious phenomena *leads* one to questions of a philosophical and metaphysical nature, but the history of religions as such cannot deal with those questions philosophically.

Wach believed that the history of religions was a discipline to be taught in a university, ideally simultaneously in a department of theology and in the humanities. He himself taught primarily in the Divinity School but he had an intellectual, outlet in the Committee on the History of Culture. He devoted much time as well to the social sciences, participating, for example, in an interdisciplinary seminar called "The Birth of Civilization', under the direction of the great anthropologist Robert Redfield. But basically he was happiest when surrounded by his own students, the so-called Sangha. He was convinced, in fact, that each of his students would be an important emissary for the history of religions.

In retrospect, I wonder how happy Wach was in Chicago. He lived in the twentieth century, but he was more at home with the nineteenth, academically speaking. Cosmopolitan though he was, he had, after all, been driven out of Germany, and his intellectual gaze never wandered very far from Dilthey's *Erlebnis* (experience), *Ausdruck* (expression), and *Verstehen* (understanding). Be that as it may, Wach remained quite sure about the nature of his calling. As he once stated:

The need for *understanding*, understanding people and peoples, their thought and affections, their words and deeds, has impressed the author from his youth. He chose the problem of hermeneutics—the theory of interpretation—as the subject of an extensive historical study [meaning *Das Verstehen*, 3 vols.]. He has tried to carry out his work both as a scholar and as a teacher, in two continents, with a view to practicing and teaching understanding. Two wars brought home to him even more clearly the urgency of helping to create the conditions for understanding among nations. Wach was delighted to deliver the Barrows Lectures on Comparative Religion in India in 1952 and the American Council of Learned Societies Lectures in the History of Religions in 1954-55. In late spring 1955, he attended the Congress of the International Association for the History of Religions (IAHR) in Rome. His later travels confirmed for him a statement made early in his Chicago days: "The European centres of learning, nearly all of which were affected by war, continue to devote great interest to the study of Eastern civilizations and religions. But the handicap under which they have to work places an increased responsibility upon American scholarship and initiative." And, true to his own words, Wach was determined to do his share of teaching and scholarship in America. Just before his death in August 1955, he received the coveted invitation from Marburg University offering him the chair once occupied by his mentor, Rudolf Otto. Tempting though this offer was, especially since he felt the kind hand of his former teacher, Friedrich Heiler, in the invitation, Wach declined the offer because "my vocation is to develop what I have started at Chicago."

This volume contains representative essays from each of the major phases of Wach's scholarly career. From the first phase we have chosen two essays. The first, "Master and Disciple," was originally published as *Meister und Junger: Zwei religionssociologische Betrachtungen* (Tubingen: J. C. B. Mohr, 1925). The English translation by Susanne Heigl-Wach and Frederick Streng first appeared in the *Journal of Religion* 42, no. 1 January 1962), 1-21. The second, "Mahayana Buddhism," was originally published as *Mahayana, besonders im Hinblick auf das Saddharma-Pundarika-Sutra* (Munich-Neubiberg: Schloss, Untersuchungen 16, 1925). The English translation by Nancy Auer Falk has not appeared before. Also included are two essays from Wach's second phase: "Wilhelm von Humboldt" (which was found in Wach's desk after his death) and "Sociology of Religion," written at Brown University and published first in George Gurvitch and Wilbert E. Moore, eds., *Twentieth Century Sociology* (New York: Philosophical Library, 1945). Four essays represent Wach's third and last phase: "Radhakrishnan and the Comparative Study of Religion," which appeared in P. A. Schilpp, ed., *The Philosophy of Sarvepalli Radhakrishnan* (New York: Tudor Publishing Co., 1952), pp. 443-58; "Religion in America," which was based on notes from lectures given at various universities in the United States; "On Teaching History of Religions," which appeared in a memorial volume to honour G. van der Leeuw called *Pro Regno Pro Sanctuario* (Nijkerk: G. F. Callenbach, 1950), pp. 525-32; and "On Understanding," which appeared in A. A. Roback, ed., *The Albert Schweitzer Jubilee Book* (Cambridge, Mass.: SCI-Art Publishers, 1946), pp. 131-46. All are reproduced here with proper permission. These selections will, we hope, provide readers with some understanding of Wach's intellectual pilgrimage.

Joachim Wach's spirit lives among his former students, to whom this volume is dedicated. I wish to take this opportunity to thank Charles E. Smith, Paul Bernabeo, and Elly Dickason of Macmillan Publishing Company for their advice and assistance in bringing together this collection.

Thanks also are due to Dean Franklin I. Gamwell of the Divinity School of the University of Chicago; to my secretary, Martha Morrow-Vojacek, and to Peter Chemery, my present research assistant, upon whose extensive care and attention my recent work has depended.

Lastly I wish to express my special appreciation to

Professor Gregory Alles of Western Maryland College, co-editor of this volume and of this book's companion volume (also published by Macmillan this year), entitled *Introduction to the History of Religions*, consisting of Wach's 1924 habilitation thesis, *Religionswissenschaft* and six articles which appeared in *Religion in Geschichte und Gegenwart* (1930). In both Professor Alles has cheerfully carried a heavy burden because of my poor health.

MASTER AND DISCIPLE: TWO RELIGIO-SOCIOLOGICAL STUDIES

Only there man's nature is sustained where the darksome offering is retained. —Der Stern des Bundes

The disciple is not above his master. —Matt. 10:24

The Master and Disciple—The Teacher and Student

The disciple is always associated with a master, the student with a teacher. Let us speak of an ideal teacher-student relationship based solely on subject matter and not on the personalities of the teacher and student. The bond is constituted through common interest in the object of study; the student respects the teacher as the possessor and mediator of certain crafts, a body of knowledge or an accomplished skill; he considers him worthy when this treasure is great and significant and when the teacher is willing to give of it freely.

It is not the person who is admired and esteemed, but a certain faculty, a skill, knowledge, or capability. The human prestige is entirely dependent upon the inherent relevance and respect, the importance and value of the object of study. The student admires in the teacher the greatness and significance of his learning; and his merit consists in his willingness to give freely of this treasure.

The student is dear to the teacher to the extent that he is willing to open himself to the teacher's communication; the student's value depends on his individual success or failure to appropriate the subject matter. This entire relationship is born and lives by means of the common interest in the object of study. A diversion from it results in the disintegration of the relationship between them. From this we can understand the replaceability of the person; any given teacher like any given student is replaceable; if he is not, it is merely that none can actually be found to take his place.

The relationship of the master to the disciple is found where the tie is personal—not based primarily on subject matter; the individuality of the master and the disciple consequently gains central significance. The master does not enjoy this esteem because he conveys something useful, something transferable from his possession to the disciple; it is not the result of the fortunate possession of a particular artistic skill. Rather, the significance for the disciple rests in the master's personality, whose very character and activity are individual and irreplaceable. Corresponding to this the choice of the disciple is grounded in the master's inclination, which grows out of a deep conviction regarding his "calling" to discipleship. The favourite disciple is not he who advances or shows promise of advancement toward mastering the common subject matter (which may also be there but is not decisive in this relationship); he is the one with whom the master cultivates a profound personal relationship. The disciple understands the master; the student understands the teaching—the skill of the teacher. A student makes himself what he is by his own individual effort. A disciple is chosen; he is called to understand the master. The disciple must be touched to the core by his personality. The beloved master must be an essential part of his own existence.

The teacher and student, united through a bond of work on a common task, form a series of links in which the student in his own proper time will also become a teacher. Conversely, the master and disciple in themselves represent the beginning and the end, a cosmos in itself; the disciple will never become a master. Accordingly, the teacher heads a school; the master forms a circle around himself. The teacher gives of himself to the student without receiving anything in return; personal relationship means nothing to the teacher, but the master-disciple relationship at its very core is one of mutual significance. The master becomes a master only in relationship to a disciple. Here we are not emphasizing a merely verbal correlation but rather a profound fact: that the master only becomes fully aware of the sense of his mastership in its highest and final form through a perceptive and comprehending disciple, and it is the disciple who ordains his master to mastership. The master reads his calling in the eye of his disciple, just as the disciple hears destiny speak in and through the master.

The teacher gives of his knowledge, of his ability; the master gives himself. What the master is to the disciple, he is through his existence, that is, if he is to be master, he must be himself. What he is, he had achieved through his own development; and what he has become through this development is always actually present in its totality. Therefore, what he has to say is always existentially significant; it must be understood from the standpoint of existence, for it pertains to the total man. The disciple understands the master only when he understands him in the context of existence. Fundamentally this means that the master must renounce all hope of being fully understood, because to understand him fully would mean to become the master, to know the great mystery of renunciation, to know that the highest fulfillment is possible only in another person. This is the melancholy awareness of all masters—that no heirs are provided for the master, that the sweetest and best fruit which ripens for him never can be given away, because whoever comes to himself indeed comes only to himself. This characterizes the attitude of the master: a touch of gentle resignation, of understanding kindness, and of silent grief.

The most sacred moment in the relation of the master to his disciple comes when the master finally turns the disciple back to himself; it reveals the significance of the master for his disciple; it is the moment in which the relationship is most intimate. Yet, at the same time, it is that moment in which the master appears most remote: above the relationship of master and disciple is written the word "farewell." It is the specific tragedy of the master's life that he is destined to direct everything toward this parting. Instead of completely drawing to himself, he must completely thrust away; instead of moving from distance to the intimate unity, he must move in the opposite direction.

Therefore the master can only love his disciple with a tinge of sadness. The disciple does not understand the master, though the master means everything to him; he loses himself in the greatness of the master and seeks to comprehend him existentially. His highest goal is to be most intimately related to this master. So "he follows after him," until the hour of decision comes, which always must be the hour of parting; then the disciple despairs either of the master or of himself. He must choose either himself and take leave of the master, who was dearer to him than all things, or he must deny himself, continuing to love the master, and so destroy completely the master's labour. The master will love this disciple because of this devotion, but the disciple who left him will not be forgotten by him. This is the double recognition which is earned by the master's character. On the one hand, his sacrifice, even though not understood, is still effective and bears fruit, for what has proceeded out of the existence procreates and remains living in existence; and, on the other, the consequences of love remain even into solitude, reverence, and faithful service, enjoying the severity of the task. Therefore, when the evening of life comes for the master, and the friends of his best years go their ways, the disciple remains with him. The disciple performs the service of love for him, not because he knows what really constitutes the mystery of the final loneliness which no love shares and no understanding can brighten, but because he has fully realized that his place is here.

The teacher survives in his work; the master survives in those who have experienced his influence and bear witness to him. All others can only surmise it. The disciple testifies to what the master was to him when he speaks of his master: as he has seen the master, so he paints his picture that it might be imprinted on the memory. He alone possesses the full value of the image, and others are dependent on him for their view of the master. And as he, in order to make known the beloved figure, tries to transmit the features of the master's character to others, so also the other disciples do it, in fact all who surround the master. In them burns the desire to share what they have known by firsthand experience, and they are eager to tell others. But the secret of the master is really the influence of his personality; and only he who has experienced it can evaluate it. So from the beginning the labour of the disciple carries the germ of the tragic necessity that it must fail. Whoever saw the master cannot communicate the experience which he alone had; any talk of it is bound to fail. Each story concerning the master is a legend which has its own action and time. The legend itself changes when it is once established along more universal lines and has received a form that is easily apprehended; as such it reaches those who come after, for whom it becomes tradition and history. But what passes between men in life must be experienced directly.

The teacher knows that his work remains; the master lives in the knowledge that nothing of what he gives can remain. The teacher gives a definite subject matter; the master provides only stimulus. In the disposition of the master, the significance of the moment is important; as for his attitude, the whole problem of time is of prime importance. From the recognition of transitoriness and of change comes the understanding of the need for the right moment. "Kairos" is the key term here: therefore no eternity can bring back what was missed before; only the sacred hour begets the sacred knowledge; therefore many hours must be nourished from this one. The teacher, carefully measures his time and dedicates as much as he is able to the task of teaching—worry for fear that his task will not be accomplished would never occur to him, since he knows that after him his students will become teachers in turn, and so he will live on. But the master would never worry about his time or his own security in any sense. Now and then, at ease, he gives all he has. All the sweetness of the moment, with its immediate demands, its unending horizon, the weight of a thousand possibilities, the apprehension of death and perishability, loosens the heart and tongue; and it is as though nothing had been before, and as though nothing will ever be again.

It can happen only once; it is unique. And as only one being can produce *this one* thing in this one particular moment, so it is possible to produce it only in one person, in the disciple who is awake in the decisive hour. Then both the world and all time around them are swallowed up; through the transitory human frailty shines the eternal, before which all humanity and human accomplishments are futile. A faint notion of the divine is dawning, which never is revealed to mere effort, not even the most persistent.

This means that the master's life is filled with activity and unrest, while that of the teacher moves along in serene security. This is indeed the distress and mystery of this disposition, the fact that it can never be permitted "to forget itself"—neither in surrender nor in service, so that it is continually giving of itself. Whenever it gives, it gives out of a depth in which living powers are always operative and in which there is always life, which means that there is continual conflict. The teacher is consumed by his task, his work; the master consumes himself. "And as you consume yourself, you are full of light." The teacher has the truth which he wants to promulgate—or else he is on the way to finding it; but the master has nothing which he can give to all.

The teacher meets the student in the area of the subject matter: he teaches him to cultivate the soil, and they work on the ground together. Or the student sits at the feet of the teacher, who speaks to him from his lofty height. The master would raise his disciple up to himself; he would raise him higher, even above himself: they never meet on the same plane. The teacher and student have something in common on which they work together and which unites them. The master and his disciple are either completely united or not at all, and they live with each other in this relationship day in and day out. The teacher praises the swift foot, the skilled hand, the sharp eye, and the keen intellect of the student; while in the master's eye there are no such distinctions. For him, body and soul remain undivided. A standard and a measure are held up to the disciple: to exist, which means to live from a central norm; and this norm is the very living body of the disciple. Such is the meaning of the master's requirement, that the body also love beauty.

To be the typical student and to belong to the same school as one's teacher is a unifying experience. The point of contact which expresses the common bond between teacher and student also provides the foundation upon which the school is established. In this joint enterprise everything that is primarily objective is in the foreground, and where subjectivity plays a part, it is only accidentally interwoven in this relation between person and thing. Everything individual—all personal effort and striving—recedes to the background and is of no validity or interest.

Discipleship is different: being one of a group of disciples under a master is no basis for mutual love; rather it is often the basis for hate. From the beginning it seems impossible that someone else should have a part in the relationship that ties the disciple to his master (it is a condition which has its foundation in the incomparability and uniqueness of individuality), so, in principle, no way leads from one of them to another. Convinced that he is devoted to and open to the master as no other is, the disciple feels a passionate conviction to claim his master's love in preference to all else and all others. Thus, the human, the all-too human emotions of envy and jealousy arise. Of course such emotions are also known among students, but they are not intrinsic to scholarly activity. The sinister act of the disciple, who from jealousy betrays the master, is the most shattering expression of this impulse, and it is conceivable only in such a relationship. Let us compare now discipleship with the school when each is deprived of its head: here the situation is nearly reversed. Within the school, embittered disputes are raised concerning the "authentic interpretation" of the legacy left by the teacher; a contest concerning a successor sets in; the fellow student who becomes the opponent will be fought more desperately than the most wicked enemy. But this is not so among the disciples who are deprived of their master. In the true spirit of their master those who are left behind—who often possess entirely different individualities—are brought together through the image which is sacred to each of them. Moreover, the personal distress, common loneliness, and concern over the future produce a great unity. The work of the master will not continue, since no one can continue it except he who began it. And where it appears as though this did occur, a new master has arisen or a school has been assembled about a teacher.

The name of a powerful teacher is associated with his work, and in it his reputation is secured. The personality of the master lives on as an effective force. Of both, however, the word of Daniel has been spoken: They shall shine as the splendour of the heavens.

ON THE MEANING OF THE MASTER'S LIFE

This essay is about the master and disciple. Our concern is not with the specific content of the teachings proclaimed by the exalted masters. Rather, the following discourse will deal with the meaning and value of the master's life, the "existence" of the master.

First let us consider the tradition of Buddhism regarding its master. We are told that one night, in the forest of Urvela, Gotama—while he was lost in solitary meditation, going through continually higher states of ecstatic self-renunciation—attained release and revelation of this release. In this sacred moment he grasped the knowledge about the suffering of the world, the sources of suffering, its annihilation and the way to its annihilation. The night in which the Buddha attained this knowledge—as he was seated under the tree—is the holy night of the Buddhist world; in this night Gotama became the Buddha. The creatures of all the worlds were elated; gods and men shouted with joy. As the saving wisdom in the blessed and most holy Buddha appeared, the radiant sunrise of release became manifest for all creatures.

Four times seven days the fasting Buddha relished the bliss of release. Into this period of time, tradition places a temptation. Underlying this story is a profound thought—the Buddha is tempted to keep his insight to himself:

Why disclose to the world what I won in difficult struggle?

The truth remains hidden from those filled with craving and hate.

It is laborious, mysterious, deeply hidden from ordinary wit.

It cannot be seen when earthly striving darkens the mind with night.

Note, while the exalted one was considering this, his heart was inclined to persist in peace and not to proclaim the teaching. With profound insight and wonderful psychological understanding the great temptation is recognized and described here—the temptation which will at one time face everyone who is enlightened (*Wissenden*): to remain silent, to lock within his innermost being that which he has attained through tedious struggle and to remain in the joy of enlightenment. It is not only the fear of exposing himself or of being misunderstood and misinterpreted which suggests this; it is the concern regarding those who are not able to grasp it, who would be utterly destroyed by having knowledge to which they are not equal. For as it is said in one of the texts: The preacher rescues those who believe him and annihilates those who do not believe him.

The tradition of Buddhism reveals that in this moment, in which the destiny of millions upon millions is decided, Brahman Sahampati himself came down from heaven to beg the conqueror to preach the truth. Finally the Buddha complies with this request.

Let the gate of eternity be opened to all.

Whoever has ears let him hear the word and believe.

In order to avoid vain effort, I have not yet proclaimed the noble word.

Later tradition held that Mara, the Buddhist Satan, appeared to the enlightened one after the latter spent the first seven days in silent contemplation. The evil one knew that earthly pain and pleasure could no longer seduce the Buddha, so he tempted him to enter Nirvana immediately. Then the Buddha alone would escape him; but all other beings would remain without release and would still belong to him.

The cunning and strength of the tempter, however, came to nought; Buddha turned him away; Mara left "the perfected one." The later texts report that the prince of darkness again drew near to the Buddha when he was an eighty-year-old man—this same Mara who, following other tempters, had attacked the pious one while he was toiling in ascetic discipline before his enlightenment. The Buddha, so reports this remarkable tale, was staying with Ananda near the town of Vesali. There the old man was moved by a longing for the beauty of the world. He showed his disciple the loveliness of nature, saying that if he wanted, he could remain alive for a world-period. Ananda did not understand the hint because Mara darkened his understanding. Though he implored the master to remain, the enlightened one had previously decided differently; nothing was able to hold him back any longer from entering Nirvana at the appointed respite. But he also rejected Mara's wish to depart from the world immediately before his task was entirely accomplished.

The older texts know about ever new attacks by Mara; in the later ones it is different. There the divine master with that single decisive victory attains the *sambodhi*, the highest enlightenment—henceforth nothing can tempt him. This is the conception of a time which recognized the perfect one as a mediator, a redeemer in a specific sense. That moment has an uncanny world-shaking significance: the resolution of the Buddha is conceived to preach to all beings the revelation in which he has found peace. The Mahayana Buddhists have built a religion of belief on that solemn promise of the redeemer.

Immediately after he had resolved this, the enlightened one began his teaching activity. The first disciples appear. Is it possible to tell more impressively and stirringly the first episode of the master's life than does the religious biography of the Buddha—to describe the beginning of that blessed, yot painful, time which appears in the master's existence as the growing consciousness of sacrifice? With the consciousness of his mission this existence begins—with the moment of enlightenment in which a higher and more difficult calling, the task, become recognized as destiny. In this sense the master's existence implies an understanding won through lonely, difficult struggle: the understanding of the mission to be called to a special task. This consciousness of a particular mission may be a sudden inspired enlightenment, or it may come as a realization gained by painful, laborious struggle.

This involves, first, a knowledge of the essence of things and the destiny of the world, and, second, a knowledge of his personal mission, the activity through which the chosen one should influence human destinies. The decisive point, we repeat, is the call to "understanding." Everything works together to lead "the called-one" to this understanding: earthly and heavenly powers, the natural and physical modes of existence, the driving psychical powers, the inner impulse and outer guidance, the perception of the world and its experiences, the secret revelation which lies in the consciousness of his own being. Here we are not concerned with the specific contents of that knowledge which in each instance will be an experience of the ultimate religious and metaphysical mysteries. Before all else we should keep in mind a double truth, already mentioned—that with the objective knowledge of the structure of the world, something subjective is given, namely, the nature and function of one's own being in it. It is meaningless to ask which comes earlier or later; both are knowledge of the first order; neither of them is derivable from or follows the other. Rather, of decisive significance is the nature of that interpenetration [of subjective and objective cognition]. It is primarily the consciousness of a unique metaphysical significance which makes this connection so intimate.

Hereafter we will distinguish the master from the prophets. Both fulfill a "mission," so this characteristic, by which one often characterizes the prophets, does not entirely separate the prophet from the master. But while the person of the prophet in itself is not of decisive significance for the proposed mission, the master is the carrier of a metaphysical meaning. In view of the continual process of the world, more people are dependent on the master than on the prophet, in whose place—according even to his own conviction—another person could have been called just as well. The significance of the master is certainly not always a metaphysical one in a strict sense.

It is very often only one of eminence, as could be said, for example, of the figure of the Buddha. He was destined to be the one who would discover and proclaim the holy truth. In Buddhism particularly, we can discern a growing tendency to absolutize the significance of the master's person: he became divine in the "northern" schools; pious believers even multiplied his person *ad infinitum*. According to them, there had always been "enlightened ones," Buddhas; and there are continually those who are predestined to be such, Bodhisattvas. Indeed, we experience the strange spectacle that, after passing a certain point, this absoluteness again became relative through the introduction of a Bodhisattva mythology. This mythology in itself was intended to serve the purpose of glorifying the unique one [Buddha], but it finally associated countless greater and lesser gods and holy beings with him. As in Buddhism so in Islam (though in itself viewed from the self-consciousness of the prophet-founder—which we see so clearly) there were [at first] only a few suggestions of this nature. Then the development took a similar direction in making the person of the prophet absolute; especially in Sufism his cultic veneration stimulated fantastic and unusual results.

Here we do not have to inquire into the factors which together and in particular forced the development in this direction. For Islam this examination has been done through Andrae's portrayal of "the person of Mohammed." Here we see that the development of the prophet-cult in Islam does not conflict with the view of two originally and essentially different types: the prophet and the master. The opposition against the prophet-cult, which attributed a metaphysical significance to Mohammed within the Moslem religious community itself, is certainly important; yet the justification regarding our essential distinction can hardly be doubted. The consideration of the particular kind of *charisma*—upon which Max Weber has placed special emphasis in his religious-sociological treatise—is not decisive for us. We proceed from the experience of the respective personality; we will not only analyze it psychologically but understand it in its full intention by showing its meaning for the master's whole existence and the consequences of the master's life.

Instead of recognizing the meaning and role of each person in light of his effectiveness in providing a metaphysical value, let us consider the crucial element to lie in the consciousness in itself. It is the peculiar driving force in the master's existence—the ground out of which his whole attitude toward the world, his whole thought and activity, must be understood.

The knowledge which "the called-one" receives is a tragic one. Its content is tragic; the nature of the world and his own being are felt to be full of sorrow. But this knowledge can also be called tragic in its effect on the existence itself of the master. Because this knowledge is tragic, the struggle in which the calling becomes evident is so hard; in it the thought of sacrifice is affirmed for the first time. The chosen one knows that he struggles, discerns, suffers, and succeeds by renouncing himself; he struggles, suffers, and succeeds for others. As it was stated by the poet: The fruit of the tree is not for the tree. Therefore, as expressed in the words of the Buddhist teachings, the last great temptation is to remain a saviour for one's self, a *pratyeka-buddha*, and to reject the terrifying call of the *samyaksambuddha*—to become a redeemer for all. A grandiose thought! In the midst of a suffering, fighting, turbulent world caught in tumultuous struggle, there is this one man who grasps the great thought of peace and knows about redemption in the midst of the chaos of meaninglessness and despair—one man who has found a meaning. This is the picture which the buddhist legends portray for us. The Buddha, surrounded by the fury of the elements and hosts of assaulting demons and spirits, is sunk in deep comtemplation while beholding the secrets of the holy truth.

To have this insight means loneliness. The beatitude of this tremendous knowledge is balanced by a dreadful, exalted, echoless silence. Four times seven days the Buddha continued to delight in the perception which he had gained. Again and again the sermons, which are handed down to us in the holy texts, make reference to this loneliness.

Knowledge creates loneliness and abandonment; but this does not incite the decision to share it. The chosen one feels sorry for the erring and searching men whom he henceforth sees in the light of the full perception. The desire to be a deliverer moves him: he would bring peace to them, for which they yearn; he would teach them. Will they be able to comprehend what he has to say to them? "It is difficult, mysterious, deep, hidden from the crude senses," thought the Buddha. We understand the struggle in which the impulses contend with each other: to remain silent or to speak out. But the thought of sacrifice is so intimately merged with the very nature of the master's existence, it hardly seems possible that the decisive "Yes" could not emerge, sealing the master's sacrificial path.

When Jesus knew himself as the Messiah, he knew the necessity of his own sacrificial suffering. We do not know the exact point in his life in which this consciousness came upon him, unless we would accept the baptism in the Jordan—where, according to Scripture, the Spirit of God came upon him—as the breakthrough of this consciousness. From the earliest beginning of his public appearance he is conscious of his particular mission; from the first his words and work are overshadowed by the destiny which he took upon himself in an unknown hour, by the knowledge which preceded this resolve to sacrifice.

To this hour, as also to that other mysterious copa (hour), point all those profound words—for example, concerning the ransom money in Matthew; and the words of deep suffering found in John: "I give up my life for the sheep," and "No one takes it from me, but I give it up by myself." Up to the climax in which he realized a singlemindedness with his destiny—as it is expressed in the so-called High-priestly Prayer (John, chap. 17)—is a high resolve whose confirmation is the fulfillment: "It is finished."

But between those two moments, the unknown first and this last, temptations continually seized the Chosen One. We know about it from the story of the temptation according to Matthew and Luke; we learn of it in that short, most clearly delivered story of Matthew about Peter's request: "Lord, preserve yourself...." (This is the memorable situation corresponding to the conversation of Buddha with Ananda near Vesali.) But above all it is in the shattering account of the struggle in Gethsemane and the confirmation in the Letter to the Hebrews. The cognition of the nature of the world and of the metaphysical significance of one's own self in it; the knowledge about the mission; the "Yes" to destiny; the sacrificial thought; and the last struggle and hesitation are clearly portrayed in that passage from Luke's Gospel: "I am come to cast a fire upon the earth; would that it were already kindled.

I have a baptism to be baptized with; and how I am constrained until it is accomplished!"

Let us consider antiquity: Did not the Greeks know about Chiron, the wise centaur, who instructed Achilles in playing the lyre; who introduced the mortal son of the immortal gods to the knowledge of the mysteries, guiding him out of the darkness of the Dionysian natural existence into the Apollonian kingdom of light; who showed him the way of transitoriness to immortal existence, himself a delivered deliverer?

Before us stands Empedocles, the old philosopher of Agrigentum, who has ever and again found admiring disciples up to the present time: the prophetic thinker and seer, the leader of those pious ones, whose heart longs for the redemption—whom Hoelderlin, a man very close to the Greeks, has given to us anew. In this magnificent poem everything that is decisive for the existence of a master becomes clear to us: the knowledge about the suffering of the world, the recognition of the calling, the "Yes" to it, the "Yes" to destiny, the thought of sacrifice, the temptation, the anxiety and hesitation before the final decision. Indeed, here it is expressed in the ancient Greek idiom:

Divine nature is manifested
Divinely only through Man; thus again
The race which attempts so much recognizes it.
Yet when the mortal, whose heart divine nature
Filled with its delight, has announced it,
Oh, let it break that vessel in pieces
Lest it serve to other uses
And divine things become human works.

There is no more profound expression of the masterdisciple relationship than that given by Hoelderlin in the relation of Empedocles-Pausanias. Hardly anywhere is the tragic aspect in the master's existence brought to a more moving expression. Or let us consider Socrates, who, according to Nietzsche, is an ambiguous figure in antiquity. Is not also Socrates a "master" in the sense we are attempting to develop? Something of the exalted sorrow is spread over his being and works, which comes from the knowledge of the metaphysical condition of the world, the calling and the end.

The later thinker Soren Kierkegaard, who probably most profoundly understood him, spoke once of the midwifery "of Socrates as the highest relationship between men." "Because," according to him, "between man and man [midwifery] is the highest, the [engendering] belongs to God." This throws a light on the inner existence of Socrates; one side of the master's life is profoundly characterized: the resignation in the highest sense, the sacrificial thought. Certainly Socrates specifically rejects thereby all claim to a metaphysical significance of his person; but is he not Greek? He is not only teacher, mediator of knowledge and capability, adviser, leader in ethical and political concerns, but, as his death shows—which must be interpreted as the emerging of the master's sacrifice—he is also a master in the highest sense of the word. In this way Plato had also understood him.

The melancholy and gentle sadness which characterize the life of the master show his readiness for sacrifice; it appears even in the serenity of fulfillment, as in the ancient piety of Empedocles, toward destiny. It shines through the irony of Socrates. It forms the dark-gold background against which the radiant words of Jesus are set off. It is the "Yes" to destiny—the once-spoken; yet, ever again in the master's life it must be repeated, until the end, until the fulfilment. It is this "Yes" which is ever present and which surrounds every deed and word of the master with a touch of deep sorrow. Thus we learn that the master also is bound; the task which he undertakes acquires ultimate dimensions from God, from destiny. The whole existence of the master signifies a growing-up to this call; through his entire existence the argument with the highest authority continues; the hour of the call is only its most intense concentration.

This "Yes" implies the renunciation of the splendour and happiness of the world, of home and of love, of all ties and associations; to offer one's self for sacrifice is, in a higher sense, necessary; to participate in the coherent development of events as destiny has determined. This renunciation is expressed most comprehensively by the Buddha. Ever and again in the Holy Scriptures we meet the explicit abandonment of all earthly happiness, symbolized in the story of Prince Gotama's encounters with, and his flight from, the world. At first sight this seems to be no painful resignation, since everything from which the Enlightened One turns away is indeed empty, vain, and idle. Here psychological interpretation must go deeper, for it is precisely this which is the difficulty of the knowledge to which the chosen one is called: that before its gaze all the glitter and glory of the world became nothing. The Chosen One sees that mankind lives cheerfully and painlessly; the old world sprouts and blooms continually ever anew; life goes on, in the ups and downs of its natural rhythm. But he also knows that all this is not the "true," not the decisive; it is not that upon which all depends. In the hour of his calling he experiences the mystery that from now on raises his existence to the tragic level, which makes it lonely. From the time this knowledge is awakened in him, he is excluded from this eternal play, from the cheerful thoughtless pleasures of everyday life, from ordinary happiness. It is very profound that the tradition had the Buddha grow up in worldly splendour and earthly delights; he must know them before they become shallow to him.

Profound and beautiful also is the late story, which we have previously mentioned, concerning the temptation at Vesali. Here life itself seduced the aged man; the beauty of the world threatened to draw him into its spell. But the world can be no enduring place for him. The master's existence is one of loneliness. "The foxes have holes, and the birds of the air have nests, but the Son of Man has nowhere to lay his head." He does not know the intimate fellowship in which the members of the family circle gather; he is homeless also in this sense. To become a disciple of Buddha means to renounce everything: parents and kindred, wife and child, house and home. Jesus said to the disciples: Whoever leaves his house, or brothers and sisters, or father or mother, or wife or child for my name will receive a hundred fold and inherit eternal life. It sounds even harsher in Luke: Anyone who follows me and does not hate his father, mother, wife, child, brothers, sisters, and also his own life—he cannot be my disciple. And from the same we read: Whoever does not renounce all that he has cannot be my disciple.

Even the love of women cannot bind the chosen one. Neither condemnation nor contempt of a woman and marriage is thereby expressed—although such features are found—but it is the renunciation in favour of the noble task resulting from the knowledge of the reality of things. Once Ananda asked the Buddha—who himself left behind a wife and a small son in order to reach his aim, and who according to Udana explicitly praised

Sangamaji when he had deserted his wife and child—"How should we, Lord, behave in regard to a woman?"—"You should avoid seeing them." Ananda: "If we, however, do see them, Lord, what should we do then?"—"Do not speak with them." Ananda: "If we must, however, speak with them, Lord, what then?" "Then you must be watchful of yourself." The master himself had rejected all passion of worldly love when the daughters of Mara tried to seduce him. One cannot fail to recognize that those passages in the holy texts, which unwittingly and without intent touch this relationship, keep the woman disciple both inwardly and outwardly at a certain distance from the master. None of the women disciples, as the texts tell us, is near to the dying master. The Divyavadana tells us a temptation story of Ananda, who is blamed because—as the Cullavagga reports—he permitted women at the corpse of Buddha, who by their sorrow defiled the corpse. "O Criton, let someone take this woman home," said Socrates, as Xantippe appeared in the prison to take her final leave of him. Empedocles, according to the magnificent poem, also removed himself from his female disciples before he entered his final course; nothing is left to them but the mourning of his departure and the realization of their loss.

We know from the Gospels the appreciation that Jesus had for the womanly disposition. There are many episodes reported, especially in John, concerning his relationship with women, which a later time changed to the ascetic. This later tendency is found in the well-known expression, attributed to John by the so-called "Apostolic Church Regulation":

When the master prayed over the bread and the cup, and blessed them with the words: This is my body and blood, he did not permit the women to stay with us (Martha said, on account of Mary, because he saw her smiling. Mary said: I laughed no more). And he said this to us before, when he taught: The weak are saved through the strong.

Next to him, Peter, above all, is portrayed in a later time as having particular hostility toward women. "I am afraid of Peter," expressed Mary in the gnostic writing Pistis Sophia, "because he threatens men and hates our sex." But we do not have to reduce ourselves to the apocryphal writings of the New Testament to observe the basic thrust of this onesided emphasis. As the master was without a home, so he never fell in love with a woman. This the Church Fathers, knew: Justin, of course Tertullian (who emphasized this to its fullest), Clement, and Origen. ("The power of the self-controlled, the victorious crown of the virgins, the good judgment of the once married.") So Jesus is called. We have seen already that a later period portrays him as recommending this asceticism to others. Thus, to the Record of John, the Lord himself through his appearance prevented John, who was in the process of entering matrimony, from getting married—one story which is parallel to the account of Ananda's temptation and the intervention of Buddha. The mysterious saying in Matt. 19:12 may have given a point of reference permitting such an interpretation. From the Gospel of the gnostic Marcion we learn that the Jews in their court proceedings rebuked Jesus because he broke up marriage and destroyed the bonds of family life. "The ascetic Gotama," said the people, "has come to bring childless times, widowhood, and ruin of the racial stock."

All this cannot surprise us. The master rejects even this earthly bond for himself. Through his call to knowledge, he steps out of the ever continuing cycle of reproduction in which nature knows itself as being eternal in its creatures. In nature all things call to one another—as Schopenhauer says: Today as yesterday, we are always all together.

The renunciation is joined at bottom with the mission. It is not important whether and how far the master systematizes it and makes it a requirement; it is imminent in the master's existence. From this perspective it is also proved once more that loneliness is essential to this existence.

No one can share this loneliness with him; even the disciples cannot. For an instant—as we saw—the temptation to hold back his knowledge, to side-step the difficult path together with all misunderstanding and disappointment, overcomes the master. Nothing like this is reported to us concerning Jesus. But is it false to suppose that he, who in the final hour prayed: "Lord, if it is possible, let this cup pass from me," also knew the desire to be freed from this path of sacrifice—he who continually experienced with deepest grief how little those closest to him understood? Nevertheless the master knows that everything—all his suffering, his agony—is in vain and that his sacrifice is futile unless he succeeds in planting the truth in one soul that has opened itself to him. In the cases of Jesus and Buddha, the election of the disciples followed immediately after the decisive experience of the call. Buddha enlisted his first disciples in Benares; they were the five pious devotees who before his enlightenment had practiced asceticism with him. "In that time there were six holy men in the world, Buddha himself and the five disciples." Jesus went out and called those whom he wanted to draw unto himself: "Follow me!" It has been justifiably emphasized—that by using this means of selection, Jesus promoted a principle of selection in which the choice was not based on personal worth but in which a fellowship of destiny predominated. He did not choose the most distinguished, the best, the most able; he chose those to whom his heart turned out of a deep sense of inner affinity. Despite the character of the fellowship which developed around the master, there existed a definite relationship between the master and each of the disciples which was determined by the individual nature and personality of the disciple. The image which one disciple forms of the master is necessarily different from the image formed by any other; it is coloured through his "relative a priori"—regarding individuality, temperament, and disposition. On the other hand, seen from the point of view of the master, the disciples constitute a unity. There are, no doubt, types of disciples: a type of Jesus-disciple, of Buddha-disciple, and there is a type of Hellenic, or Sufist, discipleship.

The disciples have a threefold significance for the master. They are first of all the "representatives of mankind"—ignorant mankind. In spite of all initiation and all association with the master, they remain in need of instruction to the end: they can never understand the master, never basically comprehend the idea of sacrifice. In part they belong to the master; in part to "the world"; and therefore a cleavage continues to exist between the master and themselves which makes the master lonely. He knows about it, but he is glad that those whom he loves are spared from the gravity and, burden of the knowledge which is laid upon him. Therefore he blesses them; but in difficult hours of temptation he suffers.

Second, the disciples are the master's companions. Insofar as they are capable, they are near to him. They share his outward existence and try to make it easy. They are always in readiness, and in some particularly high and choice hours we find them in closest association with the master. Then he discloses part of his being and his knowledge to them—as much as is possible for them to grasp. Out of this human need for men who are near him, the Jesus of the Acts of John says to the disciples: "I need you, come to me"—a word which almost sounds blasphemous to a person who sees only the representative character of the disciples.

Third, the disciples are the apostles of the master; they are the proclaimers of his "teaching." As such they do not interest us here, because this essay deals with the relation of the master and disciple primarily in regard to the master's existence.

The varied significance of the disciples is clearly distinguished in the historical individuality of each of Jesus' disciples—as we learn to know them from the canonical and apocryphal writings of the New Testament. Nowhere do we find the "representative" aspect of the disciple stronger, deeper, and more impressive than in the figure of Peter.

We shall recall only two of those unforgettable episodes between the Lord and the follower disciple which illustrate what we have been saying: the rescue of the sinking Peter (Matthew, chap. 14) and Peter's betrayal (Luke, chap. 22). John the Evangelist appears in the incarnation of the conception of the companion, the disciple friend. We know from Scripture that the Lord loved him: "John," the Lord says to him according to the Acts of John (chap. 98), "there is one who must hear this from me, because I need one who should hear it."

Once more let us turn back to the figures of antiquity. Certainly in regard to the crucial elements there is a similarity in the significance of the disciples for the master.

It appears clearly in the touching and beautiful

characterization of Pausanias, whom Hoelderlin has depicted as a companion to Empedocles: the only person who is close to the master, to whom the master inclines himself lovingly and trustingly, and yet whom he must so often instruct and correct, who cannot understand the highest and final thing—the necessity and the loneliness of the sacrifice. Yet he calls him "Son! Son of my soul"—the only human being he loves. It appears in Socrates, from whose circle of disciples so many a character and name are known to us. And like Socrates, also in Zarathustra—as has been shown to us again recently in a profound manner—and in whom the last of our great thinkers [Nietzsche] envisioned for himself the "ideal master."

Concerning the *sravakas*, the circle of disciples which assembled about the Buddha, it is said that there were only types, not individuals—as in the following account:

Each of the great disciples is just like another so that each

is hard to distinguish from the other; each is a model of highest

purity, highest inner peace, highest devotion to Buddha.

The representatives of the suffering and erring world are the ones whom the enlightened one instructs ever and again.

Some of them, however, come to life for us: Condanna, the confessor; Sariputta, one of the disciples who is allowed to hear a word similar to that spoken by the Lord to Peter: he compares him to the eldest son of a world ruler, who, following the king, together with him sets in motion the wheel of rulership which this king lets roll over the earth; his friend Maha-Moggallana, the possessor of mysterious miraculous power, whose beautiful account of being called is passed on to us in the Mahavagga.

Further, there is Kassapa, the former barber of Upali, a true apostle; Rahula, the Buddha's son; Devadatta, the Judas Iscariot of Buddhism; and Ananda Upatthaka, a friend and companion of the exalted one as no other, of whose temptation and confirmation the texts tell us, as in the great sutra concerning the end of the master.

A later period put the most varied teachings and sayings into the mouths of these disciples. Ever and again the well-known figures appeared and preached their sermons to the honour of the master or for the conversion of the ignorant and wavering. As in a chorus, their voices are heard in the Theragata, the "Monks' Hymns." The disciples' words which are handed down to us in the Sutta-Nipata sound like a common confession:

To him my spirit looks, as if my eyes could see him

By night by day, fixed without fatigue.

Reverently dedicated to him, I wait for the morning.

From him, I feel, I cannot be separated,

There has been far too little interest in the disciples of Jesus. At all times the most earnest, the most impressive, and the most fruitful concern for them has been shown by artists. These—especially the German masters of the high Middle Ages, but also the later Italians—have understood the wonderful fascination of those figures, who, coming out of and disappearing into the dark, surround and accompany the figure of the Redeemer. The disciples remain halfway between individuals of flesh and blood and impressive, carefully stylized types. In the first century after the coming of the Lord there was a strong interest in those who had surrounded him during his lifetime, and a rich and interesting literature testified to it. Thus we follow Peter and participate in his struggle with Simon, the magician; we hear of the tragic fate of his daughter and experience his cruel crucifixion. We follow John, the eternally pure apostle of Asia, in his wondrous deeds; we get to know the extraordinary illumination which he received, and we see his joyful end.

We accompany Bartholomew in his struggle against the Indian idols; we see James the son of Zebedee contending with a sorcerer and converting the Spaniards, and James the son of Alphaeus, the courageous and upright witness, hurled down from the pinnacle of the temple, praying for his enemies in the words of his Lord. We see Matthew suffer the most terrifying tortures for his Lord's sake. We are led into the dangerous and difficult situation into which Andrew brought himself by his strict asceticism; we experience the terrible martyrdom of Philip, the apostle to Asia Minor; and we travel with the apostle Thomas way over to India in order to learn of his wonderful experiences and deeds. We follow Simon the Zealot to Babylonia and Persia—Simon, who already as a boy was permitted to hear the promise of the future master. Thus many things are communicated to us concerning life of the master and his intimate relationship with his disciples. We learn much that is believable and unbelievable—the repulsive and the attractive. Who could not but be grasped by the descriptions which the Acts of John—the most beautiful and profound of those mysterious writings—gives to us of the last gathering of the Lord with his disciples, culminating in the account of the magnificent hymn which those intone who are united in the ecstatic cult dance. The writings of the heretical groups, particularly, know how to tell the most miraculous things. The disciples enjoy high, indeed extraordinary, esteem in these circles; they are given a kind of metaphysical meaning as it is already indicated in that passage which the Ephraim Commentary passes on to us: "I have chosen you before the existence of the world"; and this esteem is expressed in the gnostic Pistis Sophia in the most elaborate manner. All this is late stylization as it is active in the developing legends of the masters.

More beautiful and true than those superhuman exaggerated miracle workers and saints are the infinitely more lifelike figures of the disciples in the Gospels. In the former we find a parallel to the description of the disciples as seen in the Mahayana Sutras (I mention only the *Saddharma-Pundarika*, the Lotus of Good Religion). A later apology, which did not understand the importance of simplicity, believed that it must excuse its humanity. Compared to the simple account of Luke, how clumsy and inwardly untrue rings the report of the Acts of Peter, seeking to interpret the denial by Peter, explaining that "godless dogs" had duped him and lured him into a trap. The idea of "disciple" demands that the pure "humanness" be expressed. The Lord himself, according to the Acts of Peter, said in regard to the disciples: "*qui mecum sunt, non me intellexerunt*," We understand the deep necessity of this incomprehensibility (cf. also Luke 9:49 and 50). It is very possible that occasionally sorrow and bitterness came upon the master when he called to mind the human, all-too-human, nature of, those about him; but he knew that it could not be otherwise—and therefore was good. "I have yet many things to say to you," says the Christ of St. John, "but you cannot hear them now."

With an understanding gaze of love the master embraced these men who were permitted to share one destiny with him. He blessed their purely human nature; but in the pangs of his loneliness when thinking of the sacrifice, he felt their distance from him; he longed for their sympathy—which he could not have. There is no deeper, no more moving, illustration of this situation than the story of the struggle in Gethsemane as Matthew has given it to us. The master asks them: "Could you not watch with me one hour?" And then it reads: "and again he came and found them sleeping, for their eyes were heavy. And he left them and went away from them again and prayed. But the third time he called to them: 'The hour is at hand.'"

In the anticipation of his destiny the Lord spoke again and again about his suffering and the mystery of the sacrifice. "But they understood none of these things; this saying was hid from them, and they did not grasp what was said." All discipleship is blind. Beside the denial of Peter and the flight of the disciples at the capture stands the confession of Peter and the communion of the last supper. The magical and compelling appearance of the master is always for the disciple the last support and the highest challenge; therefore, the proud triumph and the deepest fall are always so close together. The master can do everything in order to acquaint the disciples with the mysteries of the teaching; but one thing he cannot do: he cannot produce the impetus for them, the stirring of the soul by which they will be free. For Socrates, the [midwifery] is the highest activity; the [engendering] belongs to God.

From this we learn a new tragic element in the life of the master—the knowledge that everyone has to walk the last stretch, the hardest way, alone; that he, who gives the best which he has to the men whom he loves, must leave them here—yes, even drive them away. The master takes upon himself that which is most difficult. No one is permitted to sense how difficult that is. The mysterious word of Mark sounds like an allusion to it: "Can you drink the cup which I drink? Can you be baptized with the baptism with which I am baptized?" The master waited for this impetus in the soul of the disciple. This is the interpretation of the mysterious relation between the Lord and the one who betrayed him, a silent understanding which is expressed in the imploring words of the master: "What you must do, do quickly." It belongs to the task which the chosen one undertakes in the hour of his call to keep this greatest difficulty secret. Bertram, in the chapter significantly called "Socrates" of his beautiful book on Nietzsche, also explores this problem with reference to his hero; he discusses the final silence which is laid upon the existence of the master; indeed he goes further and speaks of the deception involved.

This is a Greek twist, but it points out a feature in the life of all masters. The power of the example depends upon this deception, which is, in the deepest sense, instructive. It is the secret of his power to redeem. The nature of the world, the somber truth, is recognized—and banished. The sadness, which must overpower everyone who encounters it unarmed, is checked; a redemption is found. But no one must know how difficult the struggle was, or how deep the suffering: *Bis die Lasten der Lotse zuehll, die Leichen nicht mit* (Klopstock). There is something of deception, of a tender, careful deception, in this knowing kindness, in the melancholy wisdom which the disciple experiences with the master. As the profound word of the Lord proclaims it, which he says in the Acts of John to the favourite disciple: "What you are, you will see—that, I will show to you. But what I am, that alone I know, no one else. What is mine, let it be mine; but what is yours, receive through me!"

Also in this aspect, the master's existence makes a

demand; and as his whole existence is only the progressive manifestation of a deep and mysterious tragedy, there is no "master-figure" which does not disclose this in both large and small respects—this demand is dialectical from the very beginning. It is the master's will to draw close to himself and rise above himself.

Therefore he demands the self-delivery of the disciple: the sacrifice of the body, of the spirit, of all his possessions. He guides him on the way; he is—here we see the transition to the teacher, indeed to the mystagogue and head of a school—the leader, the father, the rescuer. In this sharply defined characteristic we understand the relationship in the ancient mysteries, in Sufistic union, and in the Hindu, especially Shivaistic, *guru*-practice.

The (father), the sheik, the *guru*, the zaddick: as a guide of souls, as a door to salvation, they demand the complete devotedness of the disciple, of the "son." The Murid is the son of the sheik, which signifies here more than a simple simile: "As the body is conceived in the womb of the mother through the father's seed"—so it reads according to Ibn Arabi—"so also with the heart in a spiritual birth." The spirit of the Murid is conceived in the womb of his soul, through the "in-breathing" of the sheik. It is at this birth that Isa—Jesus—was aiming with the phrase: "He who is not born twice will not enter the kingdom of heaven." The Murid must obey his spiritual father *perinde ac cadaver* [as through the body]. "The true disciple," says Dhu'n Nun, "must obey his master more than God himself."

However, here we immediately meet that other dimension: the master points not only to himself; he also directs the disciple away from himself. We think of Socrates, whose harsh and severe method of wonderfully invigorating irony provides a beautiful example of the effect on his disciple, whereby he directs the disciple away from himself and to the disciple himself. This is evident also when in the activity of Buddha's instructing the disciples, a strict distance is kept which seems to deny the later interpretation which the members of the "Great Church" were inclined to apply to the master. How otherwise are we to understand the synoptic accounts of the majestic authoritative words of Jesus: "Why do you call me good? No one is good but God alone"; even unto the requirement of faith, which implies the highest spontaneity and activity of the soul.

Up to now our investigation has led to the consideration of the relation between master and disciple with special regard to the life of the master. We will now point out the two great possibilities which a master can realize. As the most significant historical expression of these possibilities, one might, on the one hand, consider the ancient Greek master of the Empedocles-Socrates type and, on the other, the master of the Gospels who perhaps remains the most sublime example.

Søren Kierkegaard has seen the precise difference more clearly than anyone else and expressed it with the eloquence and depth peculiar to him in his Philosophical Fragments. It is preceded by the motto: Is a historical point of departure possible for an eternal consciousness? How can such a point of departure have any other than a mere historical interest?

Is it possible to base eternal happiness upon historical knowledge? The figure of the master lives in the heart of the disciples. So long as he dwells in their midst, the image grows and takes on form. Through this image each disciple is able to focus his own experience, which is enriched stroke by stroke from a living centre. This growth occurs according to the law and rhythm of the natural reciprocal influence and the dynamic of the relation between man and man. With the exhaustion of the living fount, the process of the formation does not stop; but along with this continuing process, from now on, a petrification occurs under a different law of construction. Imagination and personal experience are replaced by productive fantasy, which continues to shape the further development of the image. The magical circle of individual life is broken through. In the interchange of dialogue and in the proclamation it becomes expanded.

The "objective" character of the image, its social reception, demonstrates that it is on the way to becoming myth. With its reception it is modified in new ways: just as the individuality of the disciples was decisive for the selection, combination, and elaboration of the objective facts, so now the same conditions are effective in the contribution which everyone who seeks to perpetuate the image makes to its alteration.

Love and hate shape it. Continually, this image is active, and out of its action it receives a new splendour. The enemies continually oppose it and produce thereby the "black myth," the opposite to the glorification. Jesus is a son of the Devil according to Mandaren. Schools and factions are built. The basic reason for the separation and union of adherents is the nature of the image of the master which lives in the heart. In addition to these, in a strict psychological factor, objective factors operate: tradition, inertia, assimilation, deterioration, etc. All the combining factors which are necessarily connected with the verbal and written formulation—the misunderstanding and new meaning, interpretation and stylization—enter in.

Let us illustrate this by recalling the variation, the characteristic similarities and differences of the images of Jesus according to Matthew, Mark, Luke, and John. How decisive for Paul's image of Jesus—besides the individuality of Paul—is the fact that he is a "disciple at second hand"! Is it necessary to remind one's self of the memorable example of the Platonic and Xenophonic Socrates?

Not only do the individualities influence the change of the images; it would be an important problem of the philosophy of history in the study of the history of religions to search out the influences, the categories, through which a precise "relative a priori"—to use Simmel's expression—acts upon the shaping of the "images": national, tribal, race, class, sexmembership. The wise Buddha becomes the world-savior of Mahayana, the Japanese Amitabha, the Chinese Fo; the Christ of Aryan Christians is certainly a different one from him who belongs to Syrian or Egyptian Gnosticism.

Rules always govern the change of these images. Certain basic elements persist; certain features are drawn more heavily here or there. From the history of the portrayals of Christ we can perceive the fluctuation of rationalistic and mystical, worldly and eschatological, theomorphic and anthropomorphic conceptions. But all these are later speculations which presuppose the myth upon which they act in an expanding, deepening, enlarging manner and whose change they influence.

Decisive, on the one hand, is the history of the origin of the myth; it falls into the period which circumscribes the first attempt at fixing the image, on the other. Here, again, the first appearance of the disciple-at-secondhand, the follower, marks the division of the "original" fellowship from later times. To a certain degree, the first experience always remains esoteric; with the arrival and solicitation of followers, the esoteric experience becomes more or less an exoteric event. At the time of the first written formulation, however, something entirely new—a minimum criterion, so to speak—is created, to which the most daring allegories and stories, the most addicted to miracles and fantasy, must still have to conform through danger of being expelled. From here on the distinction of historical and unhistorical becomes important—a distinction which in a second stage becomes identified, emphasized, and limited by the canonical and non-canonical. We observe a similar development in the artistic portrayal, the gradual evolution of a canonical type, which always showed a differentiation effected by relative a priori as to race, epoch, country, etcetera.

The disciple's experience of the master is a social one; however much it may be differentiated in other respects, it is a form of social experience. It exhibits the laws of communities as such. The corresponding sociological category is the group (der Bund), as we lately have been so beautifully shown. Certain attitudes which determine the action of the members of this circle either for or against one another are applicable only out of a background of communal character. The movements of the members of the circle toward or away from one another find their meaning only in the meaning of the group. Such were the relations of the disciples as told by Mark and Luke, which have wrongly been interpreted solely as a shameful competition for supremacy.

The realization of the outward constitution of this association here—be it loose or very strict—is unimportant. There will always be disciples who are closer to the master than all others, as were John and Ananda and the witnesses of Jesus' transfiguration or his last struggle. And around the smaller and smallest circle there will be another one. On a higher level the circle has the same double meaning for the master as for the disciple; it represents humanity, and it is the union of friends in which the master, finds the comfort and strength which allows the lonely one to experience human fellowship. The circle is the supporting and nourishing ground out of which everyone who belongs gains his strength; it is the concrete revelation of the "power" of the master. Attracted by this power, moved by it, and defined through it, the disciples assemble in a circle around the master; followers and helpers assemble in ever wider circles. This is the power of which Goethe spoke when he said that God continually remains active in higher nature in order to draw the inferior near unto himself.

2

Christian Ethics and Culture

We come now in this concluding chapter to some observations about the relations of the Christian ethic to our total environing society. Had our approach been essentially empirical rather than theological and biblical, this chapter should have stood first in the book. However, it may help to draw together various threads, as well as to state some things not heretofore discussed, if we consider this theme last.

The procedure will be first to define the term, for culture is an unusually slippery and ambiguous term, and to outline the nature of the problems. Then we must look, as we have done in other chapters, at the biblical and theological foundations for their solution. The chapter will conclude with a look at some of the concrete contemporary issues involved in the fields of science, art, and education.

What is Culture?

The word "culture" has two meanings, not sharply separated but not identical, and we shall have to consider both of them. Both present difficulties and opportunities for the Christian approach to life.

In the broader meaning of the term, culture is synonymous with civilization. Every people has its culture, whether primitive or advanced, and this culture is discerned in the folkways and moral standards, forms of family life, economic enterprises, laws and modes of dealing with lawbreakers, forms of recreation, religion, art, education, science, and philosophy that constitute the social aspects of human existence as contrasted with the bare biological fact of living.

There is, however, a narrower use of the term which is related to but not identical with this inclusive meaning. In ordinary speech, who is a cultured person? By what canons does one judge another to be uncultured? Superficially but with widespread potency, one's degree of culture is judged by his manners and conformity to correct social usage, good taste in dress and appearance, cleanliness and freedom from offensive odours or habits, ability to converse agreeably and to fit smoothly into any social situation. If a person is cultured, he is not a boor! On a deeper level, one's degree of culture is to be judged by the extent of his education, the breadth of his interests, and his knowledge and appreciation of such "cultural" pursuits as good art, literature, and music.

Culture in this second sense has many manifestations, but all converge to constitute the secularism of the modern world. Social conformity plays a major part in it, even though at the point of education and the arts the right of individual differentiation is recognized. Culture in this more limited sense, as defined by the attributes of a cultured person, is an important formative factor in the total culture of a people but cannot be identified with it. For example, the prophet Amos was an uncultured person by the standards of either his time or ours, yet an important contributor to Hebrew culture. Abraham Lincoln is lauded in the American tradition because from such a lowly and uncultured background he rose to such heights of greatness.

In whichever sense the word "culture" is used, it is a distinctly human phenomenon. There is nothing like it in the instinctual organization of the anthill or beehive or in the gregarious impulses of animal life. Though its roots may indeed be traced to defensive, acquisitive, or reproductive traits which the human shares with the subhuman world, its manifestations are very different. Only men form civilizations, and only men insist on adaptation to the patterns of the cultural community.

It is always a social phenomenon. This is self-evident from the definitions given. Individuals may conform to or reject the prevailing social patterns, and thereby shape the direction a culture takes. But this never happens except in response to a social situation.

It is, furthermore, always in some measure a spiritual phenomenon. This does not mean that it is always a direct outgrowth of religion, though religions are always to be found in interplay with culture. Rather, every culture is the product of the human spirit, as the spirit of man wrestles with its total environment and seeks to work out a satisfactory adjustment to the material world, to other men, and to such invisible powers as are believed to control its destiny.

It is always rooted in a concern for values. That is, every culture presupposes in some sense a "kingdom of ends." These ends may be high or low by other standards, but to the people who live within a given culture, prize it and seek to preserve and exalt it, they are always high.

There may be room for differences of individual opinion, as democracy preserves the right of minority dissent, but no culture can endure without general support by its people of the values central to it. This is why patriotism and group loyalty, though subject to perversion, not only are but ought to be regarded as virtues of great worth.

Is culture an "order of creation"? The existence of culture as a whole may be so regarded. The framework within which cultures develop is God-given, as are the foundations of family, economic, and national life which constitute so large a part of any civilization. It is apparently the will of God that men live together in civilized societies. Yet this is far from saying that any particular society or cultural group is as God would have it, or wholly the product of divine activity. The particular form a culture takes is the product of many forces, in which geographical location, economic resources, historical contingency, the pull of tradition, and voluntary human effort all play a part. This fact, with the resulting intermixtures of good and evil, is clearly illustrated by differing attitudes toward racial segregation in the North and South of the United States, or the presence of nontheological social factors in the creation of the various denominations of the Christian Church.

A culture, even one of long duration, is modifiable by human effort under the impact of a new ideology — witness the radical transformation of China under Communist influence or the other revolutionary changes now taking place in the Orient from an emergent nationalism. This malleability is what makes both advance and decline in civilizations possible. Yet there is always a "raw material" of culture which no amount of human effort can erase. The eternal human problem, as man seeks to change his status and that of his group, is how to deal with the intransigence of nature and the inviolability of the divine order in that interlocking structure of natural, human, and divine forces which Constitutes a given culture.

The Christian faith must come to terms with culture in both the senses in which I have defined it, and with full regard for all these considerations as to the nature of culture. Because there is so much in Western civilization that is good, and that can be and ought to be made better, it would be fatal to withdraw in isolation from it or condemn it as wholly evil. Nevertheless, the perennial problem of the Christian is how to be a Christian within "the world," that is, within one's total environing society. When this surrounding culture is at the same time "worldly" — cultured in the narrower sense, demanding conformity at the peril of loss of social status — the problem is intensified. The American Christian of today lives in a nominally Christian but largely worldly culture. What shall he do with it?

Biblical and Theological Foundations

The Bible as a whole is the record of man's effort to conform to, and to transform, his culture under the impact of spiritual insights conceived to be God-given. That these were in so large measure actually God-inspired is what gives the Bible its "holy" character as the bearer of universal and timeless truth. Yet at every point it must be read in reference to the culture within which it emerged, so that its "situation-conditioned" and temporal elements may be seen in their true perspective. To disregard this surrounding culture is to nullify much of the Bible's spiritual meaning by reading into it what is not there but is imputed to it from the thought patterns of a different day.

We cannot at this point go into the whole matter of the relation of the Bible to its cultural setting. This was attempted in its main elements in Chapters 2, 3, and 4. But a further word is needed as to the relations of Jesus both to his own culture and to culture in general.

It has often been charged that by focusing attention away from "the world" to God, the kingdom of heaven, and eternal life, Jesus introduced an ascetic and otherworldly element that nullifies human culture. The Jewish scholar Joseph Klausner, for example, holds that the Pharisees and Sadducees were justified in their attacks on Jesus because he imperiled Jewish culture at its foundations, and that by ignoring everything that belongs to wholesome social life he undercut the work of centuries.

Others within the Christian tradition have felt considerable uneasiness lest the words of Jesus about nonresistance imperil the civil power of the State, or his words about having no anxiety for food or drink or other material possessions curtail an economic motivation essential to society. Sometimes in direct attack, as in the Roman persecutions of early centuries and the Nazi and Communist movements of our time, sometimes through sneers and the opposition of hostile public opinion, Christianity has had to defend itself against those who believed the false or utopian ideas of its founder to be dangerous. This opposition has been most overtly urged on political but often on intellectual grounds, and Schleiermacher's defence of Christian faith against its "cultured despisers" is a procedure that has again and again proved necessary.

This struggle to coordinate Christian faith with culture is not temporary but has lasted through twenty centuries of Christian history. The fullest and most accurate analysis of it is found in H. Richard Niebuhr's *Christ and Culture,* which any reader will do well to consult. There he points out that the answers given have taken five main directions:

Christ in opposition to culture, Christ in accommodation to culture, Christ as transcending culture but with some elements of synthesis, Christ in paradoxical relation to culture, and Christ as the transformer of culture. He also says wisely that "when one returns from the hypothetical scheme to the rich complexity of individual events, it is evident at once that no person or group ever conforms completely to a type." I shall attempt to outline a view which follows most closely the third and fifth of these types, but adopts none of them in entirety.

It is true that Jesus said little about "the world" except to warn against letting its claims usurp the place of first loyalty to God, and had almost nothing to say about particular features of contemporary Jewish or Roman culture. Nevertheless, the message of Jesus has vital relevance, in elements which have been pointed out in all the preceding chapters. It bears upon the world to challenge culture at some points, to encourage it at others, to transform it at many. This is so for these reasons:

> *In the first place, Jesus' supreme concern was with persons, not in any humanistic sense of man's self-sufficiency, but because persons are of supreme worth as the recipients of God's love. Moreover, he cared about persons in their total bodily-spiritual unity, and with their life on earth as well as in heaven. Both his deeds of healing and his words repeatedly attest this fact. Whatever impulse his followers have had to labour for the amelioration of human life in ministering to the sick, the weak and helpless, the ignorant, the poverty-stricken, the imprisoned by any kind of chains, owes its primary origin to the love of God for persons as this was manifest in Jesus.*

Cultures are of many types, and some have much and

others little concern for the individual person. Yet as we noted, every culture is a human, social, and spiritual thing in which the values precious to the persons comprising it are exalted. Those cultures which approximate the view of Jesus as to the worth of every person are high cultures, democratic in political organization, peace-minded in international outlook, altruistic toward those in need, person-centred in education and a wide range of social services. These are the goals of a Christian civilization, imperfectly realized, to be sure, in any society but sufficiently manifest in Europe and America to make it evident that a Christian democracy is not merely a utopian dream.

Second, Jesus called his followers to faith, hope, and love. This particular conjunction of terms is Paul's, but what they signify abounds everywhere in the message of Jesus. And these are very important foundations for the stabilization or the progress of any culture. With faith in God people can endure dark days, even the jeopardy of their nation or personal martyrdom, and know that all is not lost and their cause is not in vain.

With hope for the future, not in any illusory "progress of mankind onward and upward forever," but in the confidence that the issues for time and eternity are in the hands of God, remarkable staying power is generated even in the midst of what appears to be social retrogression. With love as a basic conviction, not even the awful carnage of war can wholly erase human sensitivity, and foundations remain for building in love beyond it. Every age has had need of these qualities, but ours more than most has cried out for them as indispensable. "In God we trust" has taken on new relevance in the darkness of our times.

Third, Jesus called his followers to challenge evil and to transform the world. It is impossible to say precisely what Western civilization would have been like without the influence of Jesus, but it most certainly would have taken a very different course. Few would question the judgment of H. G. Wells, "His is easily the dominant figure of history.... A historian... without any theological bias whatever, should find that he simply cannot portray the progress of humanity honestly without giving a foremost place to a penniless teacher from Nazareth." Cultures, even with all their values which their people do well to prize, need to be challenged and transformed through the influence of Jesus as this is mediated through his followers in every age.

More than once this has happened through the work of a devoted and persistent minority when the Church as a whole, enmeshed as a social institution in its surrounding culture, lagged behind. This happened with reference to the abolition of human slavery, and it is happening now in regard to race discrimination and war. Often this comes about in conjunction with other agencies, as in the factory legislation which has made obsolete the twelve-hour day and the seven-day week, established minimum wage levels, and eliminated the grosser forms of economic exploitation.

New evils emerge, and these too must be challenged with wisdom and patience. New forms of work, of recreation, and of social organization bring both opportunities and perils to the human spirit. Both intelligence and persistence are required to cope with these problems, and the use of the best types of secular knowledge in a Christian framework, as in the growing convergence of Christian faith with psychotherapy in pastoral counselling. Christians in many matters must act with others outside the Christian fellowship. Where political action is required, it is not often that Christians alone bring it to pass. Yet Christians who keep witnessing to their convictions and thereby molding opinion contribute vitally to the fashioning of a better society.

In view of these facts, it cannot justly be said that either the message of Jesus or the Christian ethic derived primarily from Jesus is irrelevant to culture. In fact, nothing else is so relevant to the preservation and growth of right social attitudes, and from these attitudes the establishment of the "good society."

Science, Art and Education

At the beginning of this chapter I defined culture first as synonymous with civilization, and then in a narrower context. What has been said so far applies chiefly to its broader meaning.

Previous chapters in the book have dealt with the relations of Christian ethics to the culture of our times in reference to family life, economic relations, race relations, political structures, and the problems of war and peace in the international scene. These issues cover a large part of the terrain of culture in the inclusive meaning of the term. Certain other issues, however, need to be looked at both to round out this picture and to point up some special aspects of culture in the narrower connotation.

It is not necessary to say much about culture in the sense of "polish" or good manners, except that this is an important asset to Christian character and a dangerous substitute for it. Nobody ought to suppose that conformity to the accepted canons of good taste is inconsequential, for disregard of such niceties limits seriously one's acceptability to others and hence the persuasiveness of one's witness. But neither ought one to suppose that suavity and a superficial politeness are all that is needed. True politeness comes from the heart, in sensitivity to the feelings of others and adaptability to their need. The more vital one's own Christian experience and love of people, the more naturally will he reach out to them with a tact and gentleness no superficial good breeding can generate. No veneer of soft and pleasing words can ever take the place of Christian depth of character.

The major issues with regard to the cultured person are at a higher level, and are epitomized in his attitudes toward science, art, and education. At each of these we must look briefly as the book is brought to a close.

(a) *Science:* It is most unfortunate, though not surprising, that there has been such a long battle between science and the Christian faith. It is unfortunate because the exponents of each have had to expend energy needed for other things in defending their position against the assaults of the opposing group. In this process neither has lost the battle, as is evident from the vigour of both at the present time. Nevertheless, at specific points such as the time and manner of creation and the expectancy of divine intervention in an established order, the defenders of traditional Christian belief have had to make more adjustments than have the exponents of the scientific spirit. This is not to say that science has remained unchanged — it obviously has not — but only that its course has been affected less by Christian belief than the reverse.

This is natural, and not to be deplored if these two great interests of the human spirit are kept in proper coordination. Both are modes of the pursuit of truth about one world, God's world, and therefore to the degree that their affirmations are true, they cannot contradict each other. Science, however, is a partial, objective attempt to discover facts about the empirical aspects of existence;

Christian faith is an inclusive, committed approach to the totality of life's meaning as this comes to us through the revelation of God in Jesus Christ. The modifications in Christian belief above referred to in no sense discredit this revelation; they are modifications only in man's interpretation of it, and in particular, they arise from new ways of looking at the Bible as this is seen in its historical, prescientific setting.

Though science has reached phenomenal heights in our time, it has at no point invalidated anything basic to Christian faith, and at no time in human history has the revelation of God in Christ shone upon the human scene with greater clarity and power. There have been more obviously religious eras, as in the medieval "age of faith" or the periods of the great revivals under Jonathan Edwards or Dwight L. Moody; it is doubtful that there has ever been a period of such general high Christian intelligence or deep commitment to Christian social ethics as in our own time.

This can be said in spite of the fact that it must also be said that secularism is a very widespread phenomenon of our culture, and secularism means conformity to the world, the organization of life as if God did not exist. How, then, shall we sort out the strands with reference to science and the Christian faith?

Science is the pursuit of truth in any particular field of observable reality, and the attempt to discover facts and formulate the laws of structure and behaviour within this area. This pursuit, when an adjective is needed, is designated as pure science or descriptive science. There is, however, another use of the term to cover the application of scientific discovery to the satisfaction of human wants. This is applied science, with a meeting point in the research laboratories of most of the great industries.

Applied science is sometimes called technics, but since it covers also a vast range of studies affecting human life, as in nutrition and dietetics, medicine and surgery, psychiatry, pedagogy, geriatrics, social casework, penology, and the like, it is hardly accurate to classify all of these under the heading of technology. Whatever terminology is used, science cannot be fruitfully discussed unless we know whether we are talking about the quest for knowledge in objective detachment from personal interest, or an attempt to make hydrogen bombs, bigger and better automobiles, wonder drugs, or a million gadgets because men desire them to satisfy some real or fancied need.

Both types of science have their relations to Christian faith within our culture, but these are not the same relations.

Science as the quest for knowledge, for reasons suggested above, cannot contradict the Christian faith if it keeps to its own field of inquiry about the visible, tangible, experienced world. What it does is simply to shed new light upon the world created by God, and upon the orderly processes by which Cod works within his world. The evidence for biological evolution can contradict belief in a six-day creation, but not in God the Creator; astronomy can put an end to belief in a heaven "up in the sky," but not to eternal life; knowledge of the regularities of nature can recast interpretation of some of the biblical miracles, but it cannot eliminate belief in divine Providence or discredit grateful reverence before God's wonderful works.

It is only when descriptive science grows arrogant, and, not content with describing what lies within its province, makes naturalistic pronouncements which eliminate or belittle God and the human spirit, that Christian faith is affronted. When science claims that its methods and its knowledge are the only methods and knowledge to be trusted, it becomes not science but "scientism." Scientism and its usual accompaniment, scientific humanism, are serious rivals of Christian faith in the modern world. This point of view flourishes on many university campuses, and not infrequently sucks the vigour out of Christian experience by undercutting its foundations. Where this happens, the culture accompanying it may be kindly, law-abiding, and even altruistic, but it is not Christian culture.

It is at the point of the applied sciences that the more widespread and the more formidable attack on Christian ethics and culture can be found. This is true in spite of the fact that the products of applied science have been instruments of great good in physical healing, improvement of living conditions, and social services of many types, in which the Christian believes that it is the will of God for persons to be helped. Furthermore, from the invention of the printing press to the wide use of radio and television, from sailing schooner to ever-faster airplanes, the applied sciences have been essential instruments in the spread of Christian witness. Some things viewed formerly as luxuries, such as telephones, automobiles, electric lighting, and refrigeration, are now so common in the Western world as to seem virtually necessities, and none would wish to do without them.

Yet, it is just at this point that idolatry becomes dominant in our culture. Partly because of a real need for what technology supplies, more because of artificial wants aroused through a constant, competitive barrage of advertising, modern man's attention is inevitably focused on the things science produces and money can buy.

To live simply, unconcerned for the "cares of the world and the delight in riches," which Jesus said so often choke the word (Matt. 13:22; Mark 4:19), has become a possibility only for the stanchest soul. Most men feel that they must "lay up... treasures on earth," or they and their families cannot have the things other people have and all want. As a consequence, the word is choked, and Christian witness persuasive to a thing-centred and hence idolatrous generation becomes very difficult.

Here, then, is the real point at issue between science and Christian ethics within our culture. There are other points of great seriousness, as in the widespread production and advertising of alcoholic beverages and hence the encouragement given to their consumption, and in the doubtful validity of the production of implements of atomic destruction.

The Christian conscience needs to be aroused and active upon these points, and because the issues are concrete, people are apt to take sides upon them. We are prone, however, to be far more lethargic at the point of our gadget-minded culture, not even recognizing that a moral issue is involved. It is here perhaps that our greatest difficulties lie, for we cannot revert to the pattern of the penniless teacher of Nazareth, and we cannot follow him in opulence without major temptations to the soul.

(b) *Art:* A second sphere in which the claims of Christ and of culture both converge and diverge is art. This is a broad term, but we shall use it to designate the expression of the human aesthetic impulse, in both the creation of works of beauty and a love for and appreciation of beauty. Only the genius creates true art, and there are few geniuses in any generation, but many can enjoy and be lifted in spirit by their work.

There is a secondary sense in which we must speak of art also as craftsmanship, the work of a skilled artisan, to satisfy a desire for that harmonious blending of line and colour and texture that makes a commercial product attractive, or gives one pride in the ability to construct something. This is related to art in the deeper aesthetic sense much as applied science is related to pure science, as based upon its principles but produced for another reason and with a different kind of creativity. Just where to draw the line between the artist and the craftsman is not easy, but it must be drawn. So, as we speak of the relations of art to Christian culture, we must again speak in two categories.

There is a natural kinship between art in the first sense and religion, yet each has its own autonomous sphere. Both come out of the inner spirit of man and speak to that spirit for release, reinforcement, and challenge. In both there are "new eyes for invisibles," and the "vision of something which stands beyond, behind, and within the passing flux of immediate things." Whether or not divine inspiration is claimed by the artist, in his work he surrenders to something beyond his ordinary self and produces some expression of inner meaning capable of evoking purer feelings in those to whom he communicates.

"In any case, whether it be in poetry, painting or music, the work of art is the expression of something inward, passing on that inwardness to the one who enjoys it. Art, therefore, in all its branches, is expression capable of impressing." The artist need not of necessity be a religious person, or the religious person an artist. Yet so similar are the sources in the human spirit that through all ages, and not in Christianity alone, the worship of God has found natural expression in music and song, poetry and the graphic arts, the drama of sacrificial rites, and where not inhibited by convention, the dance. Man has always given to his deity, not only gifts laid upon the altar, but the gift of his soul in temples of great beauty and rituals of soul-stirring depth. What Christianity would have been like without its great hymns and oratorios, the poetry of the Bible, the time-transcending liturgies of the sacraments, and the distinctive beauty of Christian houses of worship is hard to contemplate.

Yet at this point two aberrations appear from opposite directions. One is the suspicion of art at some periods because of the prohibition of "graven images," and the rejection not only of painting and sculpture but of instrumental music as worldly and idolatrous. Fortunately, this has never been a dominant note in Christian practice, and is seldom encountered today. There are vestiges of it in the rejection by some of liturgies and any formal patterns of worship as inhibiting the work of the Holy Spirit, but the rejection is seldom made on the basis of the Second Commandment.

The other, very widely prevalent, aberration is the substitution of beauty for holiness. Again and again the quality of a service of worship is judged by the kind of music the choir renders, the aesthetic fitness of the minister's voice or vestments or manner, the beauty or ugliness of the sanctuary, the general decorum with which everything is done. That at all of these points there ought to be "comely praise" is indisputable, but that any or all of them is a guarantee of or a substitute for the presence of the Spirit of God must be questioned.

Ours is in general a beauty-loving age. Music appreciation is taught in the public schools; much good music and other forms of art are readily available. This is as it should be, but when it is carried so far in our culture that beauty becomes a substitute for righteousness and churches are bypassed unless they appeal to the aesthetic, this accent on beauty is not wholly gain. A word needs to be said about art in the second sense, which like the products of applied science to which it is closely related, is a dominant note in our culture. It is well that the things we possess, from automobiles to kitchen equipment, are made for beauty as well as efficiency. No people in any age ever had so much that was good-looking as well as useful.

Yet this too has another side, for there is much that is raucous and blatant. There is a bizarre element in contemporary taste which corresponds to, and probably at bottom is derived from, the nervous, jittery temper of our times. One has only to turn on his radio or television — our best indexes of "what the people like"—to discover how much is directed to the amusing or lulling or startling of jaded nerves, as the commercials that accompany such presentations pull at our purses and entice us to buy what we do not need.

It will not do for Christians simply to inveigh against this state of affairs. Not all of it is bad, and what is bad cannot be cured simply by complaint. But until tastes as well as moral acts are subject to the spirit of Christ, we shall not make our best use of the high potentialities for beauty in the modem age.

(c) *Education:* Education is so vast and many-sided an enterprise that it will obviously be impossible at this point to make more than a few observations upon it. It is fundamental to any culture, for the form a culture takes is shaped mainly by the way in which the people are moulded in the educative process.

The processes of education are, of course, much broader than the specific instruction given in the public or private schools or the universities. It is a truism that the home is the first, and often the most potent, educative influence. From early childhood to senility, the play group, the work group, and many other types of informal group association are moulding attitudes. V/hat one reads, hears, sees, or otherwise experiences leaves in varying degrees its stamp upon both consciousness and conscience. Not all of this is educative in the sense of constructive growth; some of it promotes miseducation or retrogression. Yet in the broad sense in which education means the shaping of ideas and ideals, it never ends as long as any mental flexibility remains.

The institution devoted essentially to education is the school. What, then, are basic points at issue between the schools and Christian ethics?

That Christian education must be given in the churches and through church schools, if the Christian heritage is adequately to be transmitted, can be taken for granted without argument. Whether under the name of church school or Sunday school, this is indispensable. In general, the quality of both curriculum and instruction is much better than in former years. Three observations only I shall make in passing. First, that the time available on Sunday morning is totally inadequate for transmitting all that is vital to knowledge of the Bible and Christian faith. Second, that what is taught must not conflict with the accepted facts of science, or the pupil is bound to be in trouble as he senses the disparity. Third, that much more theology can and should be taught at every level as the undergirding foundation of Christianity.

This last point, in particular, requires far more attention than it has generally received. To teach the Bible as factual knowledge is better than not to teach it at all, but without attention to both its historical setting and its theological implications, its richness for Christian experience can be missed. Too frequently the attempt is made to teach Christian morality without foundations other than the ordinary assumptions of our culture. When a person does not know what he believes as a Christian or why he believes it — and this is true of many adults as well as of young people — he is likely to act on the assumptions of this secular culture and not on the principles of Christian faith. But what of religion in the public schools? Can we teach the Bible there? Or must we as in the past go on permitting an intellectual vacuum to exist at the point of the Judeo-Christian heritage which has done more than anything else to shape our culture? Shall we teach our children Homer and Vergil, Shakespeare and Milton, but not the words of Amos, Isaiah, Jesus, or Paul?

It is apparent that sectarian instruction cannot be given in the public schools, and that no proselyting activities can be permitted. Since it is not easy to draw the line between proselyting and evangelism, it may also be asserted that no teacher ought to evangelize for his faith in the classroom except through the silent witness of what he (or she) as a Christian is. But this does not necessitate the alternative of the religious and biblical vacuum.

It is commonly assumed that our Constitution guarantees the separation of Church and State, and this has been invoked repeatedly to ban all forms of religious instruction from the public schools. Yet this is not just what the Constitution says. The relevant article is the First Amendment, which reads: "Article I. Congress shall make no law respecting an establishment of religion, or prohibiting the free exercise thereof...The Constitution prohibits the establishment of a State church and guarantees religious freedom in the exercise of one's fa

Yet it does not prohibit the tax exemption of churches, or the employment by the federal government of chaplains for the armed forces.

It does not prohibit the giving of nonsectarian courses in religion for academic credit in the state universities, and this is widely and increasingly being done. America is not a Godless nation. We place upon our coins "In God we trust," and by an official act of Congress the words "under God" have been placed in the salute to the American flag. Those who framed the Constitution apparently intended, rightly, to preserve freedom of religion. But that this should be interpreted as freedom *from* religion, and used as a means of sealing our culture against the imparting of religious knowledge, has no justification in fact.

What must be done is to keep insisting on the right to teach the Bible as history and as literature in the public schools until this not only is permitted but becomes as widely practiced there as in the state universities. Presumably, as in higher education, this needs to be on an elective basis to avoid infringement of religious freedom. However, the real issues lie (1) in the opportunity to teach religion at all, and (2) in the provision of persons properly qualified to teach it on a nonsectarian basis. For the present, the Supreme Court decision in the McCollum case of 1948 interposes barriers, but this need not be final. In the meantime, the churches should seize every opportunity to give weekday religious instruction on released time outside the public schools.

Ought public funds to be used to aid parochial schools? Ought public money to go to a church to pay for the services of its nuns as public-school teachers? The answer is No, though this need not be pushed to the lengths of denying such services to the children in parochial schools as rides in school buses or access to school lunches. Services to children or their parents are not identical in principle with grants to churches as ecclesiastical institutions. About the former, opinions differ; the latter must not be tolerated.

To return to the public schools, a less controversial but still a focal matter is the teaching of moral and spiritual values. This obviously needs to be done, but it is no substitute for more specific instruction in the Hebrew-Christian moral and spiritual heritage. It is essential that teachers who take seriously their obligations in character building should be protected from attack from those who cannot distinguish between democracy and subversion. Charges of indoctrination are too often levelled at those who try to lift the sights of their pupils above prevailing culture patterns, and thus the mediocrity born of fear stifles creativity and progress.

There is remaining space in this chapter only for a brief look at the relations of Christian culture to higher education. Here the same opportunities for moral and spiritual building and the same dangers to academic freedom are found as are suggested in the preceding paragraph. Yet the situation as a whole differs both in the general recognition of the right of religion to a place in the curriculum and in the existence of many church-supported and independent as well as state institutions.

The first observation to be made is that the church-related colleges, of which many were founded in the early days of the frontier, can justify their existence only by being distinctively Christian. Through their departments of religion, in the selection of Christian faculty members, and by their general atmosphere they have an important contribution to make. When a church college seeking prestige or financial support simply imitates its secular neighbours, it has lost its birthright. Standards of scholarship ought not to be lowered, but scholarship is not all that makes a training ground for the leaders of the future.

Second, much can be done on campuses not church-related. As it is the total environment that educates, so it is the total personality of a faculty member, not his presentation of specialized subject matter only, that determines the degree of Christian influence he exerts. It is a hopeful sign that responsibility in these matters by faculty persons outside the departments of religion is being increasingly recognized. The Hazen and the Danforth Foundations have done much to encourage such interest, and the Faculty Christian Fellowshipmerits warm support.

Third, the student must be kept in touch with the church during his college years. The student foundations, like the Wesley, the Westminster, and those of other denominations, are valuable links in keeping alive both church contacts and Christian service at a time when preoccupation with the multitude of other interests pressing for attention might leave the church far in the rear.

And finally, Christian theology — first, last, and always — is important. Moral standards rest on basic beliefs, and the moral standards prevalent in the culture of the future will rest in no small degree on those implicitly accepted or consciously formed during the college years.

The intellectual climate of institutions of higher learning is apparently less naturalistic and humanistic than a decade or two ago, but where this mood still is found, the counterclaims of Christian faith must be persuasively though never dogmatically set forth. As both the numbers and the influence of college-trained persons within our culture increase, so does the vital need of having the right foundations laid within those years in which not only life attitudes, but vocational and family relations, are so often determined.

Here we must stop. The unknown author of the *Epistle to Diognetus,* writing in the second century AD, said of the Christians of his time. They spend their existence upon earth, but their citizenship is in heaven. They obey the established laws, but in their own lives they surpass the laws... In a word, what the soul is in the body Christians are in the world... The soul is enclosed in the body, and itself holds the body together; so too Christians are held fast in the world as in a prison, yet it is they who hold the world together.

So it is today. To the degree there are vital Christians in any culture that culture is strong in inner fabric and high in possibilities for human good. Christians who really follow Christ "hold the world together"!

3

Christian Ethics and Moral Philosophy

The keynote in the life and teaching of Jesus with regard to man's moral duty is found in "obedient love." This means that with faith in God as the energizing centre of one's being, one is required to seek to do the will of God by loving God supremely and one's neighbour as one's self. However, as the total impact of Jesus' teaching makes evident, to love one's neighbour as one's self is not to be understood as any precise balancing and equating of love for others with self-love. Still less does it mean loving others for the sake of receiving love or other benefits in return. Agape love means, rather, an uncalculating, outgoing spirit of loving concern which finds expression in deeds of service without limit.

Such "obedient love" is defined for us in the Gospels less by specific statements than by the whole tenor of Jesus' ministry, culminating in his own death upon the cross in fidelity to it. Yet it is implied throughout his recorded words from the Sermon on the Mount to the Last Supper discourse. It is basic to his central teaching, the obligation to "seek first his [God's] kingdom and his righteousness." Its supremacy over any ordinary love comes to clear expression in the words:

> *For if you love those who love you, what reward have you? Do not even the tax collectors do the same? And if you salute only your brethren, what more are you doing than others? Do not even the Gentiles do the same? You, therefore, must be perfect, as your heavenly Father is perfect. (Matt. 5:46-48.)*

How does this differ from the focus of reference in the various systems of classical moral philosophy? Though this is not the place for an extended exposition of them, even a casual glance may suggest that there are both affinities and differences. Platonic thought makes much of eros, and eros means love. Yet agape love, and Bishop Nygren has shown this at length in his now classic *Agape and Eros*, is not the same thing as eros. Eros (which must not be confused with its modern derivative, "the erotic') means a quest for the highest values, the harmonious adjustment of personality in a well-rounded life, self-fulfilment through seeking the good. This is achieved in the individual only through promoting the well-being of others. It therefore involves mutuality in love. Its modern correlate is the quest for "the good life" through self-realization.

But is not this what a Christian ought to desire? It has much to commend it, and no Christian ought to disparage it. But to the Christian is *eros* enough? That is our problem.

Aristotle's eudaemonism, with its emphasis on a life of moderation with every man fulfilling the function for which he is fitted by nature, and thereby ensuring happiness, is a practical and down-to-earth system which still has much modern relevance. The hedonistic, or pleasure-seeking, ethics of Epicurus was by no means the crass sensualism suggested by the oft-quoted 'Eat, drink, and be merry; for tomorrow we die"; it centred in a refined enjoyment of congenial friends, simplicity of living, and freedom from tension in a cultured and unstrenuous life. Stoicism, on the other hand, with its appeal to courage in the face of life's vicissitudes and the pursuit of virtue solely for virtue's sake, was both a more serious and a more religiously grounded ethic. Its doctrine of an all-pervasive World-Reason, or Logos, and of a natural law of morality fundamental to all existence and embracing in its scope all men, had a note of universalism which made Stoicism particularly open to amalgamation with Christian thought. These, of course, are not the only classical systems of moral philosophy.

There is the formal, duty ethics of Kant with its categorical imperative, or unconditional demand, to treat all persons as ends, never as means, and to act only in such a way that one's conduct could be universalized. There is the utilitarianism of Bentham and Mill, centred in the "greatest happiness of the greatest number" and the measurement of all courses of action by their usefulness toward this end. And there is the modern, but in its elements very old, "social adjustment" philosophy of John Dewey which measures right conduct by the ability to take one's place as a good citizen in an ordered, democratic society.

It is apparent that there are good elements in all of these systems. But are they Christian?

From the early days of Christianity to the present, various courses have been followed with regard to the relations of Christian ethics to moral philosophies stemming from other sources. One has been the process of incorporation and amalgamation. In practice, this has often meant the accommodation of Christian principles to what was incorporated. Starting from a laudable desire to propagate Christianity by finding points of contact with the non-Christian world, it has tended to de-emphasize what is distinctive in Christianity in order to stress common ground.

At its worst, this has meant the complete subsuming of Christian ethics within philosophical ethics even to the point of disclaiming that anything to be called Christian ethics exists. At its best, it has bred a form of "coalition ethics" in which natural law and the insights of Plato, Aristotle, and other great philosophers are drawn upon to supplement Christian ethics in areas where the gospel gives no specific directives. Examples of such incorporation and amalgamation, with varying levels of success, are seen in the incorporation by Clement of Alexandria of the best in Greek philosophy, the Thomistic assimilation of Aristotle, and the present-day tendency to adjust Christianity to a workable synthesis with the rationalistic, scientific, and humanitarian ideals of modern culture.

A second course follows as a reaction from the first. In alarm at the tendency to accommodate Christianity to the accepted standards of the secular world, there is a repudiation by Christian leaders of all sources of moral decision not specifically grounded in the Bible. This is seen in the familiar Barthian mood of the present. In general this movement in ethics has gone along with the rejection of philosophical theology in the attempt to base Christian theology solely on the Bible. It was illustrated in the early Church by Tertullian, who refused to give any credence to Greek philosophy, asking scornfully, "What has Athens to do with Jerusalem?" It is illustrated today by the neo-orthodox school in its suspicion of not only liberal theology but the liberal social gospel, though the tendency is not uniform throughout neo-orthodoxy.

Some of its exponents, notably Emil Brunner, have a large place for "middle axioms," or practical social directives, derived in part from the Christian ethic but less than a full expression of Christian agape. Christian ethics is on unsafe ground if it either sells its birthright by accommodation to secular standards or refuses to respect and learn from the moral wisdom of the ages. The third possible approach is less easy to define, for its centre lies more in attitudes than in specific procedures. These attitudes may be characterized as those of mutual understanding and critical appropriation.

What is involved is that Christian moralists must familiarize themselves as thoroughly as possible with the history of philosophy, seek to understand other world views in their best forms as well as their worst, give them sympathetic but critical evaluation — then appropriate what is worth appropriating if it is not at variance with Christian faith. But in this process, there must be no amalgamating of what is different, no surrender of what is distinctive in Christianity. If this process is followed faithfully, there can be some hope of mutuality, with some appropriation of Christian insights into secular philosophy, as there is not apt to be on any other basis.

To state in barest outline what can result if this procedure is followed, there can be a partial acceptance by Christians of the insights of Plato and the Stoics, but no identification of eros with agape, no substituting of stoic fortitude for devoted submission to the will of God. From Aristotle's ethics not a few elements of practical wisdom can be taken, but not their humanistic foundations. The self-centred hedonism of Epicurus must be rejected because it is squarely opposed to Christian agape, while the duty ethics of Kant the utilitarianism of Bentham and Mill, and the contemporary emphasis on social adjustment may well be used as instruments for carrying out some aspects of the Christian moral imperative but ought never to be confused with its goals.

If this third position is accepted, we shall neither scorn moral philosophy nor identify Christian ethics with it. We shall rejoice that God has found many channels for the disclosure of truth to men and that these channels include the best rational thought of the ages on the nature and aims of the good life. Yet while we thus rejoice, we shall not substitute them for what God has disclosed to us in Jesus Christ or admit any to be true which stands clearly at variance with his gospel.

This third position, which I believe to be the only valid one, is what we shall attempt to maintain in this study. For its wider philosophical basis, the reader is referred to my earlier book in this series, *Foundations of Christian Knowledge, and* for its historical backgrounds insofar as they relate to Greek and Roman thought to *The Sources of Western Morality.*

Christian Ethics and the Ethics of Christendom

By Christendom we mean those geographical areas and those types of culture which have been largely influenced by Christian ideals. It is nearly, though not fully, synonymous with "the West." Two important elements prevent it from being synonymous. The first is the expansion of Christianity into the Orient, so that there is now a world Church and a large penetration of Christian influence into areas predominantly non-Christian. The second is the ambiguous situation in those areas under Communist domination, wherein a political regime officially atheistic includes within its scope millions of persons who are still Christians. Should Communism succeed in stamping out Christianity, these areas would no longer be a part of Christendom; fortunately, this appears not likely to occur.

The identification of Christian ethics with the ethics of Christendom is more subtle, and hence more dangerous, than its identification with the various schools of moral philosophy. As one element it includes the latter, as is illustrated by the wide permeation of the social and educational philosophy of John Dewey within current American culture. Yet it is something more diffuse and usually more binding than the thought of any single philosopher or school. It involves the whole "climate of opinion" within which one is reared, lives, and does his work. And because there is so much that is good about this climate of opinion and environing structure, it is easy to identify it with the best and hallow it with the name of Christian.

There is not space here to canvass in any detail the ways in which Christian ethics gets mixed up with the ethics of Christendom. This I have tried to do in *The Modern Rival of Christian Faith,* particularly in Part 2, where under the general caption of "Rival Secular Faiths" I have indicated elements of agreement and difference between Christianity and scientism, humanism, democracy, nationalism, racism, fascism, capitalism, and Communism. Further observations will be made on specific questions as we come to them later in this book. It may be noted in passing, however, that there is little danger of an identification of Christian ethics with humanism, racism, fascism, or Communism when these are recognized for what they are, since their foundations are so clearly opposed to those of the Christian faith. Even racism, widely practiced by Christians, is repudiated in principle.

It is at the point of the other four—scientism, democracy, nationalism, and capitalism—and their diffusion into an exaltation of scientific and technological achievement, the American way of life, patriotism, and free enterprise, that the identification becomes most common. Add to these a sense of the dignity of man, humanitarian concern for the weak, the helpless, and the suffering, a wholesome respect for law, and in general, attitudes of kindness, generosity, and responsible citizenship — and one comes out with what most Americans regard as "acting like a Christian."

Is this judgment mistaken? It is, and it is not. All the achievements and virtues above mentioned have in them large elements of goodness. Some of them—particularly humanitarian concern for others and a sense of the worth of every person—can be traced directly to Christian roots. Yet taken as a whole, they do not add up to Christian agape. One can believe in every one of them and be a decent, respectable, even admirable citizen, and still not be a Christian. A major, and perhaps the most difficult, task of Christian leaders is to induce people who are virtuous in all these respects to see that such goodness is not good enough. As long as one identifies Christian ethics with the ethics of Christendom, one does not cry out, "God, be merciful to me a sinner!" or lay hold in humility upon divine grace, or seek in costly self-surrender to follow the path of obedient love.

Christian Ethics and the Churches

The ethics of the Church, and individually of the churches, stands midway between the ethics of Christendom and the ethics of the gospel as it comes to us in Jesus Christ. The Church, insofar as it is faithful to its mission as the carrier of the gospel and is a fellowship of persons sincerely trying to follow Jesus, sees more clearly what is right than does the surrounding society. It is for this reason that it is called to be the "conscience of the State" and is obligated without falling into a trite and secularistic moralism to proclaim and practice the principles of Christian morality.

Its official pronouncements, whether in a papal encyclical or a statement of the World Council or National Council of Churches, or an action of a General Conference, are likely to be on a plane above that of current practice. This is not to say that any human document is flawless, but when the Church through its leaders tries to speak from a Christian frame of reference, it both indicts current practices and sets higher goals. This is as it should be if the Church is to be effective in applying the principles of its eternal gospel to the changing temporal scene.

Nevertheless, except in such authoritarian churches as the Roman Catholic and Eastern Orthodox, it is seldom contended that the voice of the Church is to be equated with the voice of God in Christ. Even In Roman Catholicism this claim is not made except when the Pope speaks ex cathedra. It is the genius of Protestantism to recognize that any Christian may grasp something of Christian moral truth, and comparably, that no Christian, or group of Christians, has a monopoly upon the gospel and its ethical demands.

The Church exists to be the carrier of the gospel in a fellowship of Christians. But the Church exists also as a human institution, a social group with a common centre of professed loyalty to Christ, yet a social group made up of fallible human beings. These fallible human persons "who profess and call themselves Christians," who are of varying degrees of ethical insight and fidelity to Christ, are also enmeshed in a network of other human institutions, political, economic, domestic, recreational, cultural. It is only natural, therefore, that the standards current in these other social institutions should impinge upon their life as Christians and so find access into the structure of the churches. Hence, the churches are always in danger of themselves becoming secularized and conforming to the standards of the world instead of being agencies of Christian transformation.

A statement on *Christian Principles and Assumptions for Economic Life* adopted by the General Board of the National Council of the Churches of Christ in the USA puts this pointedly:

> *The churches themselves own property, invest funds, and employ labour. Often their policies have been no better than those which the Church condemns in the secular world. Its divisions often reflect and seem to give a religious sanction to the social divisions that are characteristic of society at large. In all these matters judgment should begin at the house of God." This statement, unfortunately too true to give comfort to any discerning Christian, describes a state of affairs which can be countered only by a combination of clear Christian insight and courageous, patient Christian action. Both the individual Christian and those corporate groups that make up the churches need always to keep in mind the piercing injunction: "Do not be conformed to this world but be transformed by the renewal of your mind, that you may prove what is the will of God, what is good and acceptable and perfect" (Rom. 12:2).*

It is apparent, therefore, that while churches are the natural media for Christian enlightenment, Christian ethics cannot be identified with the ethics of any of the existing churches.

But what of the past? Was not the Church once pure? And if we look to the early days of Christianity, or to the

Reformation, or to the beginnings of our denomination, do we not find there norms for action?

There is always a tendency, when we do not find things as they ought to be around us, to take this backward look. The tendency is in part wholesome, but in other respects it is bound to cause distortion. It is true that there have been at intervals great creative outpourings of the Spirit of God, which have always had ethical accompaniments, and sometimes very significant ones.

Among these, in addition to the supreme event of the life and death of our Lord, may be mentioned the era of the eighth-century prophets, the voices of Jeremiah and the Second Isaiah, the birth of the Church and the beginnings of missionary witness, the implanting of the gospel in Western Europe, the work and ministry of Francis of Assisi, the Protestant Reformation, the struggle for religious freedom, the Wesleyan revival, the emergence of the modern missionary and ecumenical movements. We do well to learn whatever lessons they have to teach us. Yet one of these lessons is that there has never been a forward movement without some mixture of human error and sin.

The Church of today is further along the road toward a true Christian ethics than was Paul in his attitudes toward women, or Francis of Assisi in regard to the care of the body, or Luther in regard to the economic status of peasants, or Calvin in regard to infant damnation, or Wesley in regard to the requirements of world order and peace. The Church through the centuries has been the carrier of the Christian evangel and of a basic stricture of Christian faith. Out of this evangel and this faith the principles of Christian ethics are fashioned.

We owe, then, to the Church of the past and to our fathers in the faith an incalculable debt. The past merits to be known and understood, to be viewed critically where necessary, but never to be treated lightly. We need to know what Augustine and Aquinas, Luther, Calvin, and Wesley believed about the Christian life, both to learn from them and to avoid their errors. Yet while we acknowledge our debt to the "faith of our fathers, living still," and to those fathers who valiantly proclaimed it, let us not suppose that the Church of the past can be our norm for the ethical decisions of today.

Christian Ethics and the Bible

We come now to a frame of reference on which we are on firmer ground. The Bible is certainly indispensable to our knowledge of Christian truth and moral obligation. Without it, it is very possible that there would be today no churches, no Christendom, no knowledge of Christ. It is, of course, conceivable that God would have found a way to propagate the faith by word of mouth without a Book through all the centuries, and the fact that Roman Catholicism could exist so long without access to the Bible by the laity makes it impossible to say categorically that the Bible is the *sine qua non* of Christianity. Yet few would dispute the fact that without the Bible we should be infinitely poorer in our Christian experience and moral insight.

Furthermore, in today's world the Bible is the common possession of all Christians, and hence serves to unite Christians across deep divisions. This is not to say that all Christians agree on what the Bible says. There are differences in translation, and far more radical differences in interpretation. Acute controversies and sometimes schisms arise from this fact. Yet the Bible is still our common possession, and it is no accident that its sales continue year after year to exceed that of any other boo[k] that it has been and continues to be translated into m[...]

hundreds of languages and dialects, that it has become so deeply embedded in our literature and culture that even those who have no personal familiarity with it daily use its phrases in ordinary speech.

The Bible is the fountainhead of Christian theology. It is not the sole source, for there is a natural theology, also called philosophical theology, which finds evidences of God throughout his total creation and in the moral and religious aspirations and experience of all peoples. There is a place for such natural theology and at points where both biblical and philosophical theology are true, they cannot contradict each other. Nevertheless, the Bible is our firmer base for what is distinctively Christian, and the movement away from the more generalized conclusions of philosophical thought about God and his world to a more Christ-centred, biblically based structure of theology is in the right direction.

If this is the case, is not the Bible all we need as the foundation of Christian ethics? The answer is Yes and No. This question may be followed by another. Are Christian ethical principles to be derived from the whole Bible or only from selected parts of it? Once more it is necessary to say Yes and No. Reviewing what has been said about the relations of Christian ethics to moral philosophy, to Christendom, and to the Church, we see that "no other foundation can any one lay than that which is laid, which is Jesus Christ." In the supreme duty of love to God and neighbour, rooted in faith, obedience, and humble acceptance of divine grace, we find "all the law and the prophets"—and enough to give a basis for centuries of ethical application. But this gives the basis; it does not give the applications. We are still left with a multitude of concrete moral decisions to make. For guidance in making them we must look—not to any ethical compendium above the Bible or beyond it in wisdom—but to other ranges of experience that may throw light on problems nonexistent in Bible times or not treated within its scope. What, for example, about slavery, birth control, juvenile delinquency, polio, speeding on highways, labour unions, stock-market manipulations, hydrogen bombs and war? The first and last existed in full force within the period covered by the Bible, but the Bible does not tell us what to do about them; the others are for the most part modern problems.

It is apparent, then, that the Bible alone does not give us all we need. The thinking and experience of the centuries, whether in philosophy or the Church, will help us at some points. But we cannot live by the past, and we must know our times and the causes and consequences of prevailing evils. We must be continually on the alert to see what a sensitive Christian conscience, responsive to the call of Christ, will hold to be right and wrong courses of action in the circumstances where we are.

Turning to the second question, we ask, "Shall we use the whole Bible, or only parts of it, as the basis of ethical decision?"

This question may mean either of two things. One angle it takes is the question as to whether we should use the Old Testament as well as the New. And if the answer is Yes, shall we equate them in value? The other angle of the question goes to the heart of biblical interpretation and separates into two camps—at times one could almost say armed camps—the literalists and the liberals. This issue is, of course, the degree to which the historical method is to be used in discerning the ethical as well as the theological truth within the Bible. Let us look at these questions separately, though they impinge upon each other.

As to whether we should look to the Old Testament for our ethical foundations, the answer is "Yes, but with discernment." I have said, and shall repeatedly insist, that the basic foundation of Christian ethics is in the ministry and teachings of Jesus Christ, as these bring to us the supreme revelation of God's nature and will.

Yet the Old Testament contains also much that is revelatory in its own structure, as well as preparatory for the coming of Christ.

We could not dispense with the Ten Commandments or the great moral insights of the prophets or the matchless devotional poetry of the psalms. Even the ups and downs of Hebrew history, with their sordid spots as well as high moments, with moral weaklings as well as giants in the story, and much that reflects the lights and shadows of the times, teach us that:

God moves in a mysterious way
His wonders to perform.

The discernment we need, if we are to see God's light in the midst of earthly shadows, is found in the measuring rod of Jesus Christ. Are the polygamy, the trickery, the vindictiveness, found on many pages of the Old Testament Christian? Unquestionably not. Are the twenty-third psalm, or Isaiah's vision in the Temple, or Micah's definition of true religion Christian? Unquestionably yes. They are not the whole of Christianity, but they are fully consistent with what Jesus taught and did. So, too, are a wealth of other passages in the Old Testament.

The Old Testament, we must remember, was Jesus' Bible. He did not repudiate it; he loved it and learned from it and often quoted it. But he did not slavishly feel bound to it. In the Sermon on the Mount the six-times-repeated "You have heard that it was said to the men of old.... But I say to you..." indicates how he used it. He took it as a foundation, but put deeper meaning into the issues involved. This we must do, drawing from his insights. On the question of a historical versus a literalistic approach to the Bible I have stated my convictions elsewhere and need not here discuss the subject in detail.It is not a question of inspiration, for one who sees in the Bible a progressive revelation of the living God as he moves in the events of Hebrew history, the coming of Christ and the birth of the Church, accepts the Bible as the Word of God as truly as does any literalist.

What he attempts to do is to hear this Word more clearly as he discerns the Spirit of God moving in the midst of the human, historical situation, and thus aims to discover in the Bible the heavenly "treasure in earthen vessels." He is likely to be called an infidel by one who believes that the Bible must be taken "letter for letter" or not at all. But that does not matter if his studies lead him to clearer vision and deeper faith.

If we are to find in the Bible dependable guidance for our own time, such a historical approach is indispensable. No situation is an exact replica of the past, and words spoken in the past to other situations take on distorted meaning unless these situations are understood. This is not to say that the literalist discerns no moral truth in the Bible.

He does, and often lives by it in his personal relations an admirable Christian life. Yet in matters of complexity and doubt as to the right thing to do, he tends to follow his own course of action and find a proof text in the Bible to support it. He usually defends a traditional point of view in which an attempt is made to preserve the status quo, not infrequently with harsh words and attitudes toward those who differ. For ethical sensitivity and responsiveness to the Christian thing to do in doubtful situations, one who sees the Bible in its total historical setting is on safer ground.

Christian Ethics and the New Testament

The final question for this chapter is a closely related but still a somewhat different one. What about the authority of the New Testament, not only in relation to the Old, but within it in the relations of its parts?

Most Christians, without rejecting the Old Testament or disparaging its many marvellous elements, find the New Testament more authoritative for their faith and living. This is as it should be, for while the Old Testament tells us much about God and foreshadows the coming of Christ, it is the New Testament that records for us the historical revelation of God in Christ. Their interrelatedness has thus been well expressed by a group of eminent scholars in the ecumenical movement:

> *It is agreed that in the case of an Old Testament passage, one must examine and expound it in relation to the revelation of God to Israel both before and after its own period. Then the interpreter should turn to the New Testament in order to view the passage in that perspective.*

It is agreed that in the case of a New Testament passage one should examine it in the light of its setting and context; then turn to the Old Testament to discover its background in God's former revelation.

Returning again to the New Testament one is able to see and expound the passage in the light of the whole scope of *Heilsgeschichte. Seeing* the Bible as a whole, we make the revelation of God in Christ our norm for understanding and for judgment. But within the New Testament, is one part any more authoritative than another? In order to answer this question, we must avoid two common courses, both of which have been responsible for error.

One of these courses is to take the New Testament as if it were all on the same level of Christian insight. Because the words are there, Paul's words enjoining women to keep silent in the churches and Jude's words contending "for the faith which was once for all delivered to the saints" have again and again been used as a bulwark against change.

That these injunctions reflect particular situations in the early Church instead of being universal principles, and stand squarely in opposition to Paul's other word, "Where the Spirit of the Lord is, there is freedom," is too frequently overlooked.

Passages attributed to Jesus which seem to predict a speedy Second Coming and a catastrophic end of the world by divine intervention are equated in importance with the Sermon on the Mount — and seemingly ranked superior to it — by eminent theologians whose conception of Christ as the hope of the world is primarily eschatological rather than ethical.

On the other hand, the recognition that the Gospels are the product of the experience of the Church in the first century, not first-hand accounts, and that Paul's early letters antedate by nearly a quarter-century even Mark, which is the earliest of the Gospels, has led some scholars to shift the focus of attention away from Jesus to Paul. There is wide latitude among New Testament scholars as to the historicity of the Gospels; there is general agreement that none is completely historical, with John the latest and least so of the four. That Paul has much to teach us both about redemption through the grace of God in Christ and about the requirements of the Christian life need not be disputed. Yet it may be asked whether it is not Jesus of Nazareth, seen clearly even though not photographically through the records we have in the Synoptic Gospels, that is our surest foundation of the Christian life, Paul was a great Christian, a great theologian, a great missionary and administrator, a great teacher, but it was not he in whom "the Word became flesh" to dwell among us.

It will be a basic assumption of this book, as it is not of some contemporary treatments of Christian ethics, that the picture we have of Jesus in the Synoptic Gospels is in essential outlines correct and that what we see there of his life and death, his ministry and teaching, is the one adequate foundation for Christian ethics. Yet to take this as our base does not mean that we can indiscriminately take every word recorded as spoken by Jesus to be accurate or authoritative. At the end of Mark, in a passage now generally regarded by scholars as a later addition to the original text, Jesus is reported as saying:

> *And these signs will accompany those who believe: in my name they will cast out demons; they will speak in new tongues; they will pick up serpents, and if they drink any deadly thing, it will not hurt them; they will lay their hands on the sick; and they will recover. (16:17-18.)*

Regardless of what we may today believe about the exorcism of demons, speaking in tongues, or healing by the laying on of hands, can we really believe that the Christian ethic requires snake handling and the drinking of poison as a proof of faith? Some of Jesus' more naive followers have tried it in our own time, and they died. We should doubt that Jesus ever said it even if there were no textual evidence to the contrary.

To cite another example, there is a verse at the end of the parable of the pounds as it is given in Luke which is generally omitted when the story is read. In Luke 19:27 appear the words: "But as for these enemies of mine, who did not want me to reign over them, bring them here and slay them before me." Why do we omit it? Because it does not sound like Jesus! It simply does not seem like the words of one who could say on the cross, "Father, forgive them; for they know not what they do." And even though the textual accuracy of Luke 19:27 is less disputed than of Luke 23:34, we still I believe it is the latter in which the real Jesus speaks.

These illustrations indicate what must be a basic procedure— a difficult but a very necessary procedure. This is to get to know Jesus from the total picture the New Testament gives of him—find our main point of reference in the first three Gospels, then interpret these Gospels and all the rest of the New Testament in the light of what we believe he was and said and did. This, of course, immediately opens the door to the charge that one is reading in what he wants to find there. But there is no other way. We cannot take the record as it stands, and we cannot discard it. Whatever interpretation we place upon it, we shall still be interpreting. And the best interpretation is that which is most faithful to the total picture of Jesus as our Lord, the Son of God, the supreme revelation of the Father and the supreme gift of God for our redemption.

What, then, is Christian ethics? It is the systematic study of the way of life set forth by Jesus Christ, applied to the daily demands and decisions of our personal and social existence.

Since Christian ethics centres in the ethical insights of Jesus, a logical "next step" might be to move directly into an examination of these as they are to be discerned from his recorded words and deeds—thence to an application to the problems of our time. The reader who wishes to follow this sequence is free to do so, and the table of contents will direct him in it.

Yet if we are to understand Jesus, or if we are to discern the centrality of his message in reference to the entire Bible, we cannot proceed so simply. Jesus had a past, and from his life and influence came the Church of which the beginnings are recorded for us in the New Testament. It is essential, therefore, to look first at the Old Testament, then at Jesus, then forward from his earthly life to the birth of Christianity. From this wider biblical perspective we shall be the better equipped to judge what is truly Christian.

4

The Economic Ethics of the New Testament

As has been noted, Jesus had very little to say about specific social institutions of any kind. His concern was chiefly with individuals in their person-to-person, face-to-face relationships. Therefore in his recorded words there is less to be found about the structures of economic life than about the family. There is, for example, nothing comparable to Matt. 19: 5-6 to undergird a particular economic system as this passage does monogamous marriage.

Throughout the letters of Paul and in other parts of the New Testament there are scattered economic references, such as the obligation to work in self-support and not become a burden to others (II Thess. 3:6-12) and the injunction to slaves to obey their masters with due docility (Col. 3:22; Eph. 6:5; Tit. 2:9). Yet there is no clear focusing on any social system as good or evil, a fact which made it possible for slavery to go unchallenged by Christians for many centuries. In the prophets there is a much more direct reference to the evils of economic exploitation with repeated, ringing denunciations of it. It is to Amos, Hosea, Isaiah, and Micah that we are most apt to turn for the biblical foundations of social and economic justice.

There are a number of reasons why the New Testament is relatively so silent at this point. First, there is the fact that the Christian message centres so largely in faith and love that justice in social relations tends to be overshadowed. In the gospel of redemption there is no overlooking of divine justice. But in the call to love one's neighbour and even one's enemy, to pray for one's persecutor and to accept injury with nonresistance, to give freely and beyond necessity to those in need, the emphasis lies on uncalculating love and not on the correction of unjust systems or the punishment of evildoers. This note in Jesus was carried on into the early Church with the further emphasis on accepting Christ and finding new life in him as all-important.

In the second place, eschatology permeates the ethics of the New Testament. For reasons given in Chapter 4, the expectancy of a speedy end of the existing world scene did not basically pervert the ethical insights of the early Church, and still less those of Jesus. But it did foreshorten the perspective and divert attention away from social systems to the individual soul. Since it was the Christian believer, and he alone, who would dwell with God in his eternal kingdom, it was the soul alone that mattered. This attitude survived long after the passing of apocalyptic expectations and has not yet been surrendered.

A third factor explains at least in part the keener social conscience of the prophets as contrasted with the early Christians.

No Christian writer of the New Testament, so far as our records reveal, ever faced the responsibility of applying high moral principles to preserving the institutions of society, administering governments, handling international relationships, prosecuting social reforms, or even mitigating by public measures the inequities of an economic system. Their life as an "odd sect" with the simplest of economic pursuits within occupied territory did not give occasion for such responsibility. The prophets as the challengers and advisers of kings in a State struggling for political survival and economic power were much closer to the perennial problems of social injustice and conflict than were the relatively detached early Christians.

Yet Jesus stood in the succession of the prophets, and there is danger of overstressing the fact that he said nothing about economic systems. From his words and spirit has come a challenge that has persistently affected the economic order. Not only does the love commandment have a bearing on property as well as every other social issue, but in unequivocal terms he denounced some tendencies still very prevalent in modern economic life.

There is nothing clearer in the message of Jesus than his indictment of acquisitiveness, and the putting of one's trust in material rather than spiritual goods. Again and again this note is sounded. "You cannot serve God and mammon." (Matt. 6.24.) "A man's life does not consist in the abundance of his possessions." (Luke 12:15.) "Do not lay up for yourselves treasures on earth, where moth and rust consume and where thieves break in and steal, but lay up for yourselves treasures in heaven." (Matt. 6:19.) To lay up treasures on earth without being rich toward God is to follow the foolish way of the rich man who, thinking he had goods laid up for many years, heard the inescapable decree, "Fool! This night your soul is required of you" (Luke 12:16-21).

Jesus was very forthright as to the perils of riches.

He did not hesitate to condemn in stinging terms those who "cleanse the outside of the cup and of the plate, but inside they are full of extortion and rapacity." In his reference to the camel and the needle's eye, it is hardly likely that he denied all access to the Kingdom to the rich, but this arresting hyperbole states with great vividness the spiritual dangers and temptations of wealth. Yet this does not mean that he thought lightly of the material foundations of life. "Give us this day our daily bread" undoubtedly means material, not spiritual bread; and in the passage in the Sermon on the Mount in which he warns against overanxiety as to what one will eat or drink or wear, it is significant that he nowhere indicates that these are unimportant. So important, indeed, are they that "your heavenly Father knows that you need them all" (Matt. 6:32). Such passages indicate a perspective on the part of Jesus which puts material goods in their proper place as the instrument, and not the end, of man's existence. Out of them has come an impulse within Christianity toward honesty in the acquisition and philanthropy in the use of economic goods which through the centuries has had great social influence, and which ought never to be disparaged or lost. Our chief lack has been, not in directive principles from Jesus, but in the scope of their application by Christians.

As has been noted repeatedly, it is not alone from specific words that we get our directives, but from the total spirit of Jesus in his estimate of the worth of persons to God. As a fuller awareness of this became prevalent among Christians, the scope of economic concern broadened. It was seen that economic conditions affect vitally every person and the whole man; hence they must be a Christian concern. It gradually became — or is becoming — recognized that personal integrity and

Christian giving to those in need will not meet the full requirement of the Christian ethic. We have today problems more complex than those of any previous age, but we have also a fuller sense of Christian obligation in and to a "responsible society."

The Christian View of Property

The basic note in the Christian understanding of material possessions is stewardship. This term is often understood too narrowly to mean personal giving, usually with an emphasis on tithing. That Christians ought to give of their material resources for the support of the Church and many worthy causes, for the extension of the gospel and the relief of human need, is indisputable. That this should be on the mathematical basis of the tithe is more open to question, not because this often indicates too much to give but because for those who are well-to-do it is too little.

The amount of personal sacrifice involved in setting aside the tithe varies greatly from the one-thousand-to the ten-thousand-dollar income, and still more as incomes go up. The Pauline observation that the Christian should put something aside "as he may prosper" (I Cor. 16:2) if taken seriously might yield larger gifts, and with more Christian dedication, than the Old Testament provision.

However, stewardship is not primarily a matter of personal giving. This is secondary and derivative. Stewardship means the recognition that *all* our goods, not some portion only, belong to God and we hold them in delegated trust.

The earth is the Lord's and the fullness thereof,
the world and those who dwell therein;
for he has founded it upon the seas,
and established it upon the rivers. (Ps. 24:1-2.)

If this principle of God's sole ownership and our stewardship, which is stated in the creation story (Gen. 1:26) and presupposed throughout the Bible, were taken seriously we should have a less acquisitive and more just society. Before it our vast disparities of wealth and poverty, wasted natural resources, and the use of God's good gifts solely for selfish ends could not stand.

But what of private ownership in the sense of each man's individual proprietorship of a portion of economic goods? Christians have not always agreed as to the answer. The main trend of thought, however, both in the Bible and in the history of the Church, reinforces the conviction that some measure of individual ownership is right and Christian. The very existence of the commandment "Thou shalt not steal" presupposes the right of ownership, and one of the offences against which the prophets had most vigorously to protest was its infringement. While there was for a time in Jerusalem after Pentecost a communal sharing of goods (Acts 2:44-45; 5:1-5), there is no evidence that this became a general arrangement.

It was apparently a product of Christian fellowship rather than a social policy. Christian monastic orders with surrender of personal possessions have existed since the sixth century, and outside of Christianity long before that, but there has been no general conviction on the part of Christians that society as a whole should be thus organized. Asceticism and voluntary poverty, where practiced, have been considered as a divine vocation rather than as a mandatory social practice.

Furthermore, quite apart from the biblical and traditional grounds, there are other reasons why private ownership is right and Christian. The most basic of these is that the fullest development of personality requires it. Economic insecurity, we noted, is very closely linked with personal insecurity. The child may find his security in his parents without personal ownership, though even a small child ought to have some things that he can call his own. No adult, unless the Church or some other institution has assumed for him a protective status, can feel secure without some ownership. Contemporary Communism has attempted to make the State assume this function, but with very doubtful results, and has been led by experience to reinstate much more private ownership than was envisaged at the beginning of the Soviet regime. In our society the "lift" one gets from owning something — whether one's clothing or furniture, a car or a home — is more than an outcropping of acquisitiveness or the prestige of possession; it is a response to a deeply embedded craving for security and a measure of personal independence.

A second factor is one about which the Bible is silent but which cannot be disregarded in the modern world. This is the greater degree of economic efficiency and the higher standard of living that has ensued where the right of private ownership has been recognized. This is not to say that "enlightened self-interest" or a policy of unrestrained economic individualism will make a society either just or as a whole prosperous. The contrary is evident. Nevertheless, it is hardly disputable that not only in the production of goods but in the development of human skills and in the increased availability of both goods and skills for the service of human need, the right to possess has played no minor role. Individual ownership has produced a more advanced as well as more opulent society than has been possible under feudalism or any form of communal ownership in ancient or modern times.

A third and closely related factor is the relation of property to work. Personal ownership is necessary for economic motivation. There are some kinds of work one delights to do regardless of pay, as Bliss Perry elaborated in his book with the intriguing title *And Gladly Teach.* Christian leaders do not ordinarily choose their vocations chiefly from considerations of salary, or they would choose occupations better paid. Nevertheless, society as a whole with all of its hard, monotonous, and disagreeable jobs could not run without private profit and private ownership. It is fatuous to say that throughout all society there ought to be glad, voluntary cooperation; the fact is that there is not! With the human impulse what it is, it is unlikely that it will be possible to dispense entirely with personal profit as the reward of labour.

Private ownership and private profit are so deeply embedded in both our Christian and our democratic heritage that few would wish to see them eradicated if this were possible. But this is not to say that all the results are either beneficial or Christian. It is essential that the Christian conscience remain sensitive to perversions and continue to challenge evils which thrive all too frequently within this view of property.

The most common evil is the encouragement of acquisitiveness, and with it all the perils of self-aggrandizement, self-righteousness, and a false trust in material possessions against which Jesus spoke so vigorously. It is a half-truth, which when cited to justify unrestrained individualism becomes an untruth, to say that the sin does not lie in the system but in the people. Only persons can sin, but in the complex structures of present-day economic life it is impossible to draw a clear line between wilful acquisitiveness and fair profit, or between individual and group sinning. Private ownership we must have, but not the amount and range of possession-centredness that dominates our current society.

An accompanying evil is the vast disparities of wealth and poverty that have developed within every country, and in particularly acute form between opulent America and the hungry Orient. It is this which gives Communism its primary appeal, and no informed person needs to be reminded that this disparity is one of the major sources of world tension. Such vast inequalities of possession have always existed, but as the instruments of potential destruction become more deadly and the underprivileged become more conscious of the possibilities of change, the ferment of revolution and unrest becomes inevitable. Whether this will lead to global destruction in the clash of competing systems or to a greater measure of freedom and justice through the lifting of the living standards of the underprivileged peoples of the earth, no one can predict.

How much property ought a person, or a group, to possess? There is no simple answer. Competition alone cannot ensure justice, for competition encourages not only effort and skill but shrewd manipulation and the scramble for power. Equality is not the answer, for whether income and ownership are measured by earning or by need, inequalities must inevitably be reckoned with. An equal wage for all would not be an equitable one, for great differences exist both in the quality of services rendered and in family obligations, cost of training, and many other factors.

In judging what one ought to receive or possess, two simple rules may suggest the answer as well as anything more complex: (1) every person ought to have enough income to meet his basic physical and cultural needs without anxiety and with some surplus for saving and for giving; (2) no person ought to have so much that possession breeds indifference to the needs of others or becomes a peril to the soul. Within these limits a Christian society will find some latitude to be both inevitable and desirable. If this seems somewhat lacking in equalitarian justice, a higher spiritual justice is established by the principle of responsibility announced in the words, "Every one to whom much is given, of him will much be required" (Luke 12:48).

A third major evil is the linkage of power with possession of economic goods. This is not wholly evil, for power may be constructively exercised. There are rich men who manage a business benevolently without its being a benevolent despotism, and who use their money constructively for great philanthropies. These facts ought to be neither overplayed nor overlooked. Nevertheless, the temptation to an irresponsible and selfish use of power is always near at hand, and only a few at any economic level successfully resist it.

One of the major causes of social conservatism is the fact that churches, schools, and other social institutions are so largely influenced by persons whose advantage it is to preserve the *status quo* and who are prone to regard any departure from it as an affront to Christian morality. Not all social change is good. Yet under the guise of preserving freedom (and in the present scene, of resisting Communism) unjust conditions are perpetuated, and any attempt at social criticism is viewed as subversion. When the attitude is joined, as it frequently is, with a deep Christian piety in personal matters, the power becomes the more impregnable. Since human motives usually "come mixed," only God is wise enough to judge how much of this resistance to social change is due to self-interest, how much to the pull of tradition, and how much to sincere Christian conviction.

Yet it is not this exercise of power by individuals that

is the most serious aspect of current society. Widespread though it is, where it can be isolated, challenged, and changed, there is the possibility of a creative use of economic power. It is corporate social sin, by great groups of persons against great groups of persons, that causes the most serious evil consequences and is hardest to reckon with. *Persons* are involved, as both sinners and victims, or it would not be sin. Unemployment, for example, is more than an inevitable, tragic fate; it is caused by circumstances for which human beings are morally responsible. When a worldwide depression occurs, as in the early 1930's, many millions of persons are made to suffer acutely, and economists can give some reasons for its occurrence. But this is not to say that guilt can be precisely allocated. In less widespread but deeply disrupting conflicts, as in a clash between a giant corporation and a giant labour union, the fault is seldom all on one side; and while some persons are more responsible than others, it is seldom possible with justice to pin the responsibility wholly upon particular individuals.

This illustrates what was said in Chapter 6 — that there is *social evil* and there is *social sin,* and the two must be neither identified nor too sharply separated. The Christian view of property is that to the degree that a person is even indirectly responsible for a misuse of it which is harmful to others, his conscience must remain sensitive and he must do all in his power to turn it to just and creative ends. Not everything is within his power, but some things are. It is in those areas where he *can* act, as these are prayerfully and reasonably discerned, that his Christian duty lies.

The Christian View of Work

We have been tracing some basic issues with regard

to property, or "capital"; we must now look at the other side of the dual structure of economic life, namely, "labour." No attempt was made in the previous section to discuss capitalism as such, though some things said have a direct bearing upon it, nor shall I in this section attempt to defend a rival system. The purpose at this point is simply to examine the place of work in the total life of the Christian.

(a) *Why Work?* To this question a variety of answers may be given, and these may be put in psychological or in normative Christian terms. A look from each angle may throw light on the issue as a whole.

Why does anyone work? The simplest answer is that one works because he has to. Economic pressures overcome the natural impulse to idleness. This fact is not universal, for there are those who through immaturity, illness, old age, indigence, inherited wealth, or for some other reason live by the product of the labour of others. Nevertheless, it remains normal for the mature adult who is able to do so to work for a living, either directly for pay and profit or, as in the case of the housewife, to cooperate in providing for the family.

Yet people work for other reasons. People economically secure still work because they enjoy it, or prefer activity to an empty leisure, or because they feel a responsibility for accomplishing something, or because they wish to please and serve someone who is loved. Work is any activity entered into for the sake of an end, and it is normal for the, human spirit, in contrast with animal experience, to have ends in view for which the immediate pleasures of idleness will voluntarily be surrendered. It is a cynical, and a false, view of man which regards economic forces as the sole determiners of human conduct.

Other reasons are less laudable but powerful. Some

people work because of the force of social approval, letting both the nature and the amount of their work be determined by prevailing social patterns. One works as little, or as much, as those around him do. Or one works under coercion, because of fear of the disfavour of "the boss," or from fear of penalties affixed or favours withheld in the case of failure to produce results.

Work habits are not easy to acquire, for children naturally prefer play to work, and this tendency if uncorrected carries over into adult life. But a work habit, once formed, is tenacious, and some people work simply because they always have and lack the will power to stop. This is particularly true of our high-pressured age, in which people work from a mixture of motives of which necessity, habit, and a feverish desire to keep busy are large components. Brunner calls this state "work-fanaticism" and says of it:

> *There is a vacuum in the soul, an inner unrest from which one escapes by work. Work-fanaticism is proportional to the poverty of the soul. As nervous people cannot keep still, man with his unrestful soul cannot but work. The modern Western world is somehow possessed with this work-fanaticism as a result of inward impoverishment.*

It is a strange paradox of the present day scene that we are suffering from a work-fanaticism and work-idolatry as well as from a lack of will-to-work.

Both these phenomena come from the same root, the loss of the sense of the eternal meaning of life. To this current state of work-fanaticism, religion has indirectly contributed. Max Weber in his famous essay *The Protestant Ethic and the Spirit of Capitalism* overstates the contribution of Calvinism to the rise of capitalism; yet it is true that in the religious sanction given to the Puritan virtues of hard work, frugality, and thrift, an emerging capitalism found strong support. Now largely divorced from its earlier moorings, a feverishly competitive society is carried along by a combination of conscience and compulsion which will not let one rest while there is still work to be done. Thus by a curious inversion the drive to incessant work which formerly came from a sense of divine vocation becomes a symptom of the loss of a sense of life's meaning.

If these are the reasons why people work, which of these motives are right and which wrong? Here the Christian ethic draws no clear-cut lines, but neither does it leave us without direction. Within the complex range of motives just outlined, not all are morally and spiritually on the same level. It is right to work to support one's self and one's family, providing for future needs as well as the present. It is right to work to express a creative impulse, contributing of one's best to "the good of the whole." Explicitly and centrally, it is right to serve God through serving other persons. To the degree that this is done, every vocation becomes a divine calling.

With equal certainty it may be said that it is wrong to work solely to gratify an acquisitive impulse, amassing more and more riches as the "chief and highest end of man." Though certain social standards must be met, it is wrong to work to secure or to maintain a superficial prestige. It is wrong to fall into a state of "work-fanaticism," finding no satisfactions through other channels and seeking escape from an inner vacuum through feverish activity.

Other motives are in a more ambiguous status. To work because one enjoys doing something or because another demands it may be right or wrong according to the nature of the enjoyment or of the demands. One has to judge the total situation in the light of the relative importance of enticing occupations or of external pressures. There is always a temptation to neglect one's main job for some trifling occupation that may soothe the conscience with a sense of busyness! Acquiescence to the demands of others is disciplinary and may be needed to curb our rebellious self-will; it may also stifle initiative and breed a rankling sense of grievance.

Is there an ideal work situation? Yes, if by "ideal" is meant not some flawless perfection but a situation that is all a human being ought to aspire to for his fullest satisfaction. A work situation is right when one works voluntarily from a service motive, under a sense of divine calling, and does the most creative job his talents permit; when one finds deep enjoyment in his work and has happy relations with his associates; when it does not overtax his physical strength or his nerves, and leaves some time for interesting and productive leisure; and when one receives for this work an income adequate to meet his needs without anxiety. So blessed is this situation, if one is blest with it, that another requirement must be added — one must know when to stop!

Such a work situation is possible. Yet few attain or possess it. Its absence is one of the major evils of our society.

(b) *Work as Vocation:* We noted above that one's daily work ought to be viewed as a divine calling, and done as far as possible in a spirit of service. This is the expression in economic life of the demand to love God and our neighbour. But to do this is no simple and easy requirement, nor have Christians always agreed as to its meaning. A brief historical review may throw light upon it.

In the Bible it is taken for granted that work is ordained of God. To be sure, in Gen. 3:17-18 work is presented as a curse for the sin of Adam, yet in Gen. 2:15 the command to till and to keep the garden precedes sin. The explicit word of Paul, "If any one will not work, let him not eat" (II Thess. 3:10), is implicit elsewhere in the Bible, though generally on a more communal basis as it is assumed that work is the duty of the "house," or family unit. There is division of labour in the Bible and there is slavery, but little suggestion of a class stratification condemning manual labour as inferior.

This was very different in Greek society, which was thoroughly aristocratic. Both Plato and Aristotle regarded the "working class" as a distinctly inferior group who must do the manual labour in order that intellectuals might have leisure for philosophy. Helots and slaves must work in order that the free man might pursue his achievements of the spirit. This stratification, along with a characteristic Hellenic dualism of body and spirit, was to have serious consequences in medieval thought.

In the Middle Ages this depreciation of manual labour was blended with the class structure of feudal society and given a religious sanction. The religious vocation of priest or monk or nun was viewed as having a higher spiritual sanctity than ordinary labour, the contemplative being ranked above the active life. Within the active life manual labour, though recognized as necessary and ordained of God, had an inferior status. In part this was due to the influence of Aristotle, in part to emphasis on the "curse" of the Fall, and in part to the ever-present tendency to give religious support to an existing social system. As a result, social stratification was tightened by the belief that every man must remain in the station in life where God had placed him and there perform faithfully its duties.

Martin Luther broke radically with one element of this medieval view — namely, the ethical dualism of the religious and the secular. His emphasis on the sacredness of the common life was a highly important new note in Reformation Protestantism. Said he:

> *It looks like a great thing when a monk renounces everything and goes into a cloister, carries on a life of asceticism, fasts, watches, prays, etc...On the other hand it looks like a small thing when a maid cooks and cleans and does other housework. But because God's command is there, even such a small work must be praised as a service to God surpassing the holiness and asceticism of all monks and nuns. Luther's doctrine of* Beruf, *or calling, gave dignity to one's daily work, however humble, and could have had a great democratizing influence. Unfortunately, however, he never surrendered the medieval idea of "my station and its duties." It was the Christian's duty and high calling to serve God in his appointed place, not to change his station in life. For this reason Luther sided against the peasants in the Peasants' War, and gave added religious sanction to a social stratification which is still much in evidence in European society.*

Calvin's view of calling did not differ materially from Luther's. Yet by his advocacy of the "middle-class virtues" of industry, frugality, honesty, and sobriety; his removal of the prohibition on the taking of interest (commonly referred to as usury); and his recognition of the right to change one's calling if one remained in humble obedience to God and his employer, he reinforced the growing ferment of free enterprise. Through a complex set of forces which cannot here be traced, Calvinism by way of Puritanism gave an undergirding to both political democracy and economic individualism.

Current society is both involved in, and divorced from, this legacy from the past. In America, far more than in Europe, social stratification has broken down, and the dignity of manual labour is recognized. The characteristic American "success" story is of the person who from the humblest beginnings by his skill and persistence has won a high place for himself in income, power, or public esteem. This climb to fame and fortune has seldom more than an incidental religious connection, if any. The advantages of democratic opportunity and free enterprise, in connection with pluck, shrewdness, and persistence under difficulties, are made focal in the telling, though there is an occasional reference to being sustained by prayer and religious faith. Seldom is there a conscious sense of divine calling in one's work, and the Reformation concept of the sacredness of the common life has virtually disappeared under the pressures of a highly competitive society.

The World Council of Churches, the National Council, and some denominational agencies are attempting to restore a sense of Christian vocation with regard to daily work. A section was explicitly devoted to this study at the Second Assembly of the World Council in Evanston in 1954. Vocational conferences of laymen to consider the implications of the Christian faith to their occupations are held with increasing frequency in Europe, and occasionally in America. It is well that this problem is coming into attention, for the frustration and loss of a sense of Christian calling in occupations other than those ostensibly religious is a serious aberration of our time.

That Christian ethics demands honesty in business dealings is still recognized in principle, however much flouted in practice, but beyond this it may be doubted that laymen often think of their religion as having a connection with their daily occupations. Yet it is in one's work and in one's family that most of one's life is spent, and it is here that both the most acute problems and the most creative opportunities of service to God and other persons are to be found.

What must be done to restore and vitalize this sense of divine calling? The principles are not difficult to state, though their application constantly confronts opposition in a secular society. There is need of a recognition not only of possessions but of the ability to work as the gift of God to be held in stewardship. Work should be chosen, where choices are open, with regard to the greatest possible service in it. If what is required affronts the Christian conscience of the worker, or if what is being produced in it is clearly not useful but harmful to society, one ought to look elsewhere for employment.

This is not to say that there is anything evil about working, as most persons must, to make a living for themselves and their families. To do this is a Christian duty, and a direct bearing on Christian service is not always easy to discover. There are dull, distasteful, routine jobs to be done, in which references to the "glory of the commonplace" are bound to seem a mockery. Yet to a greater degree than is commonly done, it is possible to look beyond the immediate task and find satisfactions in the work through its usefulness to society as a whole. One who is fortunate enough to have an ideal work situation ought to view with sympathy and understanding the plight of the many who do not; one who must earn his living under unpleasant conditions ought to try to see in his job something more than its irksome necessities.

So long as one's job is an honest, serviceable one in which one is doing the best he can, it is a divine calling, and one should endeavour like Brother Lawrence to "practice... the presence of God" within it. There are high opportunities in vocations of Christian leadership such as the ministry, the mission field, and Christian education, and many more young people should be entering them; there are also rich opportunities for Christian service and witness in an endless number of occupations to which God calls the layman.

What is Economic Justice?

We come now to an issue with which many discussions of economic ethics begin—namely, the nature of a just economic order and the principles by which such justice is to be judged. We have left it to this point, not because it is unimportant, but because the two great constituents of an economic society — property and work—must be seen in relation to God before any true perspective is possible upon their relationships.

Two cautions are in order as we move into this moot area. The first is the need to recognize that in the tangled complexity of modern society—in which not only the divergent interests of capital and labour but the pull of tradition, the uncertainties precipitated by a flood of new scientific discoveries, and the interlocking nature of the modern world are ever-present factors — perfect justice is not to be expected. This can be said without mention of sin, but when the forces of acquisitive self-interest, insistent determination to dominate others, and a deadly moral dullness are added to these other complicating factors, the result is a mixture of social evil and social sin in which no Utopia, either now or later, is attainable. A realistic economic justice is to be found in the best possible adjustment of life to life within the actual situation, not some imaginary perfection.

The second necessary caution is the need to recognize

that no situation is hopeless. No situation — however impregnated with meanness and "man's inhumanity to man" — is so bad that Christian effort to correct it is irrelevant. As the increase of love among persons is always a Christian obligation, so is the increase of justice. Furthermore, in individual circumstances, though not in society as a whole, there are situations so free from injustice that one may well "thank God and take courage." There are persons who have money enough but not too much for their personal well-being, who have earned it honestly in work serviceable to God and humanity, and who not only acquire but use it with a Christian conscience in sensitiveness to human need. This recognition ought never to induce complacency, but it needs to be made in answer to a pessimistic view of the total injustice of human society.

The most authoritative compendiums of the principles of Christian ethics in relation to the problems of economic justice are to be found in the reports of Section III of the Oxford, Amsterdam, and Evanston Conferences of the World Council of Churches, and in a statement on *Christian Principles and Assumptions for Economic Life* adopted by the General Board of the National Council of the Churches of Christ in the USA on September 15, 1954. These statements represent a surprising degree of unanimity of Christian thought in an area where precise unanimity is impossible, and where an authoritarian word even if obtainable would to the Protestant mind be undesirable. What follows is consistent with these statements, though necessarily in briefer form than even these relatively brief affirmations.

(a) *Misconceptions:* Certain misconceptions must be guarded against. Though no man living is wise enough to give a complete blueprint of the "next steps" to economic justice in every concrete situation, certain widely held errors stand in the way of these steps, and their discernment is essential to moving in the right direction.

In the first place, no economic system ought to be identified with the kingdom of God. In the past feudalism and slavery have been thus identified with the will and favour of God, and it was assumed that any change in the economic status quo was an affront to biblical teaching and to Christian morality. Not a little blood was shed to preserve these institutions with appeals to divine sanction in the process, but they had to yield to changing circumstances and a more enlightened conscience. Most American Christians now recognize the error in these particular forms of "absolutizing the relative," but new forms of idolatry have replaced them.

The most common of these identifications is the assumption that "the American way of life," meaning American capitalism and the free enterprise system, is ordained of God and any challenge to it a form of both political and religious subversion. Whether or not explicitly stated, this is the implicit assumption of many who inveigh against the "welfare state" and view with suspicion any criticism of economic individualism. On the other hand, there are those who espouse state socialism and a large measure of government ownership and control as the Christian answer. This view has had wide acceptance among religious liberals who saw in socialism an expression of the prophetic demand for social justice, but in recent years the evils in this system also have become apparent. Socialism ought not to be confused with Communism, which is clearly unchristian in its foundations and methods; yet two decades ago some Christians thought they discerned in Communism the way to economic justice.

In response to such identifications the Christian needs to be clear on two points: (1) that no system devised by man is completely Christian, or can be as long as human error and sin persist, and (2) that some systems are better fitted than others to be carriers of economic justice. Communism with its suppression of human freedom and ruthless violation of personal integrity cannot bring justice, though it can challenge injustice and possibly ameliorate some forms of it. The answer, as far as we can see it, lies in a blend of free enterprise and state control in accordance with certain positive Christian principles.

A second misconception is that benevolent intentions justify paternalistic domination by those who have superior status or power. To be sure, there can be no justice without love, for in its absence self-interest prompts to unscrupulous domination. Yet its presence in the form of attitudes of kindness is no guarantee of justice, and is too often a cloak for injustice. "Benevolent intentions have been used with sincerity at one time or another to justify slavery, to give religious sanction to white supremacy and the continuance of imperialism, to prevent the poor from having education or the suffrage, or to discourage land reform or the organization of labour." Such attitudes perpetuate injustice more often unconsciously than consciously, but are a particularly insidious form of the moral dullness to which reference was made earlier. They injure personality both in the holders of such power and its victims, for as the passage above quoted goes on to say, "It is quite as true of irresponsible economic power as of irresponsible political power, that such power tends to corrupt those who exercise it."

A third misconception, implicit in the two preceding, is that personal evangelism will automatically take care of the economic evils of society by generating Christian character. It is to the credit of the social gospel movement in American liberal Christianity that the need of changing social structures has been persistently stressed, and however far it may be necessary to go beyond it to a deeper emphasis on human sin, this must never be lost sight of. Not even John Wesley, most socially-minded of all the great religious leaders of an earlier day, fully grasped this necessity.

One looks in vain in Luther, Calvin, Baxter, Wesley, Edwards, and all the major figures of three centuries of Protestant writing, for any more than incidental treatment of the problems of the economic, political and legal structures of life. The realisation of the fluidity of social structures and the capacity of man to alter his political and economic environment is a nineteenth century insight, which became the inheritance of liberalism and neo-Protestantism as well.b) *Positive principles.* Let us now note some general principles of which the serious and determined application by Christians could, without creating a Utopia, remake society. Obviously, Christians are not the only persons who affect economic structures. Yet without waiting for all of society to become Christian — a "far-off divine event" certainly not to be anticipated in the near future — even a devoted minority of Christians could make a vast difference in the economic scene.

First, *the welfare of persons should be paramount over all other interests.* This applies to all the conditions regarding property and work which were examined in the early part of this chapter. It means that Christians should attempt by education, persuasion, and where necessary by legal action to secure a minimum standard of income for all, commensurate with the cost of living. Conditions of employment should be such that work can be done in physical and mental health and without undue anxiety for sickness, old age, or other forms of enforced unemployment. Young people should have equal opportunities to develop their capacities and to find the employment best suited to them. Enough economic security should be provided to permit marriage and the rearing of children in adequate housing and educational facilities, without undue luxury and without slums.

The ramifications of this primary principle are endless, but some because of frequent violation need special mention. There must be no racial discrimination in employment or housing, or in opportunities for education and for medical care. This alone, if taken seriously, would bring about a vast reconstruction in American life! And while racial prejudice creates the most obvious form of discrimination, a Christian conscience must be on guard also against economic injustices caused or perpetuated by family status, social stratification, political "pull," or even by church connections. Much as we stress democracy, democracy is affronted on every hand by factors such as these.

Second, due consideration *must be given* to the realities of economic life. It is customary to stress "hard facts" as cancelling out the considerations put forward by a Christian conscience. "One must live," and to live one must compete, and to compete one must do what others do. There are both rationalization and reason in this plea, and where to draw the line is an exceedingly difficult but basic need. To repeat what has been said earlier upon compromise, sin appears at the point of disparity between the actual and the best possible. To discern the highest possibility of Christian justice in a very complex world, not only a Christian conscience but technical knowledge is required. This the gospel cannot supply, though it may well provide the dynamic for acquiring and using it in a Christian frame of reference. Laymen who live close to economic realities, if they are informed and spiritually sensitive Christians, are often better equipped than ministers to judge the concrete next steps to be taken toward economic justice.

Third, *a proper balance must be maintained between individual freedom and social control*. Just what is "proper" has, of course, no easy answer. Much of the task of "Christianizing the social order" — to cite the title of an important book by Walter Rauschenbusch — lies at the point of determining this balance and putting it into effect. Some principles, however, may serve as norms of judgment. Every adult individual should have freedom to choose an occupation, exercise some creativity and initiative within it, earn an income sufficient for his personal and family needs, and determine within limits how he shall spend his money. Totalitarian control by the state is neither democratic nor Christian. On the other hand, unrestrained individualism leads neither to democracy nor to Christian social justice, but to the enhancement of acquisitiveness, an irresponsible use of power, exploitation of the weak, and to disregard of basic social obligations. It is right that by taxation and by legal restraints the grosser aspects of individualism should be curbed, and provision made for security against the hazards of illness, Unemployment, and old age. A "welfare state" or a "planned economy" can be a great step toward justice, provided an informed and conscientious citizenry insists that the welfare of all be taken into account.

Fourth, *economic justice must be viewed in a world setting*. There is a persistent provincialism which makes men tend to see political and economic issues from the standpoint of their own class or culture or nation. Few

Christians fully divest themselves of it. Yet it is rooted in the Christian gospel that *all* men are of supreme and equal worth in the sight of God. Inequality of personal endowment or of social contribution or of economic need does not cancel out this basic equality. To the degree that we are fully Christian, we shall do our utmost to see that all men, all women and children of all races and in all lands are provided with the material foundations of healthful, wholesome living and the good life. How basic this is, we must observe in later chapters.

This chapter is, and is not, finished, for economic conditions ramify throughout the whole of the world's social fabric. These principles of economic justice must be applied in the personal relations of the community and the market place, in corporations and labour unions, in' national affairs and in the world scene. If they are disregarded anywhere, evil consequences occur there and elsewhere, so interdependent is our world. And if they are persistently disregarded, there may before long be no world to talk about.

5

The Impact of a Cultural Revolutionary

No one had a greater impact on the cultural consciousness of African-Americans during the second half of the 20th century than Malcolm X. More than anyone else he revolutionized the black mind, transforming docile Negroes and self-effacing coloured people into proud blacks and self-confident African-Americans. Civil rights activists became Black Power militants and declared, "It's nation time." Preachers and religious scholars created a black theology and proclaimed God as liberator and Jesus Christ as black. College and university students demanded and won black studies. Poets, playwrights, musicians, painters and other artists created a new black aesthetics and ardently proclaimed that "black is beautiful."

No area of the African-American community escaped Malcolm's influence. The mainstream black leaders who dismissed him as a rabble-rouser today embrace his cultural philosophy and urge blacks to love themselves first before they even think about loving others. No one loved blacks more than Malcolm nor taught us more about ourselves. Before Malcolm most blacks wanted nothing to do with Africa. But he taught us that "you can't hate the roots of the tree and not hate the tree; you can't hate your origin and not end up hating yourself; you can't hate Africa and not hate yourself." A simple, profound truth; one that blacks needed (and still need) to hear. And no one said it as effectively as Malcolm X.

Who was Malcolm X? He was born Malcolm Little in Omaha, Nebraska, on May 19, 1925. His father, J. Early Little, was a Baptist preacher and a dedicated organizer for Marcus Garvey's Universal Negro Improvement Association. His mother, M. Louise Norton, also a Garveyite, was a West Indian from Grenada.

The Little family was driven out of Omaha by the Ku Klux Klan before Malcolm reached his first birthday. Another white hate group, called the Black Legion, burned down the Little's house in Lansing, Michigan, during Malcolm's childhood. Malcolm described the experience as "the nightmare in 1929." Soon after, his father was killed, thrown under a street car by the Black Legionnaires, Malcolm reported in his *Autobiography*.

With no husband, without the proceeds of his life insurance policy (the company refused to pay) and faced with constant harassment by the state welfare officials, Louis Little, a very proud woman, broke down under the emotional and economic strain of caring for eight children during the Depression. The Little children became wards of the state. Six of them, including Malcolm, were placed in foster homes. Malcolm's delinquent behaviour eventually landed him in a detention home in Mason, Michigan, where be was allowed to attend junior high. He was the only black in his class. Although Malcolm was an outstanding student and extremely popular among his peers, he dropped out of school when his white eighth grade English teacher discouraged him from becoming a lawyer and suggested carpentry as a more "realistic goal for a nigger."

From Michigan, Malcolm journeyed to Boston and then to New York where he became known as "Detroit Red." He was involved in a life of crime—numbers, dope, con games of many kinds and thievery of all sorts, including armed robbery. Malcolm described himself as "one of the most depraved parasitical hustlers" in New York—"nervy and cunning enough to live by my wits, exploiting any prey that presented itself." A few months before he reached his 21st birthday, Malcolm was convicted and sentenced to eight to ten years in a Massachusetts prison for burglary.

In prison Malcolm's life was transformed when he discovered (through the influence of an inmate) the liberating value of education and (through his family) the empowering message of Elijah Muhammad's Nation of Islam. Both gave him what he did not have: self-respect as a black person. For the first time since attending the Garvey meetings with his father, Malcolm was proud to be black and to learn about Africans who "built great empires and civilizations and cultures."

Discovering knowledge through reading raised Malcolm's consciousness. He found out that history had been "whitened" and blacks bad been left out. "It's a crime," Malcolm said, expressing his anger, "the lie that has been told to generations of blacks and whites. Little innocent black children born of parents who believed that their race had no history. Little black children seeing, before they could talk, that their parents considered themselves inferior. Innocent little black children growing up, living out their lives, dying of old age and all their lives ashamed of being black."

Malcolm pledged while in prison to use his intellectual

resources to destroy black self-hate and to replace it with black self-esteem. He transformed his prison cell into a hall of learning where he educated himself about "the brainwashed condition of blacks" and the crimes which "the devil white man" had committed against them. He was so engrossed in his studies that he even forgot he was in prison. "In every free moment I had," Malcolm reflected, "if I was not reading in the library, I was reading on my bunk. You couldn't have gotten me out of books with a wedge."

It was also in prison that Malcolm developed his debating skills. Debating, he said, was "like being on a battlefield —with intellectual and philosophical bullets." He became so effective in public speaking that even his opponents had to acknowledge his talent. Martin Luther King, Jr., and other mainstream civil rights leaders refused to appear on the same platform with him. People who did debate him often regretted it. For Malcolm there was no place for moderation or disinterested objectivity when one's freedom is at stake. "You can't negotiate upon freedom," he said. "You either fight for it or shut up."

After his release from prison in 1952 Malcolm became a minister in the Nation of Islam and its most effective recruiter and apologist. In June 1954 Elijah Muhammad appointed Malcolm the head minister of the influential Temple Number 7 in Harlem. Speaking regularly in the Temple and at many street-corner rallies, Malcolm told Harlemites that "we are black first and everything else second." "We are not Americans," he said. "We are Africans who happen to be in America. We didn't land on Plymouth Rock. That rock landed on us."

Malcolm's primary audience was the "little black people in the street," the ones at the "bottom of the social heap." His message was harsh and bitter, a "sharp truth" that "cuts" and "causes great pain." "But if you can take the truth," he assured Harlem blacks, "it will cure you and save you from an otherwise certain death." Malcolm told them that they were "zombies, walking dead people," who had been cut off from any knowledge of their past history. "We have been robbed deaf, dumb and blind to the true knowledge of ourselves." We do not even know our names or our original language. We carry the slavemasters' names and speak their language. We even accepted the slavemasters' religion of Christianity, which teaches us that "black is a curse." How can a people make others treat and respect them as human beings if they are culturally and spiritually dead?

After describing their zombie-like state, Malcolm commanded blacks to "wake up" to "their humanity, to their own worth, and to their cultural heritage." He also told them to "clean up" themselves of drunkenness, profanity, drugs, crime and other moral failings. A resurrected, morally upright black people will be able to "stand up" and "do something for themselves instead of sitting around and waiting for white people to solve our problems and tell us we are free."

Initially, Malcolm's black nationalist message was very unpopular in the African-American community. The media (both white and black) portrayed him as a teacher of hate and a promoter of violence. It was the age of integration, and love and nonviolence were advocated as the only way to achieve it. Most blacks shared Martin Luther King, Jr.'s dream that they would soon enter the mainstream of American society. They really believed that the majority of whites were genuinely sorry for what America had done to blacks and were now ready to right the wrongs and to treat blacks as human beings.

Malcolm did not share the optimism of the civil rights

movement and thus found himself speaking to many unsympathetic audiences. He did not mind speaking against the dominant mood of the time as long as he knew that he was speaking the truth. He defined the Nation of Islam as "the religion of naked, undressed truth." "You shall know the truth and the truth shall make you free" was his favourite biblical passage. "If you are afraid to tell truth," he railed at his audience, "you don't deserve freedom." With truth on his side, Malcolm relished the odds that were against him. His task was to wake up "dead Negroes" by revealing to them the truth about America and about themselves.

The enormity of this challenge motivated Malcolm to attack head on the philosophy of Martin King and the civil rights movement. He dismissed the charge that he was teaching hate: "It is the man who has made a slave out of you who is teaching hate." He rejected integration: "An integrated cup of coffee is insufficient pay for 400 years of slave labour." He denounced nonviolence as "the philosophy of a fool": "There is no philosophy more befitting to the white man's tactics for keeping his foot on the black man's neck." He ridiculed King's 1963 "I have a dream" speech: "While King was having a dream, the rest of us Negroes are having a nightmare." He also rejected as inhuman King's command to love the enemy: "It is not possible to love a man whose chief purpose in life is to humiliate you and still be considered a normal human being."

As long as Malcolm stayed in the Black Muslim movement he was not entirely free to speak his own mind. He had to represent Elijah Muhammad, the sole and absolute authority in the Nation of Islam. But in December 1963 Malcolm disobeyed Muhammad and described President Kennedy's assassination as an instance of the "chickens coming home to roost." Muhammad rebuked him and used the incident as an opportunity to silence his star pupil—first for 90 days and then indefinitely. Malcolm soon realized that much more was involved in his silence than what he had said about the Kennedy assassination. Jealousy and envy in Muhammad's family circle were the primary motives behind his silencing, and this meant the ban would never be lifted.

For the sake of black people who needed to hear the message of black selfworth he was so adept in proclaiming, Malcolm reluctantly declared his independence in March 1964. His break with the Black Muslim movement was an important turning point. He was now free to develop his own philosophy of the black freedom struggle.

Malcolm, however, had already begun to show independent thinking in his great "Message to the Grass Roots" speech, given in Detroit three weeks before his silencing. In that speech he endorsed black nationalism as his political philosophy, thereby separating himself not only from the civil rights movement but, more important, from Muhammad, who had defined the Nation as strictly religious and apolitical. Malcolm contrasted "the black revolution" with "the Negro revolution." The black revolution, he said, is "worldwide," and it is "bloody," "hostile" and "knows no compromise." But the so called Negro revolution is not even a revolution. Malcolm mocked it: "The only revolution in which the goal is loving your enemy is the Negro revolution. It's the only revolution in which the goal is a desegregated lunch counter, a desegregated theatre, a desegregated public park, a desegregated public toilet; you can sit down next to white folks on the toilet." He smiled as the audience broke into hearty laughter at this.

After his break with Muhammad, Malcolm developed

more fully his cultural and political black nationalist philosophy in a speech titled, "The Ballot or the Bullet." In urging blacks to exercise their constitutional right to vote, he made a move toward King and the civil rights movement. Later he became more explicit: "Dr. King wants the same thing I want—freedom." Malcolm wanted to join the civil rights movement in order to expand it into a human rights movement, thereby internationalizing the black freedom struggle, making it more radical and more militant.

During his period of independence from the Nation of Islam nothing influenced Malcolm more than his travels abroad. He visited countries in the Middle East, Africa and Europe, where he explained the black struggle for justice in the US and linked it with liberation struggles throughout the world. "You can't understand what is going on in Mississippi if you don't know what is going on in the Congo," he told Harlem blacks. "They are both the same. The same interests are at stake."

On February 21, 1965, Malcolm X was shot down by assassins as he started to speak to a crowd of 400 blacks at the Audubon Ballroom in Harlem. He was only 39.

Although dead for nearly 27 years, Malcolm's influence in the African-American community is much greater today than during his lifetime. His most far-reaching impact was among the masses of African-Americans in the ghettos of American cities. He told them, as James Baldwin observed, that "they should be proud of being black and God knows they should be. This is a very important thing to hear in a country that assures you that you should be ashamed of it." Saying what Malcolm meant to her, a Harlemite said: "He taught me that I was more than a Little Black Sambo or kinky hair or nigger."

There is a resurgence of interest in Malcolm in every

segment of the African-American community, especially among those who were not yet born when he died. His name, words and face adorn T-shirts, buttons and the cover of rap records. His writings, books about him and tapes of his speeches are sold by street vendors, at cultural festivals and in bookstores. Wherever black people gather to talk about their struggle for justice, the ghost of Malcolm's presence is there, reminding us of the strengths and weaknesses of our past and present efforts. The more we reflect on the meaning of Malcolm's life and message the more we realize the greatness of his legacy.

Malcolm was a cultural revolutionary, an artist of the spoken word. Maya Angelou aptly called him "a charismatic speaker who could play an audience as great musicians play instruments. "Peter Bailey said he was a "Master Teacher." Alfred Duckett called him "our sage and our saint." In his eulogy Ossie Davis bestowed upon Malcolm the title: "Our Shining Black Prince." For me, Malcolm was a cultural prophet of blackness. African-Americans who are proud to be black should thank Malcolm for creating the cultural space that lets us claim our African heritage. All Americans owe Malcolm a great debt. He was not a racist, as many misguided observers have claimed. He was an uncompromising truth-teller whose love for his people empowered him to respect all human beings. "I am for truth," he said, "no matter who tells it. I am for justice no matter who is for or against it. I am a human being first and foremost, and as such I am for whoever and whatever benefits humanity as a whole."

THE KING ASSASSINATION: AFTER THREE DECADES, ANOTHER VERDICT

In December, 1968, a jury in Memphis, Tennessee,

concluded that Martin Luther King Jr. was assassinated by a conspiracy involving Loyd Jowers and "others, including governmental agencies." Almost 32 years after King's murder at the Lorraine Motel in Memphis on April 4, 1968, a court extended the circle of responsibility for the assassination beyond the now deceased James Earl Ray, the man sentenced for the crime.

Explaining how this verdict came about requires some background. In 1969 Ray pleaded guilty to the murder. His lawyer, Percy Foreman, had threatened to throw the case if Ray let it go to trial. Before receiving his 99-year sentence, Ray answered Judge Preston Battle's question as to his guilt with a qualified, "Yes, legally, yes." He told the judge he disagreed with the government officials who denied there was a conspiracy. Three days later, Ray fired Foreman and asked Judge Battle for a new trial. For the rest of his life Ray continued to seek a new trial, maintaining that he had been set up in the King murder by a shadowy gunrunner named Raul. Ray died in prison in 1998.

William Pepper, who began investigating the King assassination in 1978, became convinced that Ray was innocent. In 1995 Pepper published *Orders to Kill: The Truth Behind the Murder of Martin Luther King,* a labyrinthine investigative work that detailed the tangle of evidence he had found pointing to a murder conspiracy that included government officials. The King family contacted Pepper in 1997 and asked to see his evidence. Convinced by it, the Kings supported Ray's request for a trial.

After Ray's death, the King family asked President Clinton to set up a commission similar to South Africa's Truth and Reconciliation Commission that would offer legal immunity in exchange for truth telling. When their proposal was turned into a "limited re-examination" of the murder by the Justice Department, the Kings tried another route to get at the evidence: they filed a wrongful death lawsuit against Jowers, who said he had been part of a conspiracy to kill King.

The complaint actually reads *King v. Jowers and Other Unknown Co-Conspirators.* As soon became evident at the trial last fall, the real defendants were the anonymous co-conspirator who stood in the shadows behind Jowers, the former owner of a Memphis bar and grill. The King family, represented by Pepper, was in effect charging US intelligence agencies—particularly the FBI and army intelligence—with organizing, subcontracting and covering up the assassination. Needless to say, this was a difficult case to make.

Many qualifiers have been attached to the verdict in *King v. Jowers.* It came not in criminal court but in civil court, where the standards of evidence are much lower than in criminal court. (For example, the plaintiffs used unsworn testimony made on audiotapes and videotapes.) Furthermore, the plaintiffs (the King family) and the defendant (Jowers) agreed ahead of time on much of the evidence.

But these observations are not entirely to the point. Because of the government's "sovereign immunity," it is not possible to put a US intelligence agency in the dock of a US criminal court. Such a step would require authorization by the federal government—which is not likely to indict itself. The civil case in Memphis laid out the strange story of the murder, and in the end 12 jurors (six black and six white) said: Guilty as charged—King was murdered by an intricate plot that included government agencies.

Jowers, 73, attended only the first three days of the

trial. He was excused by the judge because of illness. He said through his attorney, Lewis Garrison, that he would plead the Fifth Amendment if subpoenaed. However, in 1993 Jowers—against Garrison's advice and prompted by Pepper's investigation—appeared on *Prime Time Live* with Sam Donaldson and said he had been asked to help in the murder of King and had been told there would be a decoy in the plot. He was also told that the police "wouldn't be there that night."

In that interview, the transcript of which was read to the jury in the Memphis courtroom, Jowers said the man who asked him to help in the murder was a Mafia-connected produce dealer named Frank Liberto. Liberto, now deceased, had a courier deliver $100,000 for Jowers to hold at his restaurant, Jim's Grill, the back door of which opened onto the dense bushes across from the Lorraine Motel. Jowers said he was visited the day before the murder by a man named Raul, who brought a rifle in a box.

The jury in Memphis also heard a tape recording of a two-hour-long confession Jowers made at a fall 1998 meeting with Martin Luther King's son Dexter and former UN ambassador Andrew Young. On the tape Jowers says that the meetings to plan the assassination occurred at Jim's Grill. He said the planners included undercover Memphis Police Department officer Marrell McCollough (who now works for the Central Intelligence Agency), MPD Lieutenant Earl Clark (who died in 1987), a third police officer, and two men Jowers did not know but thought were federal agents.

Young, who witnessed the assassination, can be heard on the tape identifying McCollough as the man kneeling besides King's body on the balcony in a famous photograph taken right after the shooting. According to witness Colby

Vernon Smith, McCollough had infiltrated a Memphis community organizing group, the Invaders, which was working with the Southern Christian Leadership Conference. In his trial testimony Young said the MPD intelligence agent was "the guy who ran up [the balcony stairs] with us to see Martin."

Jowers says on the tape that right after the shot was fired he received a smoking rifle at the rear door of Jim's Grill from Clark. He broke the rifle down into two pieces and wrapped it in a tablecloth. Raul picked it up the next day. Jowers said he didn't actually see who fired the shot that killed King, but thought it was Clark, the MPD's best marksman.

Young testified that his impression from the 1998 meeting was that the increasingly frail Jowers "wanted to get right with God, wanted to confess it and be free of it." Jowers denied, however, that he knew the plot's purpose was to kill King—a claim which seemed implausible to Dexter King and Young. Jowers has continued to fear jail, and he had directed Garrison to defend him on the grounds that he didn't know the target of the plot was King. But his interview with Donaldson suggests he was not naive on this point.

Jowers's story opened the door to testimony on other areas:

Background to the assassination: James Lawson, King's friend and an organizer with SCLC, testified that King's stands on Vietnam and the Poor People's Campaign had created enemies in Washington. He said King's speech at New York's Riverside Church on April 4, 1967, which condemned the Vietnam war and identified the US government as "the greatest purveyor of violence in the world today," provoked intense hostility in the White House and FBI.

Hatred and fear of King deepened, Lawson said, in response to his plan to hold the Poor People's Campaign in Washington, D.C. King wanted to shut down the nation's capital in the spring of 1968 through massive civil disobedience until the government agreed to abolish poverty. King saw the Memphis sanitation workers' strike as the beginning of a nonviolent revolution that would redistribute income. "I have no doubt," Lawson said, "that the government viewed all this seriously enough to plan his assassination."

Evidence of a local conspiracy: On the night of April 3, 1968, Floyd E. Newsum, a black firefighter and civil rights activist, heard King's "I've Been to the Mountain Top" speech at the Mason Temple in Memphis. On his return home, Newsum returned a phone call from his lieutenant and was told he had been temporarily transferred, effective April 4, from Fire Station 2, located across the street from the Lorraine Motel, to Fire Station 31. Newsum testified: "I was not needed at the new station. I was needed at my old station. I was eventually told I was transferred by orders of the Police Department."

The only other black firefighter at Fire Station 2, Norvell E. Wallace, testified that he too received orders on the night of April 3 for a temporary transfer to a fire station far removed from the Lorraine Motel. The officer told Wallace vaguely that he had been threatened.

"I guess it was because I was putting out fires," Wallace told the jury with a smile. "I have never to this day been given a satisfactory explanation."

On the afternoon of April 4, a black Memphis Police Department detective, Ed Redditt, was removed from his surveillance post at Fire Station 2. Redditt had been watching King and his party across the street. Redditt testified that MPD Intelligence Officer Eli Arkin came to

Fire Station 2 later that afternoon to take him to Central Headquarters. There he was brought to Police and Fire Director Frank Holloman, a retired FBI agent. During his 25 years in the FBI, Holloman had been head of the Memphis field office (1959-64) as well as J. Edgar Hoover's appointments secretary. Holloman told Redditt that a secret service agent had just flown in from Washington with information about a threat on Redditt's life. He ordered him to go home.

"I objected," Redditt said. "Director Holloman told Arkin to take me home." When they arrived at Redditt's house, the car radio announced that King had just been assassinated at the Lorraine Motel. Redditt testified that nothing further was ever said to him by the authorities about the threat on his life.

Former MPD Captain Jerry Williams followed Redditt to the witness stand. Williams had been responsible for forming a security unit of black officers whenever King came to Memphis. For King's April 3 arrival, however, Williams was not asked to form that bodyguard. He was told that someone in King's entourage had asked for no security.

Philip Melanson, author of *The Martin Luther King Assassination* (1991), described his investigation into the April 4 pullback of four tactical police units that had been patrolling the immediate vicinity of the Lorraine Motel. When Melanson interviewed MPD Inspector Sam Evans (now deceased) on why the units were pulled back five blocks on the morning of April 4, in effect making an assassin's escape much easier, Evans said that a local pastor connected with King's party had ordered it. The pastor, however, denied this to Melanson.

Olivia Catling lived a block away from the Lorraine

on Mulberry Street. Catling had planned to walk down the street the evening of April 4 in the hope of catching a glimpse of King at the motel. She testified that when she heard the shot a little after six o'clock, she said, "Oh, my God, Dr. King!" She ran with her two children and a neighbour's child to the corner of Mulberry and Huling streets, just north of the Lorraine. She saw a man in a checkered shirt come running out of the alley beside a building across from the Lorraine.

The man jumped into a green 1965 Chevrolet just as a police car drove up behind him. He gunned the Chevrolet around the corner and up Mulberry past Catling's house, moving her to exclaim, "It's gonna take us six months to pay for the rubber!" The police, she said, ignored the man and blocked off a street, leaving his car free to go the opposite way.

I visited Catling in her home, and she told me the man she had seen running was not James Earl Ray. "I will go into my grave saying that was not Ray, because the gentleman I saw was heavier than Ray."

"The police," she told me, "asked not one neighbour [around the Lorraine], 'What did you see?' Thirty-one years went by. Nobody came and asked one question. I often thought about that. I even had nightmares over that, because they never said anything. How did they let him get away?"

Catling also told me that from her vantage point on the corner of Mulberry and Huling she could see a fireman standing alone across from the motel when the police drove up. She heard him say to the police, "The shot came from that clump of bushes,'" indicating the heavily overgrown brushy area facing the Lorraine and adjacent to Fire Station 2.

The crime scene: A 1993 affidavit from former SCLC official James Orange was read into the record. Orange said that on April 4, "James Bevel and I were driven around by Marrell McCollough, a person who at that time we knew to be a member of the Invaders, a local community organizing group, and who we subsequently learned was an undercover agent for the Memphis Police Department and who now works for the Central Intelligence Agency.... [After the shot, when Orange saw Dr. King's leg dangling over the balcony], I looked back and saw the smoke. It couldn't have been more than five to ten seconds. The smoke came out of the brush area on the opposite side of the street from the Lorraine Motel. I saw it rise up from the bushes over there. From that day to this time I have never had any doubt that the fatal shot, the bullet which ended Dr. King's life, was fired by a sniper concealed in the brush area behind the derelict buildings.

"I also remember then turning my attention back to the balcony and seeing Marrell McCollough up on the balcony kneeling over Dr. King, looking as though he was checking Dr. King for life signs.

"I also noticed, quite early the next morning around 8 or 9 o'clock, that all of the bushes and brush on the hill were cut down and cleaned up. It was as though the entire area of the bushes from behind the rooming house had been cleared....

"I will always remember the puff of white smoke and the cut brush and having never been given a satisfactory explanation.

"When I tried to tell the police at the scene as best I saw they told me to be quiet and to get out of the way.

"I was never interviewed or asked what I saw by any law enforcement authority in all of the time since 1968."

Also read into the record were depositions made by Solomon Jones to the FBI and to the Memphis police. Jones was King's chauffeur in Memphis. The FBI document, dated April 13, 1968, says that after King was shot, when Jones looked across Mulberry Street into the brushy area, "he got a quick glimpse of a person with his back toward Mulberry Street.... This person was moving rather fast, and he recalls that he believed he was wearing some sort of light-coloured jacket with some sort of a hood or parka." In his 11:30 P.M., April 4, 1968, police interview, Jones provides the same basic information concerning a person leaving the brushy area hurriedly.

Maynard Stiles, who in 1968 was a senior official in the Memphis Sanitation Department, confirmed in his testimony that the bushes near the rooming house were cut down. At about 7:00 AM. on April 5, Stiles told the jury, he received a call from MPD Inspector Sam Evans "requiring assistance clearing brush and debris from a vacant lot near the site of the assassination. I called another superintendent of sanitation. He assembled a crew, went to the site, and cleaned up the site in a slow, methodical, meticulous manner under the direction of the police department." Stiles identified the site as an area overgrown with brush and bushes across from the Lorraine Motel.

Within hours of King's assassination, the crime scene that witnesses were identifying to the Memphis police as a cover for the shooter had been sanitized by orders of the police.

The rifle: The rifle that government authorities have maintained is the murder weapon was found the night of April 4 in the Main Street doorway of the Canipe Amusement Company, one block from the Lorraine. It was dropped accidentally, they say, by Ray just before he jumped in his white Mustang and drove to Atlanta. The 30.06 Remington Gamemaster rifle was held up at the witness stand by Criminal Court Judge Joe Brown, who had presided over two years of hearings into the evidence concerning the rifle. "It is my opinion," he told the jury, "that this is not the murder weapon."

"Sixty-seven percent of the bullets from my tests," Brown said, "did not match the Ray rifle." He added that the unfired bullets found wrapped with it in a blanket were metallurgically different from the bullet taken from King's body, and therefore were from a different lot of ammunition. And because the rifle's scope had not been sited, Brown said, "this weapon literally could not have hit the broad side of a barn."

Circuit Court Judge Arthur Hanes Jr. of Birmingham, Alabama, testified that he had been Ray's attorney in 1968 (before Foreman) and had interviewed Guy Canipe, owner of the Canipe Amusement Company and a witness to the dropped bundle that included the rifle and unfired bullets. That dropped bundle was crucial to the case against Ray. Hanes said that Canipe (now deceased) provided "terrific evidence": "He said that the package was dropped by a man heading south on Main Street about ten minutes before the shot was fired."

When I spoke with Judge Hanes after the trial about the startling evidence he had received from Canipe, he commented, "That's what I've been saying for 30 years.

The mysterious Raul: In a 1995 deposition by Ray that was read to the jury, Ray told of meeting a man named Raul in Montreal in the summer of 1967, three months after Ray had escaped from a Missouri prison. According to Ray, Raul guided Ray's movements, gave him money for the Mustang car and the rifle, and used both to set him up in Memphis.

Andrew Young and Dexter King described their meeting with Jowers and Pepper at which Pepper had shown Jowers a spread of photographs, and Jowers picked out one as the person named Raul who brought him the rifle to hold at Jim's Grill. Pepper displayed the same spread of photos in court, and Young and King pointed out the photo Jowers had identified as Raul. (Private investigator John Billings said in separate testimony that this picture was a passport photograph from 1961, when Raul had immigrated from Portugal to the US)

The additional witnesses who identified the photo as Raul's included: British merchant seaman Sidney Carthew, who in a videotaped deposition from England said he had met Raul (who offered to sell him guns) and a man he thinks was Ray (who wanted to be smuggled onto his ship) in Montreal in the summer of 1967; Glenda and Roy Grabow, who recognized Raul as a gunrunner they knew in Houston in the '60s and '70s and who told Glenda in a rage that he had killed Martin Luther King; Royce Wilburn, Glenda's brother, who also knew Raul in Houston; and British television producer Jack Saltman, who had obtained the passport photo and showed it to Ray in prison, who identified it as the photo of the person who had guided him.

Saltman and Pepper, working on independent investigations, located Raul in 1995. He was living quietly with his family in the northeastern US. It was there in 1997 that journalist Barbara Reis of the *Lisbon Publico,* working on a story about Raul, spoke with a member of his family. Reis testified that she had spoken in Portuguese to a woman in Raul's family who, after first denying any connection to Ray's Raul, said that "they" had visited them. "Who?" Reis asked. "The government," said the woman. She said government agents had visited them three times over a three-year period. The government, she said, was watching over them and monitoring their phone calls. The woman took comfort and satisfaction in the fact that her family (so she believed) was being protected by the government.

A broader conspiracy: Carthel Weeden, captain of Fire Station 2 in 1968, testified that he was on duty the morning of April 4 when two US Army officers approached him. The officers said they wanted a lookout for the Lorraine Motel. Weeden said they carried briefcases and "indicated they had cameras." Weeden showed the officers the roof of the fire station. He left them at the edge of its northeast corner behind a parapet wall. From there the officers had a bird's-eye view of Dr. King's balcony doorway and could also look down on the brushy area adjacent to the fire station.

Former CIA operative Jack Terrell testified by videotape that his best friend, J. D. Hill, had confessed to him shortly before Hill's death that he had been a member of an army sniper team in Memphis assigned to shoot "an unknown target" on April 4.

After training for a triangular shooting, the snipers were taking up positions in a water-tower and two buildings in Memphis when their mission was suddenly cancelled. Hill said he realized the next day that the team must have been part of a contingency plan to kill King if another shooter failed.

Douglas Valentine said that while researching his book *The Phoenix Programme* (1990), on the CIA's notorious counterintelligence programme against Vietnamese villagers, he talked with veterans in military intelligence who had been redeployed from Vietnam to the domestic front. They told him that in 1968 the army's

111th Military Intelligence Group kept Martin Luther King under 24-hour-a-day surveillance. Its agents were in Memphis April 4. Valentine wrote in *The Phoenix Programme* that they "reportedly watched and took photos while King's assassin moved into position, took aim, fired and walked away."

Cover-up: Walter Fauntroy, Dr. King's colleague and a 20-year member of Congress, chaired the subcommittee of the 1976-78 House Select Committee on Assassinations that investigated King's assassination. Fauntroy testified in Memphis that in the course of the HSCA investigation "it became apparent that we were dealing with very sophisticated forces."

He discovered electronic bugs on his phones and TV set. When Richard Sprague, HSCA's first chief investigator, said he would make available all CIA and FBI records, he became a focus of controversy and media attacks. Sprague was forced to resign. His successor made no demands on US intelligence agencies.

Such pressures contributed to the committee's ending its investigation, in Fauntroy's words, "without having looked at all the evidence." Its formal conclusion was that Ray assassinated King, that he probably had help, and that the government was not involved.

When I interviewed Fauntroy in a van on his way back to the Memphis Airport, I asked about the implications of his statements in an April 4, 1997, *Atlanta Constitution* article. The article said Fauntroy now believed "Ray did not fire the shot that killed King and was part of a larger conspiracy that possibly involved federal law enforcement agencies," and added: "Fauntroy said he kept silent about his suspicions because of fear for himself and his family."

Fauntroy told me that when he left Congress in 1991 he had the opportunity to read through his files on the King assassination, including raw materials that he'd never seen before. Among them was information from J. Edgar Hoover's logs.

There he learned that in the three weeks before King's murder the FBI chief held a series of meetings with "persons involved with the CIA and military intelligence in the Phoenix operation in Southeast Asia." Fauntroy also discovered there had been Green Berets and military intelligence agents in Memphis when King was killed. "What were they doing there?" he asked.

When Fauntroy had talked about his decision to write a book about what he'd "uncovered since the assassination committee closed down," he was promptly investigated and charged by the Justice Department with having violated his financial reports as a member of Congress. His lawyer told him he could not understand why the Justice Department would bring up a charge on the technicality of one misdated check.

Fauntroy said he interpreted the Justice Department's action to mean: "Look, we'll get you on something if you continue this way.... I just thought: I'll tell them I won't go and finish the book, because it's surely not worth it."

In an interview after the trial, former MPD detective Ed Redditt told me his testimony before the HSCA had been a "total farce." Redditt was subpoenaed by the committee to testify about being removed from his surveillance post across from the Lorraine Motel two hours before the murder. Redditt said he was grilled by the committee for eight straight hours in a closed executive session. His public testimony the next day "was a set-up." When he arrived for the hearing, he was ushered into a room and shown a book with his testimony's questions and answers already set in print.

"So in essence," said Redditt, "what they were saying was: 'This is what you're going to answer to, and this is how you're going to answer.' It was all made up—all designed, questions and answers, what to say and what not to say.

A total farce." Coretta King explained her family's purpose in pursuing the lawsuit against Jowers: "This is not about money. We want the truth documented in a court of law. My family and I have wanted to see and know the truth, and to heal the nation."

Dexter King, the plaintiff's final witness, said the trial was about why his father had been killed: "The same thing is still happening. It can happen to anybody. If the state doesn't like what you're saying, you will be dealt with—not as in China overtly but covertly."

To the question, "What do we do about this?" he answered, "We are looking to get the truth out. We have never been interested in a criminal prosecution. Nonviolent reconciliation works. If we're saying we're willing to forgive, why can't others?" When pressed by Pepper to name a specific amount of damages for the murder of his father, Dexter King said, "One hundred dollars."

The jury returned with a verdict after two and one-half hours. Judge James E. Swearengen of Shelby County Circuit Court, a gentle African-American man in his last few days before retirement, read the verdict aloud. The courtroom was crowded with spectators, almost all black.

"In answer to the question, 'Did Loyd Jowers participate in a conspiracy to do harm to Dr. Martin Luther King?' your answer is 'Yes.'" The man on my left leaned forward and whispered softly, "Thank you, Jesus."

The judge continued: "'Do you also find that others, including governmental agencies, were parties to this conspiracy as alleged by the defendant?' Your answer to that one is also 'Yes.'"

An even more heartfelt whisper: "Thank you, Jesus!" David Morphy, the only juror to grant an interview, said later: "We can look back on it and say that we did change history. But that's not why we did it. It was because there was an overwhelming amount of evidence and just too many odd coincidences.

"Everything from the police department being pulled back, to the death threat on Redditt, to the two black firefighters being pulled off, to the military people going up on top of the fire station, even to them going back to that point and cutting down the trees. Who in their right mind would go and destroy a crime scene like that the morning after? It was just very, very odd."

I drove the few blocks to the house on Mulberry Street, one block north of the Lorraine Motel (now the National Civil Rights Museum). When I rapped loudly on Olivia Catling's security door, she was several minutes in coming. She said she'd had the flu. I told her the jury's verdict, and she smiled. "So I can sleep now. For years I could still hear that shot. After 31 years, my mind is at ease. So I can sleep now, knowing that some kind of peace has been brought to the King family. And that's the best part about it."

The 40th anniversary of the invasion of Normandy was grandly celebrated and widely reported by the media. This year also marked the 20th anniversary of another invasion, but this one was little noted. Few of its veterans returned either to celebrate or to relive the harsh experiences of the summer of 1964. Those who did were not besieged by representatives of the press. I was a small part of that exciting "Freedom Summer," when hundreds of students, lawyers, teachers, doctors and clergy descended on Mississippi. "the last bastion of segregation." My return exactly 20 years later, in August 1984, was even briefer: it was just a pass through the state on the way to deposit our youngest son (he wasn't even born in 1964!) at his college in New Orleans and to see an old friend and comrade-in-arms in Greenville.

We entered Mississippi in broad daylight, travelling south from Memphis down US 62. What a contrast to our night crossing at Vicksburg in August of '64. President Lyndon Johnson had spoken to the nation over radio and television about the Gulf of Tonkin incident near North Vietnam.

As we were on the bridge over Old Man River, the announcement came that the Federal Bureau of Investigation had found the bodies of the three missing civil rights workers. I was travelling with my fellow pastor from a little town in upstate North Dakota. Roger Smith was Methodist, I Presbyterian. As far as we knew, we were the only two pastors from our state to take part in the Mississippi Project. Each of us, independently of the other, had responded to the mimeographed National Council of Churches' letter appealing to the clergy to join the students and other professionals in voter registration work in "the most segregated state of the nation."

Today the vast flat expanse of the delta cotton fields looks much the same as then. Gone, of course, was the feeling that we were travelling through enemy territory. No need now to phone ahead to our destination and, on arrival, to phone back to home base that we were safe. The green fields stretched for miles. Few houses of any size were visible as we raced along the straight highway, just clusters of dilapidated shacks. Now that machines had replaced hand pickers, many of the falling-down houses were vacant.

Hours after entering the state we passed the small hamlet of Winstonville. Here was located the headquarters of the COFO (Council of Federated Organizations, an alliance of several civil rights groups that sponsored the Mississippi Summer Project) for Bolivar County, where Roger and I had been assigned.

We lived and worked at the Freedom Centre in Shaw, a few miles down the road, but came to Winstonville several times for meetings with project director John Bradford. John was a young man with but a year or two of college—very different from the dozens of highly educated, articulate white volunteers working under him, who often chafed at his direction. Roger and I sometimes served as buffers and interpreters between the critical white students and the frustrated black director. Today Winstonville is a small collection of houses barely discernible from the highway that curves around it.

US 62 now bypasses Mound Bayou as well. I recall when the road led us right by the large brick church where we had once attended a freedom rally. Mound Bayou was the largest all-black community in the state in 1964. You didn't need to fear the local police here. No one stood outside to take down the names of those who attended the night freedom rallies, as the civil rights meetings were called. We came up here, too, to mail letters which we did not want the Shaw postal people to open—or when we thought we were being charged too much for our mailings, as we were once or twice.

A few more hot minutes past Mound Bayou and we were approaching Cleveland. But my thoughts turned to

Ruleville as we waited for the light to change and I saw the sign pointing east to the seat of Sunflower County, home of that great lover of liberty, Senator James Eastland. It was also home to a genuine freedom fighter, Fannie Lou Hamer.

We met her a number of times, this fiery orator who could fill a church with her contralto voice leading us in a freedom song or hymn. She was often in pain due to a back injury caused by a beating in jail. Her crime: speaking out against injustice and trying to use a bathroom at a bus station.

There was a cadence to her speech that lifted the spirits of the ragged people who risked so much to come to hear her. A few samples recorded in my journal: "If you see a preacher not standing up [for civil rights], there's something wrong with him.... There's something wrong with teachers who don't teach citizenship and what it means. There's something wrong about not knowing about the history of Negroes." She could be funny in a barbed way, too: "When a preacher says he doesn't want polities in his church, he's telling a lie! The pictures on those bills you pay him are of presidents—he sure doesn't keep them out!"

We were at the outdoor party to celebrate the second year of the Freedom Movement in Ruleville the day that Hamer was served with an injunction by the sheriff. Long before the northern press was interested in covering the beatings of the black Student Nonviolent Coordinating Committee workers, Charles McClaron had come to Ruleville to begin voter registration work. There were too many people and it was too hot to meet in the little church, so we ate our chicken outside. You could still see the scorched area above the church door where local whites had hurled a fire bomb. You could also see the cars slow as they passed, their white occupants scarcely believing that whites and blacks would eat and socialize together.

The sheriffs injunction was an attempt to scare Hamer from running for the US Senate and from challenging the segregated delegation at the Democratic Convention later that month. She read it and said, "it's just a scrap of paper. It don't scare me or anything. I'll be in Atlantic City, even if I have to go by myself."

We drove on by Cleveland. It was late and my wife and son were too hot and tired to make the side trip to see the courthouse where we had fruitlessly brought people to register to vote. One woman had been a schoolteacher with two years of college, yet she didn't pass the same test that hundreds of semiliterate whites were eased through.

And what courage it took for the registrants to brave the hate-filled stares and the insolence of the courthouse staff. I wondered if the monument to the Confederate soldiers still stood, proclaiming that never had so noble a cause and nation risen so cleanly. There would be no statue of Amsie Moore, longtime National Association for the Advancement of Coloured People leader who bravely carried the torch for justice. His Amoco station no longer stood by the highway—the only place where we had been able to buy gasoline safely. He had been an eloquent speaker, lacing his speeches with quotations from the Gospels and I John about loving and praying for our enemies.

I wondered too what had happened to the white Presbyterian minister whom Roger and I had called on. He had many of the same books in his library as I, yet we were worlds apart. He knew of no poverty in his area nor of any wrongs committed. Polite to us, he nevertheless regarded us as outsiders, not fellow American Christians who could help each other. He urged us to tell the students to shave and bathe more often. We refrained from telling him how difficult maintaining one's personal grooming was, when the only running water available for a square block was a pump in the backyard of the shack we slept in.

Fifteen minutes later we were at Shaw, our home base for the two weeks and a few days we had spent in Mississippi. This I couldn't bypass, filled as I was with the memory of hot, nausea-producing (if you moved too fast) days filled with knocking on doors, talking with adults, and playing with and teaching children at the Freedom Centre.

The laundromat at the edge of town where we were bawled out by the owner was gone. I still have the slide Roger took showing the large "White" and "Coloured" signs on each side. Downtown Shaw itself looked awful—rundown and seedy. Only a few blacks were out on the sidewalk as we drove along the main street. It appeared so small now; surely it was not the home of 2,300 people! Back then, that street had seemed so long as we walked down it while trying to ignore the hostile stares of the whites who knew—and disapproved of—our reason for being in town.

I looked in vain for the library which "our" local youth had so proudly integrated. There was the railroad depot, however, where the white bus had stood, together with hordes of white, helmeted state troopers with their riot guns at the ready. I had cruised slowly down that same street 20 years ago to see how the three brave teenagers who had won the right to integrate the library were faring, since none of us outsiders could accompany them.

Fear rode with me and my companions, for a large crowd of angry whites stood on one side of the road. Held back by sheriff's deputies, they made it clear that they didn't like what was happening.

Even if black taxes also supported the facility, no "nigra" had ever entered it, except to clean up. We had called the FBI to inform them of the planned integration, and the Bureau in turn had notified the state and local authorities. All the chairs had been removed from the little storefront library, but the youths were allowed to take out the books they asked for, a small victory. On our way back down the main street I saw the new library on the opposite side.

It was still a storefront, but neat and well painted, in marked contrast to the faded appearance of most of the shops and stores in town. We passed the large Baptist church which we whites had attended one Sunday. No warm greetings or "Y'all come back" for us. Nor did we want to, so irrelevant and "spiritual" was the lifeless sermon.

The big white church faced the bayou that divided Shaw. Behind the row of fine homes on the other side was "Coloured Town." I was appalled at how dilapidated the area looked, despite a large sign proclaiming the renovations taking place. A closer look showed us that curbs had been put in. The open ditches that had served as a sewage system were gone. Even blacks could have sewers and indoor plumbing now, apparently. There were a few street lights. But the houses and the people seemed locked into a bygone era. Could this be the prosperous America that Ronald Reagan extols so often?

We felt like the outsiders that we were, so I didn't take time to find the churches where we had met to sing freedom songs and make fervent speeches. No doubt the white policeman who had stood outside taking down names had long since been pensioned off. When the black audience recited, "Yea, though I walk through the valley of the shadow...," they meant it. When they chanted prayers asking to be delivered from the "terror by night and the arrow that flieth by day," we *all* meant it. Those meetings—so filled with joy and the hope of deliverance from Mr. Charlie—and our daily work with the local blacks came as close to the church of the Book of Acts as I've ever been privileged to see. The people taught us so much about faith, hope and love.

We found the grocery where we often ate our breakfast of doughnuts and orange juice. I couldn't be positive about the present identity of what had been our Freedom Centre: a three-room house stuffed with library books, sports equipment, telephone (the only one in the black section) and mimeograph machine and a thousand posters and handbills. There we had talked with people, written reports and letters and kept in touch with the outside world.

We drove out of the black area, crossing the bayou bridge to head south again. Passing the cutoff that led to the settlement of Choctaw, I thought of our forays into the country to register people for the Freedom Democratic Party—and of the fear that we felt each time a white-driven truck, rifle resting on the rear-window rack, had slowed down to look us over. We had been stopped by one irate white and warned to get moving. As he pulled away, the teens in my car got out to write down his license plate number so we could report the incident to the FBI. The driver saw the kids, screeched to a stop, and backed into a driveway, where he got stuck in the mud. The loud laughter of the teens didn't help his temper, I'm sure—though we didn't wait around to find out.

Our day ended in Greenville. That night we dined with my companion of two decades ago, Roger Smith. Roger had returned to North Dakota for a year and then asked to be assigned to the staff of the Delta Ministry. He was now the only white person on the staff of the Delta Resources Committee, under the direction of native Mississippian Jean Phillips. This Greenville-based group provides emergency assistance, counselling, advocacy and other services for the poor blacks (and those whites who are beginning to see that they too are victims of an unjust system) of a large portion of the Mississippi Delta. I've often wondered if all the work, beatings, bombings and deaths of that 1964 summer were worth it. The World War II veterans who returned to Normandy could be proud and satisfied that their invasion had ended in total victory over the most vicious system in human history. None of us Freedom Summer vets could make such a claim. We succeeded in registering only about 8,000 new voters that summer. Fannie Lou Hamer never made it to the Senate. And some of the people Roger and I knew have been killed. Life still looks much the same: blacks are at the bottom of society and maybe even worse off than before, since machines have taken over much of their work in the cotton fields. There is no longer a government in Washington that cares whether they live or die.

When Roger and I were preparing to leave Shaw 20 years ago an old man told us, "You know why the whites here hate you so? Because you all came down here and opened our eyes. Now we see that things don't have to stay the same!" (Today they call this process "conscientization.") Two elderly women thanked us as we came out of the church on our last night there. One said, "I'm old and won't see the day of freedom. But my grandchild will." That day still hasn't come. But as Roger and Jean point out, there are now black mayors, council members and other county and state officials in Mississippi. We could enjoy our dinner together in one of Greenville's finest restaurants—whereas once, just a few miles away, we had nearly been attacked because an integrated group of us rode in the same car. Instead of the pitifully few thousand blacks registered to vote, there are now tens of thousands. And there will soon be more, if the Delta Resources Committee staff has anything to do with it.

No monuments or celebrations commemorate the 1964 invasion of Mississippi. Instead, there are dedicated people living and working here, resolved to carry on the way begun then—and largely abandoned by the rest of the country. Maybe someday, when people can again sing, "We shall overcome" with integrity, there will be celebrations and speeches commemorating slain civil rights workers Andy Goodman, Michael Schwerner and James Chaney—and all other who gave so much, yet received so much more from the quiet courage and faith of the people whom they had come to help.

6

The Relation of the Faculties of the Human Mind

The active faculty of the human mind, as the faculty of desire in its widest sense, is the power which man has, through his mental representations, of becoming the cause of objects corresponding to these representations. The capacity of a being to act in conformity with his own representations is what constitutes the life of such a being.

It is to be observed, first, that with desire or aversion there is always connected pleasure or pain, the susceptibility for which is called feeling. But the converse does not always hold; for there may be a pleasure connected, not with the desire of an object, but with a mere mental representation, it being indifferent whether an object corresponding to the representation exist or not. And second, the pleasure or pain connected with the object of desire does not always precede the activity of desire; nor can it be regarded in every case as the cause, but it may as well be the effect of that activity. The capacity of experiencing pleasure or pain on the occasion of a mental representation is called "feeling," because pleasure and pain contain only what is subjective in the relations of our mental activity. They do not involve any relation to an object that could possibly furnish a knowledge of it as such; they cannot even give us a knowledge of our own mental state. For even sensations,* considered apart from the qualities which attach to them on account of the modifications of the subject-as, for instance, in reference to red, sweet, and such like-are referred as constituent elements of knowledge to objects, whereas pleasure or pain felt in connection with what is red or sweet express absolutely nothing that is in the object, but merely a relation to the subject. And for the reason just stated, pleasure and pain considered in themselves cannot be more precisely defined. All that can be further done with regard to them is merely to point out what consequences they may have in certain relations, in order to make the knowledge of them available practically.

*The sensibility as the faculty of sense may be defined by reference to the subjective nature of our representations generally. It is the understanding that fir refers the subjective representations to an object; it alone thinks anything by means of these representations. Now, the subjective nature of our representations might be of such a kind that they could be related to objects so as to furnish knowledge of them, either in regard to their form or matter-in the former relation by pure perception, in the latter by sensation proper.

In this case, the sense-faculty, as the capacity for receiving objective representations, would be properly called sense perception. But mere mental representation from its subjective nature cannot, in fact, become a constituent of objective knowledge, because it contains merely the relation of the representations to the subject, and includes nothing that can be used for attaining a knowledge of the object. In this case, then, this receptivity of the mind for subjective representations is called feeling. It includes the effect of the representations, whether sensible or intellectual, upon the subject; and it belongs to the sensibility, although the representation itself may belong to the understanding or the reason.

The pleasure which is necessarily connected with the activity of desire, when the representation of the object desired affects the capacity of feeling, may be called practical pleasure. And this designation is applicable whether the pleasure is the cause or the effect of the desire. On the other hand, that pleasure which is not necessarily connected with the desire of an object, and which, therefore, is not a pleasure in the existence of the object, but is merely attached to a mental representation alone, may be called inactive complacency, or mere contemplative pleasure. The feeling of this latter kind of pleasure is what is called taste.

Hence, in a system of practical philosophy, the contemplative pleasure of taste will not be discussed as an essential constituent conception, but need only be referred to incidentally or episodically. But as regards practical pleasure, it is otherwise. For the determination of the activity of the faculty of desire or appetency, which is necessarily preceded by this pleasure as its cause, is what properly constitutes desire in the strict sense of the term. Habitual desire, again, constitutes inclination; and the connection of pleasure with the activity of desire, in so far as this connection is judged by the understanding to be valid according to a general rule holding good at least for the individual, is what is called interest.

Hence, in such a case, the practical pleasure is an interest of the inclination of the individual. On the other hand, if the pleasure can only follow a preceding determination of the faculty of desire, it is an intellectual pleasure, and the interest in the object must be called a rational interest; for were the interest sensuous, and not based only upon pure principles of reason, sensation would necessarily be conjoined with the pleasure, and would thus determine the activity of the desire. Where an entirely pure interest of reason must be assumed, it is not legitimate to introduce into it an interest of inclination surreptitiously.

However, in order to conform so far with the common phraseology, we may allow the application of the term "inclination" even to that which can only be the object of an "intellectual" pleasure in the sense of a habitual desire arising from a pure interest of reason. But such inclination would have to be viewed, not as the cause, but as the effect of the rational interest; and we might call it the non-sensuous or rational inclination (propensio intellectualis). Further, concupiscence is to be distinguished from the activity of desire itself, as a stimulus or incitement to its determination. It is always a sensuous state of the mind, which does not itself attain to the definiteness of an act of the power of desire.

The activity of the faculty of desire may proceed in accordance with conceptions; and in so far as the principle thus determining it to action is found in the mind, and not in its object it constitutes a power acting or not acting according to liking. In so far as the activity is accompanied with the consciousness of the power of the action to produce the object, it forms an act of choice; if this consciousness is not conjoined with it, the activity is called a wish.

The faculty of desire, in so far as its inner principle of determination as the ground of its liking or predilection lies in the reason of the subject, constitutes the will. The will is therefore the faculty of active desire or appetency, viewed not so much in relation to the action-which is the relation of the act of choice-as rather in relation to the principle that determines the power of choice to the action. It has, in itself, properly no special principle of determination, but in so far as it may determine the voluntary act of choice, it is the practical reason itself.

Under the will, taken generally, may be included the volitional act of choice, and also the mere act of wish, in so far as reason may determine the faculty of desire in its activity. The act of choice that can be determined by pure reason constitutes the act of free-will. That act which is determinable only by inclination as a sensuous impulse or stimulus would be irrational brute choice (arbitrium brutum). The human act of choice, however, as human, is in fact affected by such impulses or stimuli, but is not determined by them; and it is, therefore, not pure in itself when taken apart from the acquired habit of determination by reason.

But it may be determined to action by the pure will. The freedom of the act of volitional choice is its independence of being determined by sensuous impulses or stimuli. This forms the negative conception of the free-will. The positive conception of freedom is given by the fact that the will is the capability of pure reason to be practical of itself. But this is not possible otherwise than by the maxim of every action being subjected to the condition of being practicable as a universal law. Applied as pure reason to the act of choice, and considered apart from its objects, it may be regarded as the faculty of principles; and, in this connection, it is the source of practical principles. Hence it is to be viewed as a lawgiving faculty.

But as the material upon which to construct a law is

not furnished to it, it can only make the form of the form of the maxim of the act of will, in so far as it is available as a universal law, the supreme law and determining principle of the will. And as the maxims, or rules of human action derived from subjective causes, do not of themselves necessarily agree with those that are objective and universal, reason can only prescribe this supreme law as an absolute imperative of prohibition or command.

The laws of freedom, as distinguished from the laws of nature, are moral laws. So far as they refer only to external actions and their lawfulness, they are called juridical; but if they also require that, as laws, they shall themselves be the determining principles of our actions, they are ethical. The agreement of an action with juridical laws is its legality; the agreement of an action with ethical laws is its morality. The freedom to which the former laws refer, can only be freedom in external practice; but the freedom to which the latter laws refer is freedom in the internal as well as the external exercise of the activity of the will in so far as it is determined by laws of reason. So, in theoretical philosophy, it is said that only the objects of the external senses are in space, but all the objects both of internal and external sense are in time; because the representations of both, as being representations, so far belong all to the internal sense. In like manner, whether freedom is viewed in reference to the external or the internal action of the will, its laws, as pure practical laws of reason for the free activity of the will generally, must at the same time be inner principles for its determination, although they may not always be considered in this relation.

The Idea and Necessity of a Metaphysic of Morals

It has been shown in The Metaphysical Principles of the Science of Nature that there must be principles a priori for the natural science that has to deal with the objects of the external senses. And it was further shown that it is possible, and even necessary, to formulate a system of these principles under the name of a "metaphysical science of nature," as a preliminary to experimental physics regarded as natural science applied to particular objects of experience.

But this latter science, if care be taken to keep its generalizations free from error, may accept many propositions as universal on the evidence of experience, although if the term "universal" be taken in its strict sense, these would necessarily have to be deduced by the metaphysical science from principles a priori. Thus Newton accepted the principle of the equality of action and reaction as established by experience, and yet he extended it as a universal law over the whole of material nature. The chemists go even farther, grounding their most general laws regarding the combination and decomposition of the materials of bodies wholly upon experience; and yet they trust so completely to the universality and necessity of those laws that they have no anxiety as to any error being found in propositions founded upon experiments conducted in accordance with them.

But it is otherwise with moral laws. These, in contradistinction to natural laws, are only valid as laws, in so far as they can be rationally established a priori and comprehended as necessary. In fact, conceptions and judgements regarding ourselves and our conduct have no moral significance, if they contain only what may be learned from experience; and when any one is, so to speak, misled into making a moral principle out of anything derived from this latter source, he is already in danger of falling into the coarsest and most fatal errors.

If the philosophy of morals were nothing more than

a theory of happiness (eudaemonism), it would be absurd to search after principles a priori as a foundation for it. For however plausible it may sound to say that reason, even prior to experience, can comprehend by what means we may attain to a lasting enjoyment of the real pleasures of life, yet all that is taught on this subject a priori is either tautological, or is assumed wholly without foundation. It is only experience that can show what will bring us enjoyment. The natural impulses directed towards nourishment, the sexual instinct, or the tendency to rest and motion, as well as the higher desires of honour, the acquisition of knowledge, and such like, as developed with our natural capacities, are alone capable of showing in what those enjoyments are to be found.

And, further, the knowledge thus acquired is available for each individual merely in his own way; and it is only thus he can learn the means by which be has to seek those enjoyments. All specious rationalizing a priori, in this connection, is nothing at bottom but carrying facts of experience up to generalizations by induction (secundum principia generalia non universalia); and the generality thus attained is still so limited that numberless exceptions must be allowed to every individual in order that he may adapt the choice of his mode of life to his own Particular inclinations and his capacity for pleasure. And, after all, the individual has really to acquire his prudence at the cost of his own suffering or that of his neighbours the form

But it is quite otherwise with the principles of morality. They lay down commands for every one without regard to his particular inclinations, and merely because and so far as he is free, and has a practical reason. Instruction in the laws of morality is not drawn from observation of oneself or of our animal nature, nor from perception of the course of the world in regard to what happens, or how men act. But reason commands how we ought to act, even although no example of such action were to be found; nor does reason give any regard to the advantage which may accrue to us by so acting, and which experience could alone actually show.

For, although reason allows us to seek what is for our advantage in every possible way, and although, founding upon the evidence of experience, it may further promise that greater advantages will probably follow on the average from the observance of her commands than from their transgression, especially if prudence guides the conduct, yet the authority of her precepts as commands does not rest on such considerations. They are used by reason only as counsels, and by way of a counterpoise against seductions to an opposite course, when adjusting beforehand the equilibrium of a partial balance in the sphere of practical judgement, in order thereby to secure the decision of this judgement, according to the due weight of the a priori principles of a pure practical reason.

This holds notwithstanding the fact that the term morals," in Latin mores, and in German sitten, signifies originally only manners or mode of life.

Metaphysics designates any system of knowledge a priori that consists of pure conceptions. Accordingly, a practical philosophy not having nature, but the freedom of the will for its object, will presuppose and require a metaphysic of morals. It is even a duty to have such a metaphysic; and every man does, indeed, possess it in himself, although commonly but in an obscure way. For how could any one believe that he has a source of universal law in himself, without principles a priori?

And just as in a metaphysics of nature there must be principles regulating the application of the universal supreme principles of nature to objects of experience, so there cannot but be such principles in the metaphysic of morals; and we will often have to deal objectively with the particular nature of man as known only by experience, in order to show in it the consequences of these universal moral principles. But this mode of dealing with these principles in their particular applications will in no way detract from their rational purity, or throw doubt on their a priori origin. In other words, this amounts to saying that a metaphysic of morals cannot be founded on anthropology as the empirical science of man, but may be applied to it.

The counterpart of a metaphysic of morals, and the other member of the division of practical philosophy, would be a moral anthropology, as the empirical science of the moral nature of man. This science would contain only the subjective conditions that hinder or favour the realization in practice of the universal moral laws in human nature, with the means of propagating, spreading, and strengthening the moral principles-as by the education of the young and the instruction of the people-and all other such doctrines and precepts founded upon experience and indispensable in themselves, although they must neither precede the metaphysical investigation of the principles of reason, nor be mixed up with it. For, by doing so, there would be a great danger of laying down false, or at least very flexible moral laws, which would hold forth as unattainable what is not attached only because the law has not been comprehended and presented in its purity, in which also its strength consists. Or, otherwise, spurious and mixed motives might be adopted instead of what is dutiful and good in itself; and these would furnish no certain moral principles either for the guidance of the judgement or for the discipline of the heart in the practice of duty. It is only by pure reason, therefore, that duty can and must be prescribed.

The higher division of philosophy, under which the division just mentioned stands, is into theoretical philosophy and practical philosophy. Practical philosophy is just moral philosophy in its widest sense, as has been explained elsewhere.* All that is practicable and possible, according to natural laws, is the special subject of the activity of art, and its precepts and rules entirely depend on the theory of nature. It is only what is practicable according to laws of freedom that can have principles independent of theory, for there is no theory in relation to what passes beyond the determinations of nature. Philosophy therefore cannot embrace under its practical division a technical theory, but only a morally practical doctrine. But if the dexterity of the will in acting according to laws of freedom, in contradistinction to nature, were to be also called an art, it would necessarily indicate an art which would make a system of freedom possible like the system of nature. This would truly be a Divine art, if we were in a position by means of it to realize completely what reason prescribes to us, and to put the idea into practice. In the Critique of Judgement (1790).

The Division of a Metaphysic of Morals

All legislation, whether relating to internal or external action, and whether prescribed a priori by mere reason or laid down by the will of another, involves two elements: First, a law which represents the action that ought to happen as necessary objectively, thus making the action a duty; second, a motive which connects the principle determining the will to this action with the mental representation of the law subjectively, so that the law makes duty the motive of the action. By the first element, the action is represented as a duty, in accordance with the mere theoretical knowledge of the possibility of determining the activity of the will by practical rules. By the second element, the obligation so to act is connected in the subject with a determining principle of the will as such. All legislation, therefore, may be differentiated by reference to its motive-principle.

The legislation which makes an action a duty, and this duty at the same time a motive, is ethical. That legislation which does not include the motive-principle in the law, and consequently admits another motive than the idea of duty itself, is juridical. In respect of the latter, it is evident that the motives distinct from the idea of duty, to which it may refer, must be drawn from the subjective (pathological) influences of inclination and of aversion, determining the voluntary activity, and especially from the latter; because it is a legislation which has to be compulsory, and not merely a mode of attracting or persuading. The agreement or non-agreement of an action with the law, without reference to its motive, is its legality; and that character of the action in which the idea of duty arising from the law at the same time forms the motive of the action, is its morality.

This ground of division will apply, although the action which it makes a duty may coincide with another action that may be otherwise looked at from another point of view. For instance, actions may in all cases be classified as external.

Duties specially in accord with a juridical legislation can only be external duties. For this mode of legislation does not require that the idea of the duty, which is internal, shall be of itself the determining principle of the act of will; and as it requires a motive suitable to the nature of its laws, it can only connect what is external with the law. Ethical legislation, on the other hand, makes internal actions also duties, but not to the exclusion of the external, for it embraces everything which is of the nature of duty. And just because just because ethical legislation includes within its law the internal motive of the action as contained in the idea of duty, it involves a characteristic which cannot at all enter into the legislation that is external. Hence, ethical legislation cannot as such be external, not even when proceeding from a Divine will, although it may receive duties which rest on an external legislation as duties, into the position of motives, within its own legislation.

From what has been said, it is evident that all duties, merely because they are duties, belong to ethics; and yet the legislation upon which they are founded is not on that account in all cases contained in ethics. On the contrary, the law of many of them lies outside of ethics. Thus ethics commands that I must fulfil a promise entered into by contract, although the other party might not be able to compel me to do so. It adopts the law (pacta sunt servanda) and the duty corresponding to it, from jurisprudence or the science of right, by which they are established.

It is not in ethics, therefore, but in jurisprudence, that the principle of the legislation lies, that "promises made and accepted must be kept." Accordingly, ethics specially teaches that if the motive-principle of external compulsion which juridical legislation connects with a duty is even let go, the idea of duty alone is sufficient of itself as a motive. For were it not so, and were the legislation itself not juridical, and consequently the duty arising from it not specially a duty of right as distinguished from a duty of virtue, then fidelity in the performance of acts, to which the individual may be bound by the terms of a contract, would have to be classified with acts of benevolence and the obligation that underlies them, which cannot be correct.

To keep one's promise is not properly a duty of virtue, but a duty of right, and the performance of it can be enforced by external compulsion. But to keep one's promise, even when no compulsion can be applied to enforce it, is, at the same time, a virtuous action, and a proof of virtue, jurisprudence as the science of right, and ethics as the science of virtue, are therefore distinguished not so much by their different duties, as rather by the difference Of the legislation which connects the one or the other kind of motive with their laws.

Ethical legislation is that which cannot be external, although the duties it prescribes may be external as well as internal. Juridical legislation is that which may also be external. Thus it is an external duty to keep a promise entered into by contract; but the injunction to do this merely because it is a duty, without regard to any other motive, belongs exclusively to the internal legislation. It does not belong thus to the ethical sphere as being a particular kind of duty or a particular mode of action to which we are bound-for it is an external duty in ethics as well as in jurisprudence-but it is because the legislation in the case referred to is internal, and cannot have an external lawgiver, that the obligation is reckoned as belonging to ethics.

For the same reason, the duties of benevolence, although they are external duties as obligations to external actions, are, in like manner, reckoned as belonging to ethics, because they can only be enjoined by legislation that is internal. Ethics has no doubt its own peculiar duties-such as those towards oneself-but it has also duties in common with jurisprudence, only not under the same mode of obligation. In short, the peculiarity of ethical legislation is to enjoin the performance of certain actions merely because they are duties, and to make the principle of duty itself-whatever be its source or occasion-the sole sufficing motive of the activity of the will. Thus, then, there are many ethical duties that are directly such; and the inner legislation also makes the others-all and each of them-indirectly ethical.

The deduction of the division of a system is the proof of its completeness as well as of its continuity, so that there may be a logical transition from the general conception divided to the members of the division, and through the whole series of the subdivisions without any break or leap in the arrangement (divisio per saltum). Such a division is one of the most difficult conditions for the architect of a system to fulfil. There is even some doubt as to what is the highest conception that is primarily divided into right and wrong (aut fas aut nefas). It is assuredly the conception of the activity of the free-will in general. In like manner, the expounders of ontology start from something and nothing, without perceiving that these are already members of a division for which the highest divided conception is awanting, and which can be no other than that of thing in general.

General Preliminary Conceptions

The conception of freedom is a conception of pure reason. It is therefore transcendent in so far as regards theoretical philosophy; for it is a conception for which no corresponding instance or example can be found or supplied in any possible experience. Accordingly freedom is not presented as an object of any theoretical knowledge that is possible for us. It is in no respect a constitutive, but only a regulative conception; and it can be accepted by the speculative reason as at most a merely negative principle. In the practical sphere of reason, however, the reality of freedom may be demonstrated by certain practical principles which, as laws, prove a causality of the pure reason in the process of determining the activity of the will that is independent of all empirical and sensible conditions. And thus there is established the fact of a pure will existing in us as the source of all moral conceptions and laws.

On this positive conception of freedom in the practical relation certain unconditional practical laws are founded, and they specially constitute moral laws. In relation to us as human beings, with an activity of will modified by sensible influences so as not to be conformable to the pure will, but as often contrary to it, these laws appear as imperatives commanding or prohibiting certain actions; and as such they are categorical or unconditional imperatives. Their categorical and unconditional character distinguishes them from the technical imperatives which express the prescriptions of art, and which always command only conditionally.

According to these categorical imperatives, certain actions are allowed or disallowed as being morally possible or impossible; and certain of them or their opposites are morally necessary and obligatory. Hence, in reference to such actions, there arises the conception of a duty whose observance or transgression is accompanied with a pleasure or pain of a peculiar kind, known as moral feeling. We do not, however, take the moral feelings or sentiments into account in considering the practical laws of reason. For they do not form the foundation or principle of practical laws of reason, but only the subjective effects that arise in the mind on the occasion of our voluntary activity being determined by these laws. And while they neither add to nor take from the objective validity or influence of the moral laws in the judgement of reason, such sentiments may vary according to the differences of the individuals who experience them.

The following conceptions are common to jurisprudence and ethics as the two main divisions of the metaphysic of morals.

Obligation is the necessity of a free action when viewed in relation to a categorical imperative of reason. An imperative is a practical rule by which an action, otherwise contingent in itself, is made necessary. It is distinguished from a practical law in that such a law, while likewise representing the action as necessary, does not consider whether it is internally necessary as involved in the nature of the agent-say as a holy being-or is contingent to him, as in the case of man as we find him; for where the first condition holds good, there is in fact no imperative. Hence an imperative is a rule which not only represents but makes a subjectively contingent action necessary; and it, accordingly, represents the subject as being (morally) necessitated to act in accordance with this rule. A categorical or unconditional imperative is one which does not represent the action in any way immediately through the conception of an end that is to be attained by it; but it presents the action to the mind as objectively necessary by the mere representation of its form as an action, and thus makes it necessary.

Such imperatives cannot be put forward by any other practical science than that which prescribes obligations, and it is only the science of morals that does this. All other imperatives are technical, and they are altogether conditional. The ground of the possibility of categorical imperatives lies in the fact that they refer to no determination of the activity of the will by which a purpose might be assigned to it, but solely to its freedom.

Every action is allowed (licitum) which is not contrary to obligation; and this freedom not being limited by an opposing imperative, constitutes a moral right as a warrant or title of action (facultas moralis). From this it is at once evident what actions are disallowed or illicit (illicita).

Duty is the designation of any action to which anyone is bound by an obligation. It is therefore the subject-matter of all obligation. Duty as regards the action concerned may be one and the same, and yet we may be bound to it in various ways.

The categorical imperative, as expressing an obligation in respect to certain actions, is a morally practical law. But because obligation involves not merely practical necessity expressed in a law as such, but also actual necessitation, the categorical imperative is a law either of command or prohibition, according as the doing or not doing of an action is represented as a duty. An action which is neither commanded nor forbidden is merely allowed, because there is no law restricting freedom, nor any duty in respect of it.

Such an action is said to be morally indifferent (indifferens, adiaphoron, res merae facultatis). It may be asked whether there are such morally indifferent actions; and if there are, whether in addition to the preceptive and prohibitive law (lex praeceptiva et prohibitiva, lex mandati et vetiti), there is also required a permissive law (lex permissiva), in order that one may be free in such relations to act, or to forbear from acting, at his pleasure? If it were so, the moral right in question would not, in all cases, refer to actions that are indifferent in themselves (adiaphora); for no special law would be required to establish such a right, considered according to moral laws.

An action is called an actor moral deed-in so far as it is subject to laws of obligation, and consequently in so far as the subject of it is regarded with reference to the freedom of his choice in the exercise of his will. The agent-as the actor or doer of the deed-is regarded as, through the act, the author of its effect; and this effect, along with the action itself, may be imputed to him, if be previously knew the law in virtue of which an obligation rested upon him.

A person is a subject who is capable of having his actions imputed to him. Moral personality is, therefore, nothing but the freedom of a rational being under moral laws; and it is to be distinguished from psychological freedom as the mere faculty by which we become conscious of ourselves in different states of the identity of our existence. Hence it follows that a person is properly subject to no other laws than those he lays down for himself, either alone or in conjunction with others.

A thing is what is incapable of being the subject of imputation. Every object of the free activity of the will, which is itself void of freedom, is therefore called a thing (res corporealis).

Right or wrong applies, as a general quality, to an act (rectum aut minus rectum), in so far as it is in accordance with duty or contrary to duty (factum licitum aut illicitum), no matter what may be the subject or origin of the duty itself. An act that is contrary to duty is called a transgression (reatus).

An unintentional transgression of a duty, which is, nevertheless, imputable to a person, is called a mere fault (culpa). An intentional transgression-that is, an act accompanied with the consciousness that it is a transgression-constitutes a crime (dolus).

Whatever is juridically in accordance with external laws is said to be just (jus, instum); and whatever is not juridically in accordance with external laws is unjust (unjustum).

A collision of duties or obligations (collisio officiorums obligationum) would be the result of such a relation between them that the one would annul the other, in whole or in part. Duty and obligation, however, are conceptions which express the objective practical necessity of certain actions, and two opposite rules cannot be objective and necessary at the same time; for if it is a duty to act according to one of them, it is not only no duty to act according to an opposite rule, but to do so would even be contrary to duty.

Hence a collision of duties and obligations is entirely inconceivable (obligationes non-colliduntur). There may, however, be two grounds of obligation (rationes obligandi), connected with an individual under a rule prescribed for himself, and yet neither the one nor the other may be sufficient to constitute an actual obligation (rationes obligandi non obligantes); and in that case the one of them is not a duty. If two such grounds of obligation are actually in collision with each other, practical philosophy does not say that the stronger obligation is to keep the upper hand (fortior obligatio vincit), but that the stronger ground of obligation is to maintain its place (fortior obligandi ratio vincit).

Obligatory Laws for which an external legislation is possible are called generally external laws. Those external laws, the obligatoriness of which can be recognised by reason a priori even without an external legislation, are called natural laws. Those laws, again, which are not obligatory without actual external legislation, are called positive laws. An external legislation, containing pure natural laws, is therefore conceivable; but in that case a previous natural law must be presupposed to establish the authority of the lawgiver by the right to subject others to obligation through his own act of will.

The principle which makes a certain action a duty is a practical law. The rule of the agent or actor, which he forms as a principle for himself on subjective grounds, is called his maxim. Hence, even when the law is one and invariable, the maxims of the agent may yet be very different.

The categorical imperative only expresses generally what constitutes obligation. It may be rendered by the following formula: "Act according to a maxim which can be adopted at the same time as a universal law." Actions must therefore be considered, in the first place, according to their subjective principle; but whether this principle is also valid objectively can only be known by the criterion of the categorical imperative. For reason brings the principle or maxim of any action to the test, by calling upon the agent to think of himself in connection with it as at the same time laying down a universal law, and to consider whether his action is so qualified as to be fit for entering into such a universal legislation.

The simplicity of this law, in comparison with the great and manifold consequences which may be drawn from it, as well as its commanding authority and supremacy without the accompaniment of any visible motive or sanction, must certainly at first appear very surprising. And we may well wonder at the power of our reason to determine the activity of the will by the mere idea of the qualification of a maxim for the universality of a practical law, especially when we are taught thereby that this practical moral law first reveals a property of the will which the speculative reason would never have come upon either by principles a priori, or from any experience whatever; and even if it had ascertained the fact, it could never have theoretically established its possibility.

This practical law, however, not only discovers the fact of that property of the will, which is freedom, but irrefutably establishes it. Hence it will be less surprising to find that the moral laws are undemonstrable, and yet apodeictic, like the mathematical postulates; and that they, at the same time, open up before us a whole field of practical knowledge, from which reason, on its theoretical side, must find itself entirely excluded with its speculative idea of freedom and all such ideas of the supersensible generally.

The conformity of an action to the law of duty constitutes its legality; the conformity of the maxim of the action with the law constitutes its morality. A maxim is thus a subjective principle of action, which the individual makes a rule for himself as to how in fact he will act.

On the other hand, the principle of duty is what reason absolutely, and therefore objectively and universally, lays down in the form of a command to the individual, as to how he ought to act.

The supreme principle of the science of morals accordingly is this: "Act according to a maxim which can likewise be valid as a universal law." Every maxim which is not qualified according to this condition is contrary to Morality.

Laws arise from the will, viewed generally as practical reason; maxims spring from the activity of the will in the process of choice. The latter in man is what constitutes free-will. The will which refers to nothing else than mere law can neither be called free nor not free, because it does not relate to actions immediately, but to the giving of a law for the maxim of actions; it is therefore the practical reason itself. Hence as a faculty, it is absolutely necessary in itself, and is not subject to any external necessitation.

It is, therefore, only the act of choice in the voluntary process that can be called free.

The freedom of the act of will, however, is not to be defined as a liberty of indifference (libertas indifferentae), that, is, as a capacity of choosing to act for or against the law. The voluntary process, indeed, viewed as a phenomenal appearance, gives many examples of this choosing in experience; and some have accordingly so defined the free-will. For freedom, as it is first made knowable by the moral law, is known only as a negative property in us, as constituted by the fact of not being necessitated to act by sensible principles of determination. Regarded as a noumenal reality, however, in reference to man as a pure rational intelligence, the act of the will cannot be at all theoretically exhibited; nor can it therefore be explained how this power can act necessitatingly in relation to the sensible activity in the process of choice, or consequently in what the positive quality of freedom consists.

Only thus much we can see into and comprehend, that although man, as a being belonging to the world of sense, exhibits-as experience shows-a capacity of choosing not only conformably to the law but also contrary to it, his freedom as a rational being belonging to the world of intelligence cannot be defined by reference merely to sensible appearances.

For sensible phenomena cannot make a super-sensible object-such as free-will is-intelligible; nor can freedom ever be placed in the mere fact that the rational subject can make a choice in conflict with his own lawgiving reason, although experience may prove that it happens often enough, notwithstanding our inability to conceive how it is possible. For it is one thing to admit a proposition as based on experience, and another thing to make it the defining principle and the universal differentiating mark of the act of free-will, in its distinction from the arbitrium brutum s servum; because the empirical proposition does not assert that any particular characteristic necessarily belongs to the conception in question, but this is requisite in the process of definition. Freedom in relation to the internal legislation of reason can alone be properly called a power; the possibility of diverging from the law thus given is an incapacity or want of power. How then can the former be defined by the latter? It could only be by a definition which would add to the practical conception of the free-will, its exercise as shown by experience; but this would bc a hybrid definition which would exhibit the conception in a false light.

A morally practical law is a proposition which contains a categorical imperative or command. He who commands by a law (imperans) is the lawgiver or legislator. He is the author of the obligation that accompanies the law, but he is not always the author of the law itself. In the latter case, the law would be positive, contingent, and arbitrary. The law which is imposed upon us a priori and unconditionally by our own reason may also be expressed as proceeding from the will of a supreme lawgiver or the Divine will. Such a will as supreme can consequently have only rights and not duties, and it only indicates the idea of a moral being whose will is law for all, without conceiving of him as the author of that will.

Imputation, in the moral sense, is the judgement by which anyone is declared to be the author or free cause of an action which is then regarded as his moral fact or deed, and is subjected to law. When the judgement likewise lays down the juridical consequences of the deed, it is judicial or valid (imputatio judiciarias valida); otherwise it would be only adjudicative or declaratory (imputatio dijudicatoria). That person-individual or collective-who is invested with the right to impute actions judicially, is called a judge or a court (judex s. forum).

When any one does, in conformity with duty, more than he can be compelled to do by the law, it is said to be meritorious (meritum). What is done only in exact conformity with the law, is what is due (debitum). And when less is done than can be demanded to be done by the law, the result is moral demerit (demeritum) or culpability.

The juridical effect or consequence of a culpable act of demerit is punishment (paena); that of a meritorious act is reward (praemium), assuming that this reward was promised in the law and that it formed the motive of the action. The coincidence or exact conformity of conduct to what is due has no juridical effect. Benevolent remuneration (remuneratio s. repensio benefica) has no place in juridical relations.

The good or bad consequences arising from the performance of an obligated action-as also the consequences arising from failing to perform a meritorious action-cannot be imputed to the agent (modus imputation is tollens). The good consequences of a meritorious action-as also the bad consequences of a wrongful action-may be imputed to the agent (modus imputation is poneus).

The degree of the imputability of actions is to be reckoned according to the magnitude of the hindrances or obstacles which it has been necessary for them to overcome. The greater the natural hindrances in the sphere of sense, and the less the moral hindrance of duty, so much the more is a good deed imputed as meritorious. This may be seen by considering such examples as rescuing a man who is an entire stranger from great distress, and at very considerable sacrifice. Conversely, the less the natural hindrance, and the greater the hindrance on the ground of duty, so much the more is a transgression imputable as culpable. Hence the state of mind of the agent or doer of a deed makes a difference in imputing its consequences, according as he did it in passion or performed it with coolness and deliberation.

7

Christianity and the Race Problem

We come now to one of the most baffling and difficult of all contemporary problems. In the world scene, questions of race and colour mingle with those of national status and of economic abundance and poverty to create great restlessness and tension. In our own land, the violent reactions evoked by the Supreme Court's decision of May 17, 1954, that segregation in the public schools is unconstitutional have revealed how deep are the differences that divide us. Though integration in the schools is accepted more readily in northern states, there is scarcely a community anywhere, North or South, that does not show the marks of racial cleavage in segregated housing, employment, and social attitudes.

Even in churches this virus is widely prevalent. It was not a theological, but a racial, issue that split the Methodist Church in 1844 and kept it in sectional units for almost a hundred years, with the breach only partially healed by the formula of union in 1939. The northern and southern Presbyterians and Baptists are still separated with race in the background, though with important theological differences in addition to the racial attitudes that have prevailed in Methodism. Yet it is the existence not of separate denominations, but of segregation within virtually every denomination, that is the most telling evidence of the depth of the problem. This separateness, whether or not required by organizational structures, is everywhere present. One has but to enter almost any church and look around to discover it.

Paradoxically, it is this issue among all our major social problems on which there is the greatest agreement *in principle*. Representative church bodies have again and again called for a "nonsegregated church In a nonsegregated society." The Federal Council of Churches in 1946 declared:

> *The Federal Council of Churches of Christ in America renounces the pattern of segregation in race relations as unnecessary and undesirable and a violation of the gospel of love and brotherhood. Having taken this action the Federal Council requests its constituent communions to do likewise. Similar resolutions, including endorsement of the Supreme Court decision, have been passed by the churches again and again. One of the most significant of these is the affirmation of the Southern Baptist Convention in 1956 in view of the fact that this is the largest southern denomination and its members are widely involved in current tensions:*
>
> *We recognize the fact that this Supreme Court decision is in harmony with the constitutional guarantee of equal freedom to all citizens and with the Christian principles of equal justice and love for all men.... [We urge our] people and all Christians to conduct themselves in this period*

of adjustment in the spirit of Christ. Comparable declarations have been made by other churches even in those areas where racial tensions are most acute. "Denominational conference statements of the mainline Protestant churches in the South have almost uniformly affirmed the incompatibility of segregation with Christian principles and the need for revision of local practice." To cite one more statement from an inclusive perspective, the World Council of Churches at Evanston in 1954 issued an extraordinarily forward-looking statement on race relations which contains these words:

When we are given Christian insight the whole pattern of racial discrimination is seen as an unutterable offence against God, to be endured no longer, so that the very stones cry out. In such moments we understand more fully the meaning of the gospel, and the duty of both Church and Christian.

The skeptic is prone to say that the churches make these "ringing resolutions," yet hypocritically disregard them. That there is wide disregard is evident, but it cannot be charged simply to hypocrisy. The issues are complex, and we must attempt to sort out some of the interwoven strands that constitute the ugly net of race prejudice.

Biblical Foundations

As has been done in other chapters, let us take a look at the biblical foundations of the Christian view. This can be brief, for the directives are unequivocal.

Then God said, "Let us make man in our image, after our likeness; and let them have dominion over the fish of the sea, and over the birds of the air, and over the cattle, and over all the earth, and over every creeping thing that creeps upon the earth." So God created man in his own image, in the image of God he created him; male and female he created them. (1:26-27.)

There is no suggestion here of a white God, or even of a Semitic God. Nor is there any intimation that some who are thus to "have dominion" are to constitute a dominant race while others do the menial tasks of mankind. Even though Negroes be assumed to be the descendants of Ham, the Jews of Shem, and the Aryans of Japheth—a view which anthropologists discredit—all are equally the Sons of Adam and made in the divine image. There is not a little *religious* exclusiveness in the history of the Hebrews as it is recorded in the Old Testament, and this gave rise to a Jewish particularism which the greater prophets had to condemn as they stressed the love of God for all men. Yet the doctrine of creation that is the common heritage of Jewish and Christian faith asserts unequivocally the unity of mankind and leaves no standing ground for *racial* exclusiveness.

In the New Testament this becomes unmistakable. The equality of all persons before God was basic to the outlook of Jesus. The parable of the good Samaritan is the most dramatic challenge to racial exclusiveness, but it appears again and again in Jesus' own service to human need regardless of racial or national backgrounds and in his portrayal of the conditions of entrance into the Kingdom. In the last judgment scene, it is not one's Jewish ancestry but care for the hungry and thirsty, for the naked, sick, and imprisoned, that will determine one's place (Matt. 25:31-46).

In the great consummation, "men will come from east and west, and from north and south, and sit at table in the kingdom of God" (Luke 13:29). Jesus did not hesitate to condemn the shallow self-confidence of those who trusted in their Jewish prerogatives, or to commend the faith of a Roman centurion as being superior to theirs (Matt. 23; 8:10-13). Had Jesus been willing to be neutral toward Jewish exclusiveness for fear of causing trouble, he might have escaped crucifixion but he would not have been our Lord.

In the early Church, the contest between Jewish exclusiveness and Christian universalism was at first sharp, but the latter won out to become the settled policy. The decision recorded in Acts 15:19-21 thereby becomes a watershed in the history of the Church.

Peter's vision (Acts 10) and its bearing on the acceptance of the Roman centurion Cornelius into Christian fellowship bears directly on the issue of segregated churches today, and the truth could hardly be more forcefully put than in Peter's words that clinch the matter, "Truly I perceive that God shows no partiality" (v. 34).

Paul repeatedly declared that "all men, both Jews and Greeks, are under the power of sin" (Rom. 3:9), but that Christ died for the redemption of all, and has reconciled us to God and to one another.

"There is neither Jew nor Greek, there is neither slave nor free, there is neither male nor female; for you are all one in Christ Jesus." (Gal. 3:28.) No greater charter of race equality need be cited than that found in Ephesians, "For he is our peace, who has made us both one, and has broken down the dividing wall of hostility" (2:14).

But why multiply citations? The record is so clear that almost any Christian will admit that in principle race prejudice is wrong. But what of our practice?

The Causes of Race Prejudice

Race prejudice is a pervasive human phenomenon. Yet clearly it is not inborn. Coloured and white children will play together when permitted to do so with full friendliness. On the street where I live there is also a Negro physician and his fine family, and it is an attractive sight to see these children playing with the white children of the neighbourhood. Little Gentiles get along very well with the little Jews, or at least, as well as with other little Gentiles. It is when frightened parents erect prohibitions that the seeds of prejudice are planted. These in most cases are planted early and grow luxuriously.

By the time of adolescence, unless positive steps are taken to counteract it, segregation has emerged as a dominant pattern. So powerful are the drives toward conformity in high school and college years that it is not uncommon to find an intense and irrational cruelty toward those of other races. On the other hand, young people are more apt than their elders to break through the patterns of racial discrimination if there are democratic and Christian influences upon their thinking and friendly group contacts are possible with those of another race. Where segregation is removed in practice, its justification in principle rapidly subsides.

Confront an adult with the fact of his race prejudice, and he will do one of three things. He will deny it, he will admit it but admit also that it is irrational, or he will begin to rationalize his attitudes. The rationalizations will usually take the form of words about being different from "our kind of people"; about inferior and superior races; about dirt and smells, or dishonesty and treachery and the "yellow peril"; about the danger of intermarriage; about how those of other races are "creeping up on us" and "don't know their place." When sifted out these rationalizations indicate that psychological, cultural, social, nationalistic, and economic factors have been superimposed upon and confused with biological facts. As a result, we have a "colour caste" of which the roots are not primarily to be found in biological differences, but with its evil effects irrationally transferred to great groups loosely designated as racial.

Race is a most ambiguous term, in which many national, geographical, cultural, and linguistic elements are mixed. Though race is sometimes correctly designated by basic biological types as Caucasian, Mongolian, or Negroid, in practice it is more often indicated by colour, as black, white, red, yellow, or brown; or by nationality, as Japanese, Chinese, Filipino, Mexican; or by geographical origin, as Oriental, Asiatic, European, African; or by a combination of ethnic, national, and geographical factors, as Nordic, Teutonic, Slavic, Latin American, French Canadian. A particular problem is posed by an attempt to classify the Jews, for while they are a Semitic people who have had relatively little racial intermixture through the centuries, it is an ever-present problem as to whether the terms "Jew" and "Jewish" refer mainly to a race or to a religion.

Such adjectives give evidence that the race problem is never wholly a matter of biological distinction and stratification. Racial intermixtures have produced some very white-skinned Negroes with blue eyes and fair hair, yet the product of such a union remains a Negro. Race as the term is commonly used designates very nearly what the Germans call *Volk* — a group sharing a common cultural tradition, whether of achievement or servitude, with some measure of national, geographical, and biological affinity. Our language being what it is, we must use the term "race" in spite of its looseness.

Racial prejudice is, first of all, a psychological factor, rooting in collective egotism and pride and the pervasive human tendency to dislike the different. Though an ancient evil, it began to receive intellectual defence more recently than most evils, for it was only a century ago that Count Gobineau published in French his four-volume *Essay on the Inequality of the Human Races,* in which he contended that colour of skin determines mental and spiritual differences, and that mixture of blood produces degeneracy and the fall of civilizations. There was little, if any, racial discrimination in the early or medieval Church, the conditions of membership and fellowship being determined by faith in Jesus Christ and fidelity to the ordinances of his church. "Race and colour did not count in the early existence of the Protestant church. It was when modern Western imperialism began to explore and exploit the coloured peoples of Africa, Asia and America that the beginning of segregation and discrimination based on colour and race was initiated." Nevertheless, the *roots* of race prejudice are as old as the human race in the tendency to like those who are like oneself and to dislike those who for any reason, biological or cultural, are different.

Sometimes this psychological dislike of the different is intensified by proximity, again by separation. For example, it is not uncommon for American Christians to be quite concerned to send missionaries to the Negroes of Africa, and to admire greatly Albert Schweitzer's service to them, and yet to stand rigidly for segregation in one's own community or church, it is easy for persons in New England to be more "broad-minded" on the matter of racial integration than they would be if they lived in Mississippi. Nevertheless, proximity need not breed tension; it can create fellowship. As we shall observe in noting what the Church can do about racial tension, one of the first steps in overcoming it is to bring people together, both physically and spiritually, so that what seems to be difference can be discovered to be kinship. This calls for a mingling of the races wherever this can be done without fresh outbreaks of animosity, and a sharing of the best in every cultural tradition.

Another form of rationalization, we noted, was the *claim of "superior" and "inferior" races.* Count Gobineau's contentions were widely believed until quite recently, and are still bandied about by those who never heard his name. Yet for the past two decades they have been scientifically exploded, and no reputable psychologist or anthropologist now accepts them.

In 1938 the American Psychological Association went on record as declaring that there are no innate mental differences among races. In the same year the American Anthropological Association asserted that there is no scientific basis for the biological inheritance of cultural traits, or of any traits implying racial inferiority. These judgments have been corroborated by medical science in reference to the Negro blood bank by declaring that there is no difference in the blood of coloured and white persons, thus reinforcing the biblical word that God "has made of one blood all nations of men" (K.J.V.) to dwell together.

There are, of course, primitive and advanced groups even as there are stupid and highly capable individuals within every group. These discernible differences have lent support to the myth of natural inequality. Informed opinion, however, agrees with Gunnar Myrdal in *An American Dilemma* that there is a vicious circle at this point. Denied the cultural, educational, and economic advantages held by others, underprivileged groups tend to remain in this status, as in America the restriction of Negroes to unskilled labour and meager educational facilities has prevented their advancement to positions of leadership comparable with the more privileged. Increasingly in the world scene, as in America, it becomes evident that there are persons of extraordinary ability in every racial group, and the flowering of such talent awaits only the opportunity.

Cultural aversion to those of other races, whether in the form of depreciating their ability or in more offensive matters of name calling and the attaching of uncomplimentary labels, eventuates from the common tendency to commit the fallacy of hasty generalization. Some Negroes have grown up in circumstances where they have not learned to bathe; hence it is assumed that all are dirty. Under economic pressure for many centuries, some Jews have developed a tendency to drive a sharp bargain; hence it is assumed that this is a universal racial trait. Japan attacked Pearl Harbour, and China is held by the Communists; hence nobody from the Orient is to be trusted! The internment and relocation of 110,000 Japanese on the Pacific Coast during the Second World War, not for any acts of disloyalty but simply through a suspicion based on racial identification, was less virulent in its effect than the Nazi destruction of the Jews but equally irrational. The outbreak of violence, intimidation, and the formation of "white citizens' councils" that has come with the effort to desegregate the schools is a carry-over both from the Negro's former status as a slave and from the assumption by white persons of the Negro's general inferiority.

Such hasty generalization cannot be dealt with simply by demonstrating its irrationality. That it is irrational to judge whole peoples by mass standards of approval or disapproval rather than by individual status is certainly true, and needs to be constantly kept in mind. But since this type of judgment is basically a matter of feeling rather than reason, only a change of feeling can correct it. This is why the Christian faith, when it is made vital in terms of the equal worth of all persons to God, is a more effective solvent of ill feeling than argument, even as a sense of sin about race prejudice is a necessary prelude to repentance and change.

This cultural aversion appears in its most potent form in the *fear of intermarriage*. This is cited again and again as the all-sufficient reason why there must be no social intermingling of the different racial groups, and in particular why the young people must be kept apart not only in schools but in churches. About this two judgments must be passed. The first is that miscegenation ought not to be encouraged. Not because any biological inferiority results from a mixing of racial stocks, but because in the present state of society tensions are more often increased than abated by it, intermarriage is on the whole a step away from the solution of the race problem rather than toward it.

The second judgment is that there is no law of God against such intermarriage, and there ought to be none of the State. The World Council of Churches took a bold and true step when it declared:

> *While it can find in the Bible no clear justification or condemnation of intermarriage, but only a discussion of the duties of the faithful in marriage with partners of other religions, it cannot approve any law against racial or ethnic intermarriage, for Christian marriage involves primarily a union of two individuals before God which goes beyond the jurisdiction of the state or of culture.*

Some intermarriages have produced happy and effective Christian homes; others have not. Here as elsewhere, hasty generalization must be avoided. What can be said with certainty is that the fear of intermarriage, erected as a barrier to social fellowship, does harm and thwarts constructive effort far in excess of the actual justification of such a fear.

Ramifying through all these factors are *economic rivalry* and a fear of the loss of prestige or power through the influx or advancement of those of other racial stocks. This is evidenced by the fact that in industry, schools, and many other aspects of community life, a racial minority will be tolerated as long as it is a *very minor* minority. Let the numbers increase, or the positions other than those of unskilled manual labour be taken by those of another race, and there is an outbreak of objection which is easily stirred into violence.

Paradoxically, labour unions have gone further than any other group in America, not excepting the churches, to witness against racial injustice and try to secure equality of treatment. This is probably due chiefly to a certain sense of solidarity in injustice in protest against the dominant white, bourgeois, employing classes. Yet in both labour unions and churches, the official group pronouncements are on a higher level of insight than the actual practices of great numbers of their membership.

While the unions exercise a coercive power that the churches cannot, psychological reaction to economic rivalry follows a consistent pattern. Wherever status is touched or income is jeopardized, the liberality of attitudes tends to shrink and rationalizations of discrimination to emerge.

Racial and cultural are mixed with *national* factors to make the term "foreigner" one of opprobrium. This is evident in the tendency to speak of the Italians, Mexicans, French Canadians, or Irish as a separate racial stock, the degree of acceptance even in the "melting pot" of democratic America being by no means certain.

In the Old Testament the Jews drew tight lines between themselves as the chosen people of God and their neighbours, in the New Testament the "Jews have no dealings with Samaritans," and in every culture from the beginning of recorded history to the present there are evidences of antipathy between the "in-grout and the "out-group." Robert P. Tristram Coffin in a whimsical but nevertheless serious poem has represented the men of Ur and Akkad as telling why they do not like each other:

The Man of Akkad:

The men of Ur have heads too round.
They have to build themselves a mound
To reach their god. Their toes turn in,
They have no hair upon their chin.
They are not men. Their women wear
The finer wool and build their hair
High as towers in their pride,
The men go meekly dressed in hide.
They eat the fat part of their goats,
Their speech is low down in their throats.
To them the only proper word
Is the thin edge of a sword.

The Man of Ur:

The men of Akkad have no faces.
Their curled beards are the nesting places
Of the vermin and the flea.
They turn their toes out wantonly.
Their heads are squeezed too long for brains,
They have to ask their gods for rains.
They beat their wives, they wear soft clothes,

Their speech is high and through the nose,
Their noses are as great as plows,
They eat the udders of their cows.
The language that will suit them best
Is the arrow through the breast.
Ur and Akkad are dead sands,

But they have sons in living lands. Thus far we have been noting the merging of race prejudice with cultural, economic, and political antipathies in the domestic scene. Yet no informed person needs to be told that racism is a world-wide phenomenon and that in our interdependent world, racial antipathies anywhere endanger the security and welfare of persons everywhere.

Let us look, therefore, somewhat more briefly at the effects of race prejudice.

Effects of Race Prejudice

Racism imperils the peace of the world. Not race, which in the order of nature has been established by God that there may be variety among his children, but racism. Racism is the perversion of this variety, the injection of attitudes of domination, superiority, and enmity where there ought to be fellowship within this diversity. Since this is a moral universe, racism cannot continue without injury and peril to all — to those who dominate as well as to those who suffer from the domination of others.

In the past the major wars have been fought between those of Caucasian stock. The coloured peoples of the earth, though outnumbering the white peoples two to one, have lacked not only the incentive of hope of victory, but the economic resources and the technical skills by which massive conflicts could be waged. In the past two decades this situation has changed radically. Many millions of persons formerly in colonial status have come to a new nationhood since the Second World War— India, Pakistan, Burma, Ceylon, the Philippines, Indonesia, South Korea, and South Vietnam, with at least nominal freedom also in North Korea and Viet Minh.

Others feel the ferment of the possibility of both political freedom and release from hunger, and will no longer accept domination complacently. In two of the most troubled areas of the earth, South Africa and the Middle East, racial conflict and tension are at an all-time high, with no hope of any immediate abatement.

There is no evidence that any of the peoples just mentioned desire, or will press for, world conquest. There is, however, another power in Eastern Europe that apparently does desire world domination and with great skill manipulates the longings of these people for racial equality, economic subsistence, and political freedom. If they do not receive support from the West in these legitimate aspirations, they will look to the East to get it. The result could be a third world war and global destruction.

It cannot be said that there is complete racial equality within Communism, for Jews have been discriminated against in Soviet Russia as elsewhere. Yet there is little doubt that race equality is practiced further under Communism than is general in the democracies of the West, and it is certain that our racial inequalities, though exaggerated, are a chief weapon in the psychological war against us.

I make no claim to being a prophet. Yet in 1944, when Russia was still generally viewed as a faithful ally, I wrote these words:

Let us rejoice heartily that there is race equality anywhere, whether under a Christian or

> *Communist ideology. But let us beware. When the time comes to make the peace, the suppressed longings of the coloured and racially underprivileged peoples of the world, if they do not see freedom in prospect elsewhere, will turn to Russia to get it. The colour question cannot fail to be a powerful leverage to enhance the authority of Russia after the war. One may doubt whether Russia is altruistic enough to use this authority to increase the welfare of the world; one cannot doubt that the union of capitalism with race discrimination puts a weapon of incalculable power in the hands of Mr. Stalin. Since that time Stalin has passed from the scene and his authority as well, but what he set in motion has not passed away. Since that time also, the emergence of the atomic and hydrogen bombs has vastly increased the peril to the total world that racial conflict might fan to hideously destructive power.*

But what of the effects of race discrimination in the immediate, domestic setting?

The effects upon its recipients are so manifold in the form of hurts, frustrations, denials of opportunity, and the continuance of a rankling sense of injustice that I shall make no attempt to catalogue them.

In our own country millions of people especially American Negroes are subjected to discrimination and unequal treatment in educational opportunities, in employment, wages and conditions of work, in access to professional and business opportunities, in housing, in transportation, in the administration of justice and even in the right to vote. In recent years some advance steps have been made, as in the opening of Pullman cars and diners to Negroes, elimination of segregation in the armed forces, and the admission of Negroes to some southern state universities. Yet the attempts made to nullify the Supreme Court decision even at the cost of eliminating the public schools and passing acts of open defiance in state legislatures, to say nothing of rioting and violence and the nonviolent but intimidating acts of white citizens' councils, indicate how long a road there is yet to travel. Not since the Civil War has the internal harmony of the United States been so seriously disturbed.

Not only does race discrimination hurt those who are its recipients, but those who practice it become also its victims. As Benjamin Mays, himself an eminent Negro college president, stated eloquently before the World Council of Churches in Evanston, Usually the question is: What does discrimination or segregation do to the person segregated, to the disadvantaged person?... But we seldom realize what discrimination does to the person who practices it. It scars not only the soul of the segregated but the soul of the segregator as well. When we build fences to keep others out, erect barriers to keep others down, deny to them freedom which we ourselves enjoy and cherish most, we keep ourselves in, hold ourselves down, and the barriers we erect against others become prison bars to our own souls.

A major effect in the domestic scene is what racism does to public respect for the principles of democracy and of Christianity. In both connections there are endless reverberations, which can be touched upon only in barest mention. When one becomes accustomed to perversions of justice with reference to those of another race, these are likely before long not to seem perversions, and the democratic conscience that should be demanding "liberty and justice for all" is dulled into acquiescence. Those on the receiving end of the injustice can scarcely avoid the feeling that democracy is being flouted, and the temptation to flout it in return is strong. Both of these reactions together are responsible for not a little of the domestic unrest and incidence of crime in our society.

In the Church also there is a sheaf of bad effects. The most obvious one, by the continuance of segregation, is to negate the principle of the equality of all men before God, which even the most casual secularist recognizes to be Christian, and thus to bring the Church into disfavour.

More subtle effects, however, are found in the thwarting of the growth of Christian personality by denials of opportunity and fellowship that should be open to all, and in the deepening of the sin of moral dullness through all the forms of rationalization that have been outlined. Only God can judge fully the range and depth of these evil effects. In an issue so complex and so serious, claims of human omniscience are very inappropriate. There is need to be tolerant and understanding, to "judge not, that you be not judged." Yet there is need also to be clear-sighted and to be firm. To be neutral or acquiescent in conditions so clearly at variance with the Christian gospel is to deny our faith.

Proposals for Christian Action

The Church cannot let these conditions continue without action. The security of the world calls for the mitigation of racial tensions through justice. Yet deeper than the demand for security is the obligation of the Christian gospel to increase love in human relations.

In the first place, the Church must understand and proclaim its gospel. Vague generalities about the fatherhood of God and the brotherhood of man have often been spoken which do not cut down through our crust of convention to where the race problem is. We need to recover the insights of Jesus on this question. And one of the most amazing things about Jesus is how he met the racism of his day. Reared in a Jewish tradition that prided itself on being the chosen people of God, living in occupied territory where Roman superiority and Jewish superiority were always in uneasy tension, he lived on a plane that made a Roman centurion say of him, "Truly this was a son of God!" (Matt. 27:54). Jew, Roman, Samaritan, Syrophoenician, were to him equally the children of God. In the presence of human need, his healing knew no bounds.

If we examine the democracy of Jesus—a democracy which he never talked about but always practiced—we discover in it both the fountainhead of our democracy and certain radical challenges. We talk much about the dignity of man. This he did not deny; in fact, he assumed it, but always in the framework of man's dependence upon God and the obligation to obey God and love one another. His emphasis was not on the claim of personal rights, as so much of ours is, but on the doing of duties. This may well lead to the claiming of rights for others, but such a demand must first be expressed in the acts and attitudes of daily life. These four — divine dependence, mutual obligation stemming from love, sound judgment of human nature, and the practice of brotherhood in daily experience — are the basis of any true democracy. Not until the Church both preaches and practices such Christian democracy will it touch the fringe of the race question.

Second, the Church must put its own house in order. This means the welcome presence of coloured Christians in the membership, the worship services, church schools, discussion groups, and social gatherings of the Church. It means the presence of coloured persons in the conferences and policy-making bodies of the Church. It means the refusal to permit segregation in the living arrangements connected with church meetings. It means the sharing of the recreational, educational, and hospital facilities of the Church with all who need them.

It means the interchange of pulpits between coloured and white ministers, and much further advance in what has already been here and there undertaken, an interracial ministry. As qualified persons can be found or trained, there must be interracial teaching, medical, and administrative staffs in the institutions of the Church. In such arrangements there must be equal and nonsegregated living and working conditions, equal pay, equal opportunities of promotion, regardless of colour. Differentiation on grounds of contribution and fitness does not justify differentiation on grounds of race. If such a programme arouses opposition, as it is likely to, this calls for the tactful but courageous insistence that the house of God is a place of prayer and service for all peoples and the Church of God cannot sanction discrimination at any point.

I am aware that the relatively mild proposals of the preceding sentences, if acted upon, would be revolutionary. Already I hear someone say, "You couldn't do that in my church!" Have you tried? The ideal of race equality will not arrive all at once. But it will not arrive at all until we stop conforming to prevailing attitudes and practices and give the Church an opportunity to lead in the shaping of community standards. Even conflict, if dealt with in love, can prove a creative experience.

In bringing about such changes, there is particular need to avoid incrimination and self-righteousness and to act upon the basis of true facts and principles, not upon emotional impulse. Race prejudice, we have seen, is basically a matter of emotion, and there can be no effective challenge of it without right counter-emotions. Such depth of concern does not justify unloving attitudes toward or name calling of one's opponents. "Speaking the truth in love" is a supreme need.

It is easy for one to say this who has not personally

felt the sting of race discrimination. Yet the need becomes far more eloquent when it comes from the lips of one who bears the brunt of it, yet without hatred. It was put in words that ought to become classic by the Rev. Martin Luther King, Jr., a few hours after his arrest as a leader of passive resistance against segregation in the Montgomery, Alabama, bus lines:

> *If we are arrested every day, if we are exploited every day, if we are trampled over every day, don't ever let anyone pull you so low as to hate them. We must use the weapon of love. We must have compassion and understanding for those who hate us. We must realize so many people are taught to hate us that they are not totally responsible for their hate. But we stand in life at midnight; we are always on the threshold of a new dawn. The race problem must, for the most part, be met by person to person contacts which create understanding. This calls for more intervisitation and social fellowship, both locally and nationally, and as occasion permits, in the world community. It is hard to remain hostile toward a people whose individuals one has come to know and love. Such fellowship has been one of the major contributions of the ecumenical movement.*

In cases of racial discrimination by public agencies within the community, the Church must be willing to stand up and be counted on the side of equality. It must act in cooperation with other community forces if possible, but in any case it must act. Not alone prophetic indictment, but patient mediation, is the function of Christian leaders.

From time to time, political aspects of the question call for action. Among these are the steps to be taken toward desegregation in the schools and universities, the poll-tax issue, the passage of guarantees of fair employment practices, the removal of restrictions in housing and the use of public facilities. Segregation cannot be justified on the ground of "separate but equal" facilities, for what is separate is discriminatory and hence not equal. Though the right next steps to take are not always clear, the principle is, and Christian citizens who take their gospel seriously should lead the way.

Since the race question is a world issue, and not simply a local or national one, education and action as to its world implications are necessary. Support by citizens of such action as will lift the living standards and the human dignity of the millions of underprivileged, nonwhite peoples of the earth is imperative. Congressmen must be made to feel that their constituencies insist upon it.

Finally, the total problem must be lifted into the realm of prayer and worship. We must pray for those of other races; we must be responsive to the awareness that they are praying for us. When one enters truly into the mood of intercession, bitterness departs and fellowship takes its place. It has been the contention of this chapter that the removal of race prejudice is a duty laid upon us by God, and if it is God's business we are engaged in, we must give God an opening in our souls.

Since it is God's business, let us not despair. The solution will not come tomorrow, but it will come. In the midst of the walls of opposition erected by men stands Christ, who breaks down the "dividing wall of hostility" that separates us. It is the business of Christians to give him a chance to act.

8

Ethics of Jesus and the Old Testament

Let us now try to draw together what Jesus took from the Old Testament and what, therefore, Christians may hold to be of permanent validity.

First, Jesus shared with Old Testament thought the general structure of God-centred moral living. It apparently never occurred to him to give ethical injunctions derived from any other source. A great deal of our contemporary problem about "love perfectionism" centres in the attempt to ground ethics either in human nature or in the structure of social institutions. The biblical view — both Old Testament and New — makes obedience to the will of God the final criterion of the good life.

Did Jesus accept the idea of the covenant, and with it of Israel as God's chosen people? This question is crucial for the universality of his message. Apparently, at the beginning of his ministry he conceived his mission as to the "lost sheep of the house of Israel." It was to this group and not to the Gentiles that he commissioned the twelve (Matt. 10:5-6), and his encounter with the Canaanite woman (Matt. 15:21-28) is significant in the fact that he both at first demurred and then yielded to her entreaty for the healing of her daughter. This gives the key to Jesus' attitude. His own people were precious to him, and he never expressly repudiated the covenant relation. Yet to him so universal was the love of God, so compelling the need to serve every human being, that the covenant with its exclusive bounds was left behind. It remained for his followers in the early Church to make concrete the break which his acts and attitudes foreshadowed.

Second, his ethical principles were those of Judaism, yet with a difference in emphasis which makes their impact new. Point for point, there is nothing in the teaching of Jesus which cannot be found in the Old Testament or in the rabbinical teaching. Pharisaism, though it had its faults which called forth Jesus' rebuke, had also in it much that was great and good. Witness, for example, this passage from *The Testaments of the Twelve Patriarchs*, written toward the end of the second century BC.:

> *Love ye one another from the heart; and if a man sin against thee, speak peaceably to him, and in thy soul hold not guile; and if he repent and confess, forgive him. But if he deny it, do not get into a passion with him, lest catching the poison from thee he take to swearing and so thou sin doubly... [But] if he be shameless and persist in his wrongdoing, even so forgive him from the heart, and leave to God the avenging. Nevertheless, taken as a whole, the ethical teaching of Jesus leaves an impression which nothing in Judaism does.*

This is due in part to the conviction of Christians that Jesus fully exemplified his message, as no individual in prophetism or Phanisaism fully did. But it is due also to the extent to which Jesus always made human need the criterion of acts of obedient love to God. If the law of the Sabbath stood in the way of human service, it was to be suspended; he ate with publicans and sinners to win them to the Kingdom even at the cost of ceremonial uncleanness. Love of neighbour becomes freely given, uncalculating, unrestricted service, such as is epitomized in the parable of the good Samaritan, and this flows from the nature of the love of God. The love of God, though it appears not infrequently in the Old Testament and in the rabbinical writings, there carries with it a connotation of God's love for the people Israel which was too small for Jesus. He took the moral framework of Israel and transformed it into something so universal, so compelling, that it became new.

And in the third place, as we shall see more fully in the next chapter, Jesus took the eschatology like the ethics of his time and made it into something different. His inheritance from the prophets moralized his expectancy of divine intervention; his own sense of relationship to God gave a new turn to both eschatology and ethics.

Probably because of a conviction of the nature of his own messiahship, but certainly because of his conviction that the kingdom of God meant the righteous rule of God in a redeemed community for this world and the next, he made the kingdom of God and not the triumph of Israel the supreme note in his teaching. With all the ambiguities that surround the records of his teaching regarding the Kingdom, it is clear that it embodies the goal of God's reign over the hearts and lives of men, and thus sets forth the great hope of a better world both now and in the world to come. To make Jesus' conception of the Kingdom solely into a better society on earth is to lose its great overtones and foreshorten its vista; to deprive it of ethical content is to emasculate it into something Jesus himself would never have recognized.

Thus it comes about that Jesus, the greatest of the prophets, the fulfilment of the law, inaugurated a new covenant for the redemption of mankind. It is to him, and not to any other teaching or teacher, that we must look for our basic moral insights. It is with good reason that one is reported as saying of old, "Lord, to whom shall we go? You have the words of eternal life."

What* did *Jesus Teach?

It is not difficult to summarize with a fair degree of conciseness the principal ethical teachings of Jesus. They are not stated systematically or in a developing logical sequence, as a philosopher might state them, but over and over again they appear—in aphorism, parable, simile, striking hyperbole, in words of commendation or rebuke or in Jesus' own recorded deeds. It is only when we try to balance them one against another and ask how they are to be applied that we run into serious difficulty as to what Jesus meant. Our confusion then may be caused, as the good Bishop Berkeley put it regarding another matter, that we "raise a dust and then complain we cannot see"; yet it is also duo at points to a real lack of consistency in what the records tell us Jesus taught. Of this more will be said presently. What, now, is it clear that he did teach?

(a) *Jesus Taught an Ethic Completely Integrated with His Religion:* This is seen in its clearest expression in the two Great Commandments, where the duty of love of neighbour is not an addendum to the obligation to love God without reservation, but is an implicate of it. It appears repeatedly both in Jesus' words and in the total tenor of his life. It was his sense of calling by God that led him at the beginning of his ministry to read in the synagogue the words of Isaiah:

> *The Spirit of the Lord is upon me, because he has anointed me to preach good news to the poor. He has sent me to proclaim release to the captives and recovering of sight to the blind, to set at liberty those who are oppressed, to proclaim the acceptable year of the Lord. (Luke 4:18-19; Isa. 61:1-2.)*

These words doubtless state what he felt to be his mandate for action. Are they religion or ethics? The only answer is that they are both, and the passage loses its force if either is withdrawn. "Whatever the historicity of the Fourth Gospel, it is fully consistent with his spirit for him to have said before Pilate at the end of his ministry, "For this I was born, and for this I have come into the world, to bear witness to the truth." Is this "truth" religious or moral? It is so clearly both that only a perverted Christianity can deny their relatedness.

To illustrate by a few examples from his precepts, note the reason given for the course of action that is enjoined, "Love your enemies and pray for those who persecute you, so that you may be sons of your Father who is in heaven" (Matt. 5:44-45), or "Blessed are the peacemakers, for they shall be called sons of God" (Matt. 5:9). The term "sons of" was a familiar Semitic expression to denote likeness of character.

The same idea is borne out in the oft-debated last verse of the same chapter, "You, therefore, must be perfect, as your heavenly Father is perfect" (v. 48), and in the correlative passage in Luke, "Be merciful, even as your Father is merciful" (6:36). Omit the reference to God from these passages and they simply become counsels of perfection.

(b) *Jesus Laid Primary Stress on Ethical and Spiritual Inwardness*: This is not to say that he was indifferent to outward acts, or to the way men conducted themselves toward one another. On the contrary, his most stinging words are directed toward those who "preach, but do not practice"; to those who "bind heavy burdens, hard to bear, and lay them on men's shoulders; but they themselves will not move them with their finger"; to those who "devour widows' houses and for a pretense... make long prayers"; to those who are "blind guides, straining out a gnat and swallowing a camel" (Matt. 23:3, 4, 14, 24). Yet the same passage, as well as many others, indicates that his chief concern was with right attitudes from which right acts might proceed. Jesus was completely opposed to the substitution of either ceremonial acts or correct outward behaviour for humble obedience to God and loving concern for one's neighbour. This is the main burden of his indictment of the scribes and Pharisees:

> *Woe to you, scribes and Pharisees, hypocrites! for you tithe mint and dill and cummin, and have neglected the weightier matters of the law, justice and mercy and faith; these you ought to have done, without neglecting the others.*

Woe to you, scribes and Pharisees, hypocrites! for you cleanse the outside of the cup and of the plate, but inside they are full of extortion and rapacity. You blind Pharisee! first cleanse the inside of the cup and of the plate, that the outside also may be clean. (Matt. 23:23, 25-26.)

Note that he does not condemn ceremonial tithing or making clean the "outside of the cup"; what he condemns is the substitution of these for something more basic. In gentler tones this is also the burden of the Sermon on the Mount where, without any abrogating of the Ten Commandments, the emphasis is shifted away from legalism to those inner attitudes that determine the nature of a man, and hence his acts.

(c) *Jesus Set forth a Clear Pattern of the Demands of the God-centred Life:* By clear pattern is not, of course, meant a blueprint or easily applicable set of rules. But that we can today speak of "Christian virtues" is due to the fact that one who reads the Gospels seriously is left in no doubt as to the general structure of what a life lived in obedient love would embody. We see it in Jesus himself; we find it on every page of the record; it is epitomized in the Beatitudes. Its primary qualities are a God-centred faith and love. Its derivative aspects are purity of heart, sincerity, humility, forgiveness, love toward enemies, mercy, charity in judgment, honesty in speech and action, sexual purity, renunciation of worldly aims with the preferring of spiritual to material treasure, compassion toward those in need. The good life is that of generous and self-giving service to all men and unbroken, unworried trust in the goodness of God.

It is significant that *agape* did not have before its use in the New Testament the richness of meaning that it came there to have. In classical Greek it carries "none of the magical power of *eros* and hardly any of the warmth of *philia*.... Its meaning is colourless and indefinite." In fact, it was often used as a mere synonym for *eros* (passionate, though not necessarily sensual, desire) or for *philia* (liking or caring for another person in the ordinary sense). Jesus gave so clear a picture of what a life centred in the love of God and expressing itself in love for others would be that, when the New Testament was written in Greek, the meaning of *agape* was transformed.

A glance at the list of virtues enumerated in the paragraph above makes it apparent that, taken as a list, they represent merely a set of admirable qualities. One's reaction to them may quite reasonably be that there is nothing unique about them, for they are to be found advocated in Judaism and certain of the non-Christian religions as well as in Greek philosophy and the modern secular world. Or one may dismiss them as admirable but unattainable, and of doubtful value even if they could be attained.

To take either of these courses, and let the matter rest there, is to miss what Jesus was concerned about. He did not set out to give a catalogue of virtues, and was apparently quite untroubled as to whether he was saying something new or expressing fully attainable goals of action. His concern was to proclaim the nature of a God-centred, love-filled life lived in obedience to the call of God, and to win men to it. And this he succeeded in doing, in unmistakable terms.

(d) *Jesus had a Realistic Knowledge Both of Human Sin and of the Possibilities of the Redeemed Life:* It is significant that Jesus does not talk about sin nearly as much as Paul. A concordance shows that the word "sin" as a noun appears in his recorded sayings very few times in the Synoptic Gospels, though more in John, and with one exception (the sin against the Holy Spirit, Matt. 12:31; Mark 3:29), when he uses the term, it is in the plural. The Lord's Prayer in Luke contains the petition "Forgive us our sins (11:4), and it is perhaps unfortunate that we do not commonly use this form instead of "debts" or "trespasses." To the

> paralytic (Matt. 9:2-6; Mark 2:5-10; Luke 5:20-24) and to the woman who brought the alabaster flask of ointment (Luke 7:47-49) he said, "Your sins are forgiven." Doubtless he said it on occasions that are not recorded, and equally to the discomfiture of those who heard him. Yet if the record in the Synoptic Gospels is to be trusted, he did not, like Paul, look upon sin as an enveloping state of evil resulting from Adam's fall and corrupting man's whole being. Fuller recognition of this fact might give a more constructive turn to much of contemporary theology.

Yet this is not to say that Jesus set forth a doctrine of the natural goodness of man, such as is characteristic of Greek thought and common in present-day humanism. In the records of what Jesus said there is no doctrine of total depravity, but neither is there a sentimental assumption that if a person is well nurtured and his intentions are good, his acts will be good enough. Because "he himself knew what was in man" (John 2:25), he pierced through the veneer of "good" people to their chicanery and self-deception, and saw that the keeping of the commandments from one's youth up was no substitute for single-minded devotion to God (Mark 10:17-22). Yet, on the other hand, he never scaled downward man's possibilities, and the very virtues that have been enumerated as belonging to the life of faith and love are implicit witness to his confidence that man with the help of God could live as the "salt of the earth."

Jesus gives us no explicit doctrine of sin; what he does do is to show us what is wrong with our living and what the good life, centred in obedience to God's will, might be. But how is this to be brought about?

As with sin, Jesus gives no explicit doctrine of

redemption. Yet there is not the least doubt that Jesus viewed the sins of men with utter seriousness and gave himself with his whole being—even to the Cross—to enable men to find forgiveness and release. The ethical and spiritual insights of Jesus inevitably judge us if we are sensitive to them, yet his primary approach was a positive setting forth of the way in which men's sins could be overcome. The author of the Fourth Gospel caught perfectly the dominant mood and method of Jesus when he wrote, "For God sent the Son into the world, not to condemn the world, but that the world might be saved through him" (3:17).

What are the requirements for sin's conquest? Although these must be gleaned from Jesus' total teaching and ministry and not from systematic analysis, the directives are clear enough. God forgives in infinite love and mercy the sinner who turns to him, as is epitomized in the parable of the prodigal son. The primary focus is on God's act. But the sinner himself must do something about it; it does not happen without cost on man's part as well as God's.

These requirements are: *commitment of will* (seek first God's kingdom and his righteousness), *repentance* (repent, for the kingdom of heaven is at hand), *forgiveness of others* (for if you forgive men their trespasses, your heavenly Father also will forgive you; but if you do not forgive men their trespasses, neither will your Father forgive your trespasses), *faith* (your faith has saved you; go in peace) (Matt. 6:33; 4:17; 6:14-15; Luke 7:50). While most of the numerous occasions on which Jesus said, "Your faith has made you well," were in connection with miracles of physical healing and the casting out of demons rather than the conquest of sin, he seems to have drawn no sharp distinctions at this point. To any soul in need the promise of faith was, "Ask, and it will be given you; seek, and you will find; knock, and it will be opened to you" (Matt. 7:7).

And this could happen! Repeatedly, it has happened. Although those contemporary theologies which stress the persistence of sin even in the best Christians have a note of truth which rightly challenges complacency about the redeemed life, it is also true that there are Christian saints who attain to a very high measure of the God-centred faith and love portrayed by Jesus. It is not unreasonable to suppose that most readers of these pages will have known at least one such by whom his life has been blest. But the Christian saint, in whom sin appears to be so nearly conquered, will be the last person to claim merit for himself. For any achievement he will give humble and grateful praise to God. This is what Jesus did when he said, "Why do you call me good? No one is good but God alone." (Mark 10:18; Luke 18:19.) And it is to this spirit that he calls his followers.

(e) *Jesus Declared the Supreme Worth of Every Person to God*: He did not use the phrase heard very commonly two decades ago, "the intrinsic worth of personality," or the one now in more common usage, "the dignity of man." His idea of man was not at variance with either of these concepts, but it is not the way in which he thought. Rather, every person was of supreme worth to him because every person was beloved of God. His total ministry was a ministry of the redemption of persons—whether it was redemption from physical illness, mental disturbance, error, or sin — because he shared the love of God for every person and so gave himself completely to a ministry of helpfulness to all.

The words of Jesus make clear that he valued

personality above material things or institutions. "Of how much more value is a man than a sheep! So it is lawful to do good on the sabbath." (Matt. 12:12.) In another setting he declared of God's loving care, "You are of more value than many sparrows" (Matt. 10:31)—a graphic way of affirming the worth to God of man above the total subhuman world.

Yet it is in his attitudes and acts, rather than in specific words, that we find the charter of human equality in God's equal concern for all. Whether he dealt with women, children, or slaves, whether the persons in need were Jew, Roman, Syro-Phoenician, or Samaritan, whether he associated with "respectable" people or social outcasts, whether he was illustrating true neighbourliness by the story of the good Samaritan or declaring the principle of divine judgment on the basis of "as you did it to one of the least of these my brethren"—all persons were of equal and supreme worth to him because he saw them through the eyes of God.

It is commonly, and correctly, affirmed that democracy has its chief root in Jesus' concern for the worth of persons, though it is not true that this is its sole root. There was democracy as the political ideal in the Greek city-states before Jesus' time, and there are democratic roots — always impinged upon by aristocratic tendencies — in Greek philosophy. Still, the message of Jesus is its chief fountainhead within Christendom. What is not so commonly realized is that the democracy of Jesus in manifold person-to-person relationships was rooted in his relationship to God. He did not set out simply to exalt the dignity of man; yet he lifted the status of men, women, and children wherever his message was heard because he saw all persons as precious to God and equally the recipients of God's love.

Thus it came about that in the early Church *democracy* and *evangelism* went hand in hand. The gospel of redemption through the love of God in Christ broke down earthly barriers, and people of every occupational status, degree of wealth, or social standing saw the "middle walls of partition" melt away. In him there was "neither Jew nor Greek,... neither slave nor free,... neither male nor female," for all were one in Christ Jesus. This grounding is important to any sound preservation or extension of democracy in our own time. But of this, more later.

(f) *The Central Teaching of Jesus was the Kingdom of God!* I have thus far deferred discussion of this central theme, which was on Jesus' lips continually, because in large part its meaning is determined by the teachings already mentioned.

There are both great clarity and great ambiguity in the records as to the message of Jesus in regard to the Kingdom. Everybody agrees that it was his central message, yet there is nothing in New Testament interpretation and scarcely anything in Christian theology about which opinions differ more. The disputed elements centre mainly in the bearing of the Kingdom on the ethical demands of the present life in relation to what lies beyond it in a realm that transcends human history — that is, in the relations of ethics to eschatology. Fortunately, the matters most directly related to the practical requirements of the Christian life are those most fully agreed upon, and we shall begin with these.

First, the Kingdom means the sovereign, righteous rule of God in a redeemed society—that is, in a society of persons who accept God's rule and endeavour to live in obedience to his will. The kingship, like the lordship, of God are terms drawn from a monarchical or feudal order, but ought not to suggest to us autocracy or dictatorship. Though Jesus had a realistic sense of divine judgment, as is evident from the parable of the last judgment in Matt. 25:31-46, he never divorced his conception of the Kingdom from the forgiving mercy of God and God's loving care of the individual person. This is evident throughout and conspicuously in this same parable, where one's place in the Kingdom is to be determined by one's responsiveness to human need. Yet it is God, not man, who rules the world, and for the coming of the Kingdom his rule must be accepted by all men.

By a redeemed society—a term which Jesus did not use, though we may—is meant a community of persons responsive to the call of God in faith and love. It does not mean directly, as far as we can read Jesus' thought, a set of reconstructed social institutions. He does not have a great deal to say about political or economic structures. But he has much to say about the attitudes and motives of men in their corporate life. He was vitally concerned about sin and the harm it did, both to the sinner and to others.

Jesus' concern about social iniquities always sprang from his indignant perception of their ill effect on individuals. The victim of the bandits on the Jerusalem-Jericho road, the widow mistreated by an unjust judge, the unfortunates on whom publicans like Zacchaeus practised extortion, the destitute at a rich man's door, prisoners unvisited and hungry folk unfed— always it was wronged individuals who called out from Jesus a social message.

Therefore, while the Kingdom cannot be directly equated with the social gospel, as American liberal theology has tended to do, the impulse to social action in order to help persons—whether individually or corporately—is in keeping with his spirit and is a legitimate derivative from his message.

Second, Jesus regarded the kingdom of God as the supreme good, worth any cost. It is God's gift, yet it must be sought with all that one has. This appears again and again in such passages as "Seek first his kingdom and his righteousness" (Matt. 6:33), the treasure hid in a field for which one sells all his possessions (Matt. 13:44), the pearl of great price (Matt. 13:45-46).

It is a mistake to suppose that man by his own effort can "build the Kingdom," and it is well that this unbiblical metaphor is heard less often than formerly. Yet it is equally a mistake, if we are true to what Jesus tells us, to suppose that God will give the Kingdom without the assumption of responsibility on man's part. Although we are told, "Fear not, little flock, for it is your Father's good pleasure to give you the kingdom" (Luke 12:32), it will not do to forget that the verse before this one says "seek his kingdom" and the one after it enjoins selling all that one has for treasure in heaven.

Third, Jesus is clear as to the conditions of entrance into the Kingdom. All that was summarized as to the pattern of the God-centred life and the requirements for the conquest of sin is here involved. It is not the self-righteous moralist, trusting in his own virtue and his fidelity to the law, who enters the Kingdom; it is one who receives it with the humble trustfulness of a child (Mark 10:15). It is not everyone who is voluble about his religion who shall enter the Kingdom, but he who does the will of the Father (Matt. 7:21). The Kingdom is present among the poor in spirit (Matt. 5:3) and among repentant sinners (Matt. 21:3). The discerning scribe who saw the validity of the two Great Commandments was said to be "not far from the Kingdom of God." (Mark 12:34). The burden of

Jesus' message as of John the Baptist's, though with greater gentleness and the strength born of love, was "Repent, for the kingdom of heaven is at hand."

Eschatology and Ethics

We come now to some issues regarding Jesus' message of the Kingdom about which there is less agreement. We cannot in this brief survey go into every nuance of thought regarding them. But neither can we disregard them, for they are too central to the message of Jesus and hence to our faith. Eschatology is the doctrine of the "last things." The eschaton means the end, and eschatology has to do with what happens at the end of human history and beyond it. There is an eschatology of the individual with reference to concepts of heaven, hell, final judgment, and in general of "eternal life." There are also eschatological beliefs about the future of society and the final destiny of the human race. It is in this second framework that disputes about the Kingdom mainly centre, though the two cannot be sharply separated.

A basic question is with regard to the time of the coming of the Kingdom. Is it a present attainment or a hope for the future? And if it is both, is the full consummation of the Kingdom to be in the immediate future or at some indefinite time known only to God? Is the Kingdom to come on earth, or beyond all history? There are passages in the Gospels which seem to support all of these views.

The easiest of these questions is the first, for it is not impossible to suppose that Jesus believed the Kingdom to be in some measure already present while its final consummation was yet to come.

Being asked by the Pharisees when the kingdom of God was coming, he answered them, "The kingdom of God is not coming with signs, to be observed; nor will they say, 'Lo, here it is!' or 'There!' for behold, the kingdom of God is in the midst of you. (Luke 17:20-21.)

This may mean what through the influence of Professor C. H. Dodd has come to be called realized eschatology, the belief that Jesus had brought the Kingdom to fulfilment in his own person and he was thereby affirming his messiahship. It seems to me more probable that Jesus meant primarily though perhaps not solely to declare the possibility of entrance into the Kingdom here and now by repentance, the acceptance of God's forgiveness, and the assumption of the obligations of discipleship. The parables of the leaven (Matt. 13:33; Luke 13:20-21), the mustard seed (Mark 4:30 if.; Matt. 13:31-32; Luke 13:18-19), and the seed growing secretly until it becomes "first the blade, then the ear, then the full grain in the ear" (Mark 4:26-29) not only are parables of growth; they are indexes that what the Kingdom *will be* is already present in what is. Yet the references of Jesus to the Kingdom again and again have a futuristic note, and if there were no other reason, the fact that he taught his followers to pray, "Thy kingdom come," would be sufficient evidence that he did not regard it as having fully come.

The issues of chief difficulty arise at the point of questions as to whether Jesus expected the Kingdom to come on earth or only in some realm beyond earthly history, and in the latter event, whether he expected earthly history to end very soon by a catastrophic divine intervention when he himself would return in glory to reign over a transfigured world. Thus, the whole question of the Second Coming is tied in with the issue. These problems all come to focus in the question as to whether Jesus' view of the Kingdom was primarily eschatological or ethical and spiritual. Anyone who followed in the slightest the discussions before and at the Evanston Assembly of the World Council of Churches on the main theme "Christ — the Hope of the World" will recognize the disparities of judgment among Christians today at this point.

There are some, though it is a minority position among New Testament scholars, who think that the apocalyptic passages attributed to Jesus were interpolations of early Christian thought. This would be a comfortable way out of the impasse if we could think so, for in view of the fact that the end of the world has not yet come, it is not easy to fit into the rest of his words such sayings as, "Truly, I say to you, there are some standing here who will not taste death before they see the Son of man coming in his kingdom" (Matt. 16:28; cf. Mark 9:1; Luke 9:27), or after a vivid description of the signs of the end, "Truly, I say to you, this generation will not pass away till all these things take place" (Matt. 24:34; Mark 13:30; Luke 21:32). Nevertheless, the passages are too deeply embedded to be thus discarded. Some may have been confused by the early Church with prophecies of the destruction of Jerusalem, for Jesus saw that his countrymen knew not the "things that make for peace" (Luke 19:42) and that their doom was approaching. Some of them may have been, as Professor Dodd suggests, mixtures of references to Jesus' resurrection and his second coming. But with due recognition of these possibilities, it still remains probable that Jesus shared the apocalyptic expectations common in Judaism in the first century and looked upon himself as God's chosen agent for bringing these things to pass. The incarnate Lord lived at a particular time and place in history, and in his apocalypticism Jesus was apparently a man of his time.

What does this do to his ethics? Does it destroy the

validity of his teachings as universal principles? The answer is No.

It does not make his teachings an "interim ethic." In later Judaism it was believed that the precepts of the Torah were valid for the next world as well as this. Jesus apparently held this view with regard to what he proclaimed to be the will of God, for he never suggests that he is saying something of only temporary relevance. In fact, the contrary is clearly implied in the declaration, "Heaven and earth will pass away, but my words will not pass away" (Matt. 24:35; cf. Luke 16:17).

It does not make of his teachings counsels of perfection for the next life only. As was earlier remarked, Jesus was apparently not concerned over the exact degree of attainability of his precepts. He stated what he believed to be right — what a person would do if he loved, trusted, and obeyed God completely. It is unlikely either that he was so naive as to suppose that men could be perfect as God is perfect or that the attempt to do so was inconsequential.

It does not submerge his ethics in eschatology. Eschatology was undoubtedly present in the thought of Jesus, as it should be in ours, an eschatology of both eternal life for the individual and the hope of a final consummation of the reign of God beyond earthly time and space. Both the corruption of earthly history by persistent sin and the grandeur of a vista that transcends it lend support to the view that the kingdom of God will fully come, not on earth, but beyond this world. In this final victory:

He shall reign forever and ever,

King of kings! and Lord of lords!

and the only appropriate response of the Christian is

"Hallelujah!" But this does not mean that what Jesus has taught us of the good life here and now is set aside. Christ is our hope—now, in the earthly future, and for eternity.

The eschatology of Jesus was never the ethically barren thing that either the apocalyptists of his time or the premillennialists of ours have too often made it. Not only repentance, but sensitiveness to a brother's need, determined status in the Kingdom (Matt. 4:17; 25:31-46). There is a tension between this world and the world to come, but to Jesus its resolution lay in God's control over both realms and man's responsive, obedient acceptance of God's rule in faith and love and deeds of service.

The God to whom Jesus prayed was the Lord of heaven and earth; his will must be done "on earth as it is in heaven." Jesus' outlook was too profoundly God-centred and ethical to permit him to fall prey to pessimism regarding this world's fate, or asceticism regarding God's gifts within it, or spectacularism regarding the grand finale, or moral indifference regarding the pedestrian steps God's servants must take along the way. In short, his total outlook without eliminating eschatology transformed it.

9

Reason for Martyrdom in the Twentieth Century

In the 20th century, the Church had undergone political changes. She is stripped of political powers which she enjoyed in the previous centuries. The only power she has now is the power that emanates from the word. As for faith, she is brought back to the earth.

With regard to martyrdom in the 20th century we notice a shift: from the "heroic" to the "anonymous" martyrdoms; from the "individual" to the "collective" martyrdoms; from the "historical" to the "contemporary" reality As for the content of faith, it can be said that faith in Christ works towards liberating people from the bondage, — of all sorts. In other words, human beings have become the concern of the Church and Christian faith. Why did this shift take place and in what context?

Alarmed at the horrors of violence and threat to human life, the Church began to focus its attention on human beings. The Churches are studying this vast human identity, so often denied, ridiculed, exploited, massacred. They oppose the coalition of interests, calculations, fears or ignorance, with a concern which subordinates every principle to human dignity, and which begins with basic respect for life as such. It is in this context, Pope John Paul II, for instance, is hailed as the Pope of human rights in the five continents.

Further, the Church and Society Conference of the World Council of Churches in 1966 and the Roman Catholic Bishops' Conference of Latin America (CELAM) in 1968, both representing the Ecumenical Movement, proclaimed a message to the Christians at large in identical terms thus: they said:

> *If the Church wants to share its life with the world then it must put its weight on the side of the poor and the oppressed.*

In other words, Iraeneus' observation that "the glory of God is the living human being" sums up the aspirations of contemporary faith. Well, then, is life superior to honour? Does faith at present dictate the duty of cowardice to the faithful, inviting them to sacrifice everything for their safety? In what does my honour consist?, one might ask.

The answer is that it consists in the life of others, which calls for freedom, security, and justice; and if necessary I must defend them at the price of my own life.

Martyrdom, in the twentieth century, became inevitable in the context of totalitarian orders which quench the spirit, sow death and scorch the earth. Until recently, two super powers namely, the USA and the USSR appealed to antithetical catechism. Now, there is only one power which pretends to act as the police man of the world. At the instance of USA, the worship of the Mammon continues. While this is the context in the North, in the South, the people are weakened by misery, allow themselves to be torn by fratricidal struggles and remain defenceless in the face of those who suck them to the marrow. East against West and North against South, this way hate crucifies the world.

In the earlier part of 20th century we had Nazism, Fascism and Auschwitz. Now we have the threat from Chemical weapons, neutrons and, the bacteria, as well as giant multi-national and transnational corporations. Thus there is violence to life, human life, animal life and plant life. Mass violence characterizes the present-day situation of the world. Because of this mass violence, the notion of martyrdom has broadened out and become imprecise. Martyrdom today extends to groups sacrificed to the contemporary barbarism. Whole peoples become martyrs: Jews, Gypsies, the Cambodians, the Vietnamese, the tribals, the Dalits in India and women everywhere. In other words, torture and summary execution is the fate of many in the world today. The second feature of martyrdom in the 20th century is that though nothing was willed, everything was accepted. A definitive choice guided the destiny of the martyrs. For example, Sister Alice Domon remarked to the Archbishop of Toulouse thus: "I have already made the sacrifice of my life".

The third feature of martyrdom in the 20th century is that it takes the side of the oppressed. That is, to give in or to accept death with patience is not enough. To merit the title, he or she should be entirely swallowed up by death. What merits them? Martyrs are those who suffer but their groans, far from being a disavowal of what they were, express the noble reason for their deaths and change the apparent fatality into an absolute proof of loge. For this reason we can say that the last word which honours the martyr is not COMPASSION but EXAMPLE. That is to say, men and women, in the 20th century sacrifice their lives with a view to rescuing their brothers and sisters from scorn, from propaganda, from misery, from death and from all four at the same time. Witnesses are agreed here in spite of the fact that the circumstances and the issues are different:

Maximilian Kolbe took the place of another to perish slowly of hunger and thirst;

Martin Luther King Jr. dreamed of a children's game in which all races would hold hands;

Oscar Romero died calling on his compatriots for basic justice.

Thus, we see a claim which makes sense of all the martyrdoms of our time: Martyrs today no longer die explicitly for Jesus Christ nor for the freedom of the Spirit as was the case in the first two periods we had considered, but they die for human justice, *i.e.*, an urgent new action is needed to defend those who are overwhelmed by the weight of totalitarianism. One may ask: what is this faith if it is not explicitly for faith in Jesus Christ or for the freedom of the spirit?

The answer to that comes in the form of another question: Can faith serve God if it does not FIRST serve humankind? In other words, the contemporary martyrs are involved in political matters and are more often concerned in action than speaking, like the first Christians, or thinking as at the end of the Middle Ages. Thus, the contemporary martyrs throw themselves into the combats of the world, they denounce its impostures, seek to reduce the atrocious inequality of fortunes and classes, to uproot the cult of Mammon, the bloodiest of the gods, and dismantle the systems of oppression. By involving themselves totally in the combats of the world, the contemporary martyrs make themselves the apostles of the human person. This is clear in what M.L. King, Jr.

had said in 1961, in the context of threat to his life from the powers that were and in the context of strike by Garbage Collectors:

> *It may crucify me. I may die. But even if I die in the struggle I want people to say, "He died to make me free.*

Thus, the faith of these martyrs is totally swallowed up in the absolute urgency embodied in the oppressed and their suffering. We give prominence to the martyrs of the yester years and yester centuries. They do deserve that. But we should not overlook those others who suffer besides the martyrs. I quote Theofried Baumester who says thus:

> *The prominence given to the martyrs should not be made retrospective. But those others who suffer besides the martyrs should not be overlooked. Today they need a different theological treatment than in early Christianity. (Concilium)*

The fourth feature of martyrdom in the 20th century is that the end of these modern martyrs is very different from anything evident in former centuries. In the former centuries, the martyrs were arrested, judged, and delivered over to death; two theories were in conflict: Where is God, in an institution or in a conscience? Now there is no longer debate between a way of thinking and the supposed virtues of order. In the modern times, the persecuted person speaks in the name of his or her faith, deeply rooted in a cultural heritage. It is clear that the martyrs, embody the side of justice.

The fifth feature of martyrdom in our century is that the persecutor is often put to shame. Persecutor employs state violence, and horrible means to quench life. He or she refuses to acknowledge his or her motives in employing state violence and horrible means. The persecutor spreads lies, propagates myths and uses the media to reach the ends. For instance, the Third World theologians are branded as Marxists, drunkards, womanizers, depressed, homosexuals, lesbians, Anti-nationals insurrectionists and so on, when they in fact, are trying to live out their faith in defense of the defenceless. Again, AIDS disease is highlighted as the most urgent and serious problem in the world today. No doubt about that for, the experts say so. What about malnutrition, undernourishment, hunger and poverty around the globe — in Somalia, Ethiopia and the severe human rights violations in countries such as South Africa, Afghanistan, Sri Lanka, Pakistan and so on? In today's world, the persecutor adopts dubious means to silence the dissent voices and, silencing voice is the most atrocious crime. Therefore, there are no trials and the persecutor closes the mouth of the opponents. Public execution is avoided. Eg: Bhuto. No one may see the condemned person; no spectacle of death; his or her patience, voice or look many convey too much. Hence, the attempt to silence dissent or dissident voices who speak of freedom, truth, justice and humanity.

Thus, in modern days, not only the victim but the entire judicial apparatus is concealed, That is why the mode of killing resembles an assassination. Eg: Aquino was killed in broad day light. Thus, there is no justice, no tribunal and no scaffold, — a person is butchered! Victims fate is hidden, suppressed and in an uncertain trial, the victim remains behind the closed doors. Death perpetrated by paramilitary bands, hooligans, a militia which the state virtuously disowns after giving arms, sometimes to both parties in conflict.

Assassination is concealed behind an abduction because a bullet could be too much of a noise! However, concealment confesses the innocence of the victims and it equally points a finger at the guilty under their masks. It also pronounces the stifled message which gives the martyr his or her full significance as a witness. For it is the face of Christ that it brings out in the very act in which it seeks to deny it. Did precautions of the persecutors prevent people like Romero and Jerzy Popeluszko from becoming legends? The committed speak even after their death, perhaps even while they live out the truth in their lives. How is this possible? This takes us to the next section. Thus far, we had seen the diversity of martyrdom in three periods. Martyrdom arose for different reasons. In the antiquity in was the confession of the name of Christ which brought about martyrdom. In the second period, it was speaking on behalf of the freedom of the spirit or conscience. In the present day it is social justice which warrants martyrdom. But is there a unity in the concept of martyrdom? How fair are we in interpreting the meaning of martyrdom in three periods as we had seen thus far? The distinction made here is for the sake of clarity and because of historical development.

Thus, this distinction is an apparent one. But then, how are we to understand martyrdom with all its diversity and meanings? Is there a unity of purpose in martyrdom? yes, we will come to that shortly. But before that we should mention the two elements of constancy that we identify in the history of martyrdom in Christianity. The first element of constancy refers to the persecutors. They are the same even now, barbarians, and they expect people to call them Lords, say, the Caesar is Lord! The second element of constancy refers to the persecuted. Their faith and steadfastness is the same. They say even now: God is Lord. The different approaches adopted by the persecuted, the martyrs, stem from a single centre, belief in Jesus Christ. But this faith in Jesus is understood differently today than it was in the earlier centuries. This faith or belief in Jesus Christ, therefore, needs to be interpreted, because:

Who would dare to confess Christ without concern for his or her impoverished brothers and sisters, and without holding his or her head high before Caesar?

Who can claim to be free if they do not allow their neighbours to be because they have no food, and if they do not invoke the supreme dispenser of freedom?

Who can believe themselves to be vehicles of justice if they do not attend to the perpetrators of slavery, and taking the side of humanity, do not stand up to the powers which take only its own side; or if they do not serve, in the person of the poor, the figure of one who made himself poor to crown them with his glory?

So, what is this faith or belief in Jesus? How are we to interpret it? We need to systematize our reflections.

The Unity of Martyrdom

First of all, martyrdom should be understood in relation to the service of the humiliated. People do not die today to defend their cause as Christians. But the cause is certainly there. As Leonardo Boff says:

The martyr defends not his life, but his cause, which is his religious conviction, his fidelity to God or his brother. And he defends this cause by dying.

Neither do they fight for heavenly thoughts. But for the person of Christ in the poor. Christ is present in each one of us, especially in the person of the poor. That is why:

> *Thomas More refused to take oath which dishonoured his country and looked for the unity of the universal church. Behind the voices that Joan of Arc heard was the wounded honour of a nation.*

The Apostolic Fathers who left writings before undergoing martyrdom bear witness that they too demanded the bread that was due to the poor. For example, Ignatius and Polycarp preached "help for the widow, the orphan, the afflicted, the captive, the freedman, the hungry and the thirsty". In other words, their presence is part of the design of God for whom they die. These men and women accepted suffering because their conviction extended beyond themselves to serve the human community and to take its part on earth. In other words, their faith is focused downward, not upward, or heavenward. So, far from taking them aside into the heavens, faith nails them to these kingdoms of the earth, which are promised to the meek to inherit and the love of which they sometimes confess.

Secondly, martyrdom should be understood in relation to the freedom of the spirit. The freedom of the spirit is interior to faith. This freedom is not the monopoly of the wise or the powerful. All of us have this freedom. That is to say, the martyrdom of which it is the cause gives a hearing to the voices of people, without distinctions of class, fortune, education, age and something which is more rare, — sex. Faith invests men and women born to shadow and silence with an authority. Old men such as Polycarp and frail women like Perpetua and Felicita show it to Caesar.

But they are not rebels and there is nothing to hold against them. They are subject to those who govern them. But they are stubborn in opposing a power which glorifies itself and makes itself an end in itself. The race of freemen, the martyrs, professes political irreligion. Its slogan is: "Down with the cult of the emperors!" In other words, Christian martyrdom is based on opposition to the power which takes itself as an absolute point of reference. Christians still say that "Caesar is not Lord".

This Christian freedom, from outside, looks like rebellion within and it is confused with an obedience made an absolute, which has a name because it has a master, Jesus Christ. That is why, Joan of Arc could confidently declare thus: "I look to my judge, who is the master of heaven; yes, I look to my creator. I love him with all my heart". Polycarp echoes the same thus: "I have served him for eighty-six years" or "He has been faithful to me for eighty-six years".

In the 20th century the same obstinate voice of Romero is heard thus: "We obey the order of God before that of human beings". In a seminary in India, in the context of suppression of human rights and denial of participation in the decision-making processes, the voice of the former Moderator of Church of South of India, Bishop Anandara Samuel, was recently heard thus "It is better to obey God than the Moderators".

The last example cited here makes me to observe that martyrs need not to be only those who met with violent death and are dead, but martyrs can be still living, facing death or opposing death in their day-to-day lives. Martyrs are still there, still living but ready to die for a cause. They are numerous. These modern day martyrs explain themselves. They do not depart from the general spinelessness through personal exhibitionism or in the pride of an elitist intelligence. Further their personal drama is lost in the vastness of an eternal design into which they throw themselves without fear and sometimes without displeasure. So, martyrdom is always a confession of faith, secret or expressed.

It goes before God fri wonder. The martyrs confront their persecutors, full of humanity, if not of humour. If they protest it is at the evil done by their brothers to the "least and the last" of the humanity. The cause of the poor, the oppressed and the marginalized — secularized — is also a confession of Christ.

This broadening of the Christian vocation should not be treated as a break in the tradition of martyrdom. Karl Rahner, in making a plea for the broadening of the classical concept, asks: (with reference to Romero)

For example, why should not some one like Bishop Romero, who died while fighting for justice in society, a struggle he waged out of the depths of his conviction as a Christian why should he not be a martyr? Certainly he was prepared for his death (Concilium, p. 10.)

This question is legitimate and we will come to that later. The point to remember here is that the 20th century martyrs refuse to sacrifice men and women to Mammon, the new idol of our time. Their combat is also spiritual. To understand this otherwise would be to misunderstand and misrepresent the meaning of martyrdom. The martyrs of the present day persist in confronting oppressive power; they stimulate independence of judgement, insensitive to the seductions of money and power, and they flourish above all the faithfulness to service of the most abandoned, where faith contemplates the form of Christ in the present. Boff brings home this point powerfully thus:

Today, more and more Christians, particularly in the Third World, are carrying out actions... Which originate in faith and the Gospel. Not a few Christians... because of the Gospel, make a preferential option for the poor, for their liberation,

> *for the defense of their rights. In the name of this option they stand up and denounce the exercise of domination and all forms of social dehumanization. They may be persecuted, arrested, tortured and killed. They, too, are martyrs in the strict sense of the word (Concilium, p. 14)*

Finally, martyrdom today should be understood in relation to the Kingdom which Jesus proclaimed. Martyrs of old confessed faith in the risen Christ. But the martyrs in our times confess their faith in the Kingdom which Jesus of his own historical context proclaimed. Jesus' ministry and mission was focused on the Kingdom (Mk.1:14-15). The martyrs or witnesses of the earlier centuries, particularly those in the antiquity; awaited judgement at the end of time, they patiently awaited divine justice. Whereas contemporary witnesses have turned their eyes away from the glory of the heavens, obscured by the infinite sorrow of the world. What is this Kingdom? When is it to be fulfilled or realized? At the end of time? Does it not have two dimensions: the "already" and the "not yet"? How right is the understanding that the divine justice is to be awaited and the Kingdom to be realized here and now in time and history? When one is engaged in theological niceties, the contemporary martyrs who are dead or who are alive, raise, the following questions with enough legitimacy and justification:

> *How do we talk of God in the midst of poverty, oppression, war and meaninglessness? Should not our God-talk be meaningful in and related to the context? Should we await God's power and justice only at the end of time? If God is active in history through the Incarnation of Jesus of his own historical context, then how do we celebrate God's presence and participation in our living*

situations, in our search for meaning, in our hopes and fears, and in our anguishes and aspirations? If God is powerful and Just, then should God not intervene instead of waiting? If God is just, then should not God help instead of judging? It was in such a situation of complexity, suffering and oppression and denial of basic human rights and humanity that one martyr, our contemporary, Dietrich Bonhoffer, came up with the idea or faith reflection that "only a powerless God can help".

That is to say, faith today is oriented towards the kingdom, its value, life-style and it meditates on the scourged Christ, on the power of love bestowed, *i.e.*, on passion and suffering. Faith seeks God in Christ among the humble, the scorned in whom God is embodied. In other words, the Lord of the 20th century is the suffering servant of Second Isaiah, with wounded face and hands, which also tend the unfortunate of whom he is so intimately the brother. The important thing to remember is that God, in Christ, has made himself known in history. God is where God's people are, — especially among the least and the last, the unfortunate, the less privileged, the dehumanized, the suffering and the oppressed and the poor. Jesus did not ask his faithful to love elsewhere than on the earth where they have met him, nor otherwise than as he loved himself, dedicating himself to the liberation of our humiliated race. I close with John 12:24-25 which reads thus:

Unless a grain of wheat falls into the earth and dies, it remains alone; but if it dies, it bears abundant fruit. He who loves his life loses it, and he who hates his life in this world will keep it for eternal life.

10

The Legacy of a Loving Prophet

Modern American Protestantism has not, for the most part, focused on the lives of the saints. The psychic energy of contemporary pastors, theologians and church leaders has more often centered on the kerygmatic Word as it encounters "the problem of history," on struggles against the idolatries of fascism and Stalinism abroad and racism, classism and sexism at home, or on the development of the professional skills of ministry.

But what has been ignored at the front door has entered by the side. Both psychohistory and narrative theology have evoked a rebirth of what our grandparents called "testimony"—the stories of personal pilgrimage. People do need models; we like to tell our own tales; and we like to get the scoop on everyone else.

Some of this is little more than pious gossip, and is pernicious. When it becomes the primary focus of attention, faith is endangered: We slide easily into the conviction that theology is basically a reflection of a quest for identity, or is poetry projected onto the cosmos rather than a fundamental claim about what is true or just or holy—

just what the greatest skeptics about religion have claimed for several centuries.

The best preachers and teachers do not talk too much about the self and do not concentrate on personal experience alone. They know that psychobabble can easily become a substitute for good news, and that temptations to avoid theological insight and social responsibility in favor of self-preoccupation are all too frequent.

Nevertheless, the current burst of interest in biography may be a corrective for lopsidedness in other directions. For Christians, the divine revelation, the historic redefinition of meaning, the cosmopolitan insight—all those things that are deeper and wider than the self and that can reshape the self—have, finally, also to come to fruition in the life of persons. Even the long-expected idea of the messianic kingdom had to have a particular personal locus to be fully compelling. A testament with all the discursive writings of Paul, John and the pastorals but without the Gospels would be incomplete.

Biographical interest can be seen in the continuing fascination with the lives of modern martyrs such as Dietrich Bonhoeffer and Martin Luther King, Jr., and in the way some feminist and Third World thinkers use stories to evoke fresh modes of reflection. Consider, for example, how often Alice Walker's *The Colour Purple* is used in seminary teaching, or how C. S. Song, Kosuke Koyama and Lamin Sanneh draw on personal cross-cultural encounters to bring new perceptions to scriptural and theological themes. The pervasiveness of this emphasis can now be seen even in Christian social ethics, the field born out of the Social Gospel movement and one which in the name of prophetic spirit and social analysis has been critical of Protestantism's tendency to focus on personal piety. A refreshing effort to reflect on the intimate connection of prophecy, piety and social insight is Paul Minus's biography of the father of the Social Gospel, *Walter Rauschenbusch: American Reformer* (Macmillan, 1988, 243 pp., *$19.95)* As much as any other single figure, Rauschenbusch brought 19th-century pietism into the 20th-century world of cities, factories, immigrants, clashing classes and subcultures, and problems of housing, transportation and employment. For many, the path that led from the historic patterns of Protestant pietism to ecumenically engaged, socially involved and intellectually critical evangelicalism, and away from constrictive fundamentalism, forked at Rauschenbusch.

No one can read him deeply, or read about him, without thinking that they know him personally. Everyone is inclined to call him, as did his friends, "Rauschy." Yet, like John the Baptist, he always points beyond himself to something greater. Perhaps that is why many of those indebted to him do not take him as their final master.

The outline of his story is simply rehearsed. His father was a German Lutheran pastor who immigrated to this country and converted to the Baptist faith and the democratic polity as a young man. Born in 1861, Walter Rauschenbusch imbibed from his family a profound personal piety, a love of learning, a sympathy for the oppressed and a sense of mission. His studies both in the United States and in Germany cultivated his many gifts and reinforced his sense of having been called to a great task for God. It also gave him an abiding love of both German and American cultures.

He became a pastor in a German Baptist church in a raw section of New York City. In the course of a very successful ministry—informed by piety (he wrote wonderful prayers), pastoral experience (he cared for his flock) and learning (he regularly wrote reviews and articles for journals)—he became increasingly critical of the economic system of the late 19th century. That system seemed to undercut the democratic gains that were being made in law, politics, education 'and family life; it tended rather toward a new feudalism, dominated by robber barons and served by a new class of industrial peasants. The prophetic emphases in his thought developed roughly during the same time he discovered his love for Pauline Rother, who later became his wife, the mother of his children and a beloved companion in hard work and tender play. Previously unpublished quotations from letters between the two reveal how intense their spiritual and physical intimacy was, and how they discovered qualities of marriage that were not present in their parents'.

Such matters are significant in part because they reveal to a contemporary generation that a prophetic spirit and a passion for social justice need not be born out of suspicion, alienation or victimization. They can be, and they have been, born of an amplitude of love, in which case righteous anger can be directed against manipulators of distrust and hate and not against those who are not "like us."

With a number of fellow pastors who became lifelong friends, Rauschenbusch studied, read, talked, debated and plumbed the new social theories of the day, especially those of the non-Marxist socialists whom John C. Cort has recently traced in *Christian Socialism (*Orbis, 1988) The pastors wove these theories together with biblical themes to form "'Christian Sociology," a hermeneutic of social history that allowed them to see the power of God's kingdom being actualized through the democratization of the economic system (see James T. Johnson, editor, *The Bible in American Law, Politics and Rhetoric* [Scholars Press, 1985]) They pledged themselves to new efforts to make the spirit of Christianity the core of social renewal at a time when agricultural-village life was breaking down and urban-cosmopolitan patterns were not yet fully formed.

When Rauschenbusch became ill and lost some of his hearing, he accepted an invitation to become a professor on the German faculty, and later the English faculty, of what became Colgate Rochester Divinity School. From that position he became one of the most famous speakers on Christianity and social problems of his day, as well as a beloved teacher and honoured author of several books. Until his death in 1918, in the midst of what was for him a tragic war between Germany and America, he helped develop one of the most important theological-ethical positions of modern Protestantism.

Minus's work and its subject matter are sure to be compared with Richard Fox's recent biography of Reinhold Niebuhr, the neoorthodox proponent of Christian realism, and with the autobiography of James Luther Adams, a "liberal" with certain affinities to contemporary liberation thought, now under preparation with the help of Linda Barns. These three figures are arguably among the most influential Protestant social ethicists of 20th-century America, and in any case offer a representative spectrum of opinion.

Minus clearly has a different agenda from Fox's. In *Reinhold Niebuhr: A Biography* (Pantheon, 1985), Fox is interested in which of his teachers, Robert McAfee Brown or Michael Novak, is closer to their teacher's (Niebuhr's) legacy, and in how Niebuhr's Christian realism might influence the future of civilization. Sadly, Fox seems to lose interest in the issue along the way, perhaps because Novak seems to have the best case and Fox does not want him to. He ends up not liking Niebuhr very much and not quite caring about the fate of Christian realism. Nevertheless, his work confirms that Niebuhr stands on Rauschenbusch's shoulders and surpasses him. Rauschy's *Theology for the Social Gospel* is simply no match for Reinie's *Nature and Destiny of Man.*

Minus's concern is for recovering and recasting a creative link between populist theology and active social witness. He ends up liking Rauschenbusch very much, so much that he has to guard against hyperbole. Still, he appears to be less concerned than Rauschenbusch was with the more expansiye questions of how faith and doctrine shape civilizations and how doctrines might shape human destiny. The wider scope of history and the role of ecclesiology in it are not in his immediate horizon. This Methodist biographer is, in this respect, more Baptist than his subject.

Nevertheless, we can see that Rauschenbusch had a better sense of how grass-roots social institutions work than did Niebuhr. Furthermore, like the two-volume Adams autobiography (volume one is nearly done), Rauschenbusch's biography is studded with stories of people from every level of society. Workers and seminarians always came to hear both men speak; but they were also friends of those who did not work with their hands—like John D. Rockefeller, in Rauschenbusch's case.

Rauschenbusch remained more self-consciously rooted in Scripture than did Adams, however, and he maintained closer ties to church circles than to academic ones. While the two share a pronounced sense of the importance of the Holy Spirit, just below the surface, of Rauschenbusch's thought is a trinitarian framework and a preference for an organic society over a voluntaristic one. In comparing Rauschenbusch to Adams, the differences between a religious liberalism (Adams left the Baptists to become a Unitarian Universalist) and a progressive evangelicalism become clear; indeed, we can see how conservative Rauschenbusch really was.

A bigger difference remains in the telling of the individual story. In the Minus biography, characters do not always come alive; points are sometimes only summarized in a quotable aphorism. Of course, Adams is a constitutional raconteur. He teaches by parable, which he seems to be able to connect to systematic thought—whether it be in the philosophical-theological traditions of Whitehead and Tillich or the sociohistprical traditions of Troeltsch and Weber. Those who use Minus's book to teach the next generation how Rauschenbusch brought many in a previous generation, most of a denomination and much of ecumenical Protestantism to embrace "Social Christianity" may, want to translate his material into that kind of revealing art Which simultaneously embraces evocative parable and systematic clarification. The deeper promise of Minus's effort would then be fulfilled.

What does Rauschenbusch's Social Gospel mean for today and tomorrow? Is it the American form of liberation theology, belatedly discovered by Latin American Catholics, Third World Protestants and others who had not previously been led beyond their distinctive forms of pietism by historicism and sociology? Or is it a blip on the screen of history, born of the Progressive era among minorities in a strange land, institutionalized in the New Deal, and now left in the dust by the neoconservative revolution?

If by "liberation" people mean that Christian thought and life are to be socially engaged, committed to those forms of systemic change necessary for the greater actualization of social justice, and open to the dynamic movements of the Spirit among the people, then there is little doubt: the Social Gospel is America's indigenous form of liberation theology. It forms base communities, it overcomes resignation with greatness of soul, it ministers to those with greatest need, it empowers the voiceless. Indeed, the more one reads of Rauschenbusch, the more one sees of the Social Gospel in Martin Luther King, Jr., and even Dorothy Day.

But if by liberation theology one means other things, then differences emerge. If one means, for instance, an epistemological privilege of the oppressed, in the sense that the poor, the suffering and the dispossessed have some intuitive knowledge of God, righteousness and social reality not available to others; if one means that victims know best how to overcome their condition and build new institutions; and if one means that knowledge based on "experience" makes academic excellence unnecessary, then liberation thought and the Social Gospel diverge.

The reason for working among the dispossessed, and the reason for training teachers, preachers and missionaries to do so, while insisting on the highest standards, and the reason for fighting to get disadvantaged people access to educational and leadership resources is to equip them with epistemological possibilities not already available to them.

A similar distinction would have to be made if one means by liberation what Dorothy Solle, for instance, means when she writes that "Political Theology is a theological hermeneutic which, in distinction from a theology that interprets reality from an onotlogical or existentialist point of view, holds open an horizon of interpretation in which politics is understood as the comprehensive and decisive sphere in which Christian truth should become praxis" (*Political Theology* [Fortress

Press, 1974], p. 59). The legacy of the Social Gospel *might* challenge the notion that theology has the capacity to transcend ontological and existential questions; but it would *certainly* repudiate the social presuppositions of Solle's statement. Her view, it would say, reflects a heritage rooted in religious establishment, even if today it wants to establish a radical theology instead of a conservative one.

Rauschenbusch, like most in the Social Gospel movement, believed in the free church. He thought that Christ not only taught us how society works if we read the Scriptures deeply enough, but that Christ demanded of his followers a social theory of politics, not a political theory of society. That is, Rauschenbusch would have denied that politics, or for that matter a political economy that put production and distribution in the hands of the state, could be "the comprehensive and decisive sphere for Christian truth or praxis" without bringing tyranny with it.

Indeed, he would say that both theology and sociology require us to recognize that the church is the more decisive, and society the more comprehensive, category of the common life. Society is also more shaped by the church than modern—thinkers—including a number of church leaders, when they think about such questions acknowledge. Thus, church and society are the chief areas of Christian concern; politics and political economics are, and must be, their servants, else they will follow Mammon entirely, trailing along, often generations behind; only appearing to be innovators., That is why the church can and must speak about "social salvation," and do so wisely. On this point, Adams and Niebuhr would join with Rauschenbusch.

What most separates contemporary theology and ethics

from Rauschenbusch is his emphasis on the kingdom of God. He was one of the last great American leaders to take the kingdom of God as his governing symbol. H. Richard Niebuhr taught us in *The Kingdom of God in America* that the triune themes of the sovereignty of God over the whole world, the reign of Christ in the heart and the expectation of a Coming Kingdom in and beyond time were all embedded in the term "kingdom of God," and that these themes were decisive in the way Christian theology and ethics provided—with differing accents in different periods—a spiritual and moral rudder for American civilization, from its founding through the industrial era.

Such themes have faded. Few speak of the kingdom of God that way today. If, for the sake of biography and narrative, or for reasons of liberation or political solidarity, we leave this symbol behind, we must ask what the organizing principles of our public theology will be in the 21st century. What will become the inner guidance system for this superpower in a postindustrial era?

Those who leave the legacy of the Social Gospel behind must be sure they have something better to put in its place. Many worse options, and few better ones, stand in the wings of history.

11

Resurrected Love: The Death and Life of the Body

Caroline Walker Bynum concludes, The Resurrection of the Body with this judgment on a millennium of Christian theologians: "We may not find their solutions plausible, but it is hard to feel that they got the problem wrong." In this remarkable study, Bynum explores literary images, artistic depictions, doctrines and social contexts in which Christians affirmed bodily resurrection. She focuses on the period from 200 to 1336, the year Pope Benedict XII declared that souls experience beatific vision with the resurrection yet to come.

Bynum, who teaches at Columbia University, conducts her detailed, sympathetic treatment of patristic and medieval understandings according to the most honourable canons of historical research. But her interest is also personal. She dedicates this book to her father and daughter "because my love, for them lies at the heart of my confidence that there is, in some sense, survival and even resurrection." Bynum does not claim to know exactly what earlier understandings of bodily resurrection say to us, but she intuits that they tell us something if we have ears to hear and eyes to see.

Part of Bynum's aim, then, is to reawaken our senses. Current notions resurrection are maddeningly insubstantial affirmations proffered with" acute embarrassment":

> *Thoughts of "life after death" still conjure up for most people some notion of a disembodied soul flying, rather forlornly through pearly gates and golden streets. Preachers and theologians (especially Protestants) pride themselves on avoiding body-soul dualism, but pious talk at funerals is usually of the departed person surviving as a vague, benign spirit or as a thought in the memories of others.*

The conventional wisdom about the early church is that it was dualistic, that it denied, even hated, the body. Why then, Bynum asks, did the early church — and not we who supposedly have discovered the significance of the body and renounced all dualism — reflect so intently on the resurrection of the body? Her conclusion is refreshing and painstakingly demonstrated: "Despite its suspicion of flesh and lust, Western Christianity did not hate or discount the body. Indeed, person was not person without the body." In addition, we, more than the early church, regard the body as significant primarily as a "locus of sexuality," whereas "for most of Western history the body was understood primarily as the locus of biological process."

What was it about "biological process" that stimulated concern for the resurrected body? Change. By the end of the second century, particularly in the context of martyrdom, the issue of resurrection centered on the question of the identity of the earthly body and the resurrected body to come. In what way were these the same body?

The problem was particularly pressing because the earthly body was subject to decay—indeed it was decay. The decaying corpse was the paradigmatic biological process and the telos of all change. Christian thinkers of the late second century followed in the path of those ancient philosophers for whom "change was the ontological scandal." Their concern was to assure the identity of the resurrected and the earthly body so as to overcome the body's mutability. Resurrection's victory over death had to be a triumph over putrefaction, the scattering of the martyred body, consumption of the dead body by other animals, and even the dread of cannibalism. By the end of the second century, the resurrection of the body meant the resurrection of the flesh.

"Body" and "flesh" are not necessarily the same. Focus on the body's material identity highlights two themes. First, the interest in bodily resurrection demonstrates that Christians understood the person as composed of soul and body, not primarily as soul. If the personality were located in the soul the wasting body would present no special problem; one could even view bodily degeneration as the condition for the soul's freedom. Bynum contends that this was never the position of Western catholic or Eastern patristic theology.

During this millennium the fundamental significance of the body remains constant. Resurrection is never reduced to a question of the soul. Bynum maintains that even the beatific vision of the soul (separated from the body), affirmed by Benedict, occurs only after the soul is endowed with the specificity and particularity that had previously been associated with body. It is possible to think about the beatified soul partly because (especially in the work of women mystics and Bonaventure, and in light of the practice of dismemberment of the saints for dispersion into reliquaries) "a new use of synecdoche throbs with enthusiasm for body and for all that to which body gives us access. Bodily part becomes body; body and soul become each other; body manifests self." The moment of apparent triumph for the disembodied soul is almost the reverse: the soul becomes bodylike.

Second, the emphasis on identity tends to conflict with the original Christian expression of resurrection in 1 Corinthians: Paul's image of the earthly body as the seed of the heavenly body. This image does not emphasize identity or the continuity or sameness of the fleshy material. Although, or even because, the natural body decays, the "spiritual" body, which is not "flesh and blood," rises "in incorruption." Change is not excluded but presupposed. The Pauline image stresses the transformation of a living, changing organism.

By the late second century, a mounting fear of deteriorative change and a corresponding stress on material continuity led the church to mute Paul's language. The transformative possibilities of Paul's imagery are cancelled in favour of images of the resurrected body as a mended pot, a rebuilt temple or clothing donned anew. Fear of organic process produces preference for inorganic pictures of the resurrected body which are grafted uneasily onto Paul's organic imagery. This conflict between organic and inorganic resurrection plays through the next millennium. Bynum allows us to see that doctrinal confusions, indecisions and oppositions are grounded in a clash of images.

In the patristic and medieval churches generally, restorative inorganic versions of resurrection consistently win out over transformational, organic ones. By the early fifth century, resurrection is understood in increasingly literal ways. By the 12th century, Bynum maintains, Western thought reached its materialistic and literalistic apogee. Pauline language about what was sown in corruption being raised incorruptible is generally understood to mean that the material bits of this body are replaced and rendered incorruptible in the resurrected body.

Eucharistic theology provides part of the support for this position as early as the late second century, and continues to do so through the 12th century. Eucharistic eating reverses the usual process of nutrition. Normally, digestion transforms consumed food into the property and being of the consumer; in contrast, the body of Christ begins to change its consumer into Christ's incorruption.

Images of transformation do not disappear. Although the dominant mode of conception of the resurrection body is in terms of material continuity and reassembly, differing views abound. Bynum does not impose uniformity where she does not find it, and generally she does not find it. Bynum refuses to lead us on a unilinear path toward a conclusion that we can either laud or decry. Instead, she presents a tangle of positions, hesitations and inconsistencies that helps us feel the darkness through which theology, art and society found uneven, uncertain paths.

Thinkers not only disagreed with one another but apparently were unable to make up their own minds about the resurrected body. In their desire to remain faithful to all facets of the problem and to scriptural and traditional texts, theologians from Tertullian to Lombard sought to incorporate images of transformation even as they struggled to show that the earthly body and the resurrected body were in some sense the same. Moreover, although it is true that materialistic representations dominated the theological and artistic landscape, some theologians attempted to keep transformative conceptions at the forefront of Christian thought by emphasizing the continuing potentiality of the body. Origen, for example, prefers seed imagery to the common metaphor of the statue; Dante and Aquinas stress growth and development of body and soul. Tradition spoke with many voices.

Advocates of the reassembly of particles spoke forcefully, though their assertions took many forms, ranging from claims that bits of matter are replaced precisely as they were in life, to Augustine's hypothesis that although matter need not serve the same function or be placed identically in the resurrected body, the matter itself is nonetheless identical. Concern with material continuity also fed theological and artistic speculation about the fate of cut fingernails and hair, the condition and presence of genitals, the age and stature of the resurrected body, the bodies of the saints, the fate of relics, whether bodies in hell are reassembled as completely as those given eternal life and how and whether digested body parts are regurgitated at the resurrection.

Attention to such matters strikes the modem reader as bizarre. Yet Bynum adeptly draws us into the universe of early and medieval thought so that by the end of her book we question less why earlier figures considered these issues seriously than why we do not. She makes the problem of bodily resurrection increasingly vital—emotionally, cognitively and ethically.

Our emotional attachment to this flesh is easy to understand. Whatever pains, agonies and violations we experience, however our bodies betray us, our bodies are still the ones we love and which we hope can be perfected despite decay and infidelity. Our bodies and the bodies of others are, after all, the only bodies we know. Theologically, the demise of the body poses a basic challenge to God's omnipotence. If God cannot redeem the body that is so central to personal integrity, then God's victory over death is partial and relatively feeble. Resurrection and divine power are indissolubly linked. God must vanquish not only death but the ontological structures of change and time that make death inevitable. For Augustine, for example, spiritual rebirth is possible here and now—one does not need resurrection for that. One does need resurrection to overcome the ontology of destruction that is so obviously presented in the body. We can conceive of moral and spiritual improvement throughout our lietime, but after a point we cannot rationally believe that our bodies will improve. God saves bodily rebirth for the end of time, as the final triumphal stake through death's heart. It was early Christians' refusal of dualism, their demand that God redeem the whole person, that forced on them the question of bodily resurrection.

Ethically, because the body was the centre of personal particularity and difference, it was vital for early Christians that this flesh, which bears the marks of persecution, suffering, sainthood and merit in general, be preserved and perfected in the resurrection. Bynum claims not only that the church was not dualistic about body and soul, but that it stressed the importance of human difference and particularity. Far from being an "otherworldly" concern, concentration on the resurrected body insisted that what mattered on earth mattered in heaven, that "a rose cannot be a lily even in paradise." The beauty of earthly merit was preserved eternally. Heaven and earth kissed.

Indeed, the suspicion that less material imagery could

not guarantee the exhibition of this merit throughout eternity helped generate opposition to transformative, organic conceptions. William of La Mare and others objected to Aquinas's approach largely because of "a suspicion that his view of the soul as a single, substantial, intellective form limits soul's ability to know, and to suffer, and to contain (so to speak) our individuality." Throughout the period Bynum considers, greater stress on materiality brought attention to difference in its wake.

Of course, making eternal differences correspond to earthly ones has its drawbacks, and Bynum is not blind to them. Although she does not argue that all thought is but clever ideological cover for oppressing one or another social group, she is aware that the belief that earthly hierarchical differences are perpetuated in eternity legitimizes those earthly distinctions, both just and unjust. But there is reason to be meek in our criticism of the early and medieval worlds. They too sought to avoid dualism; they too appreciated difference. Even our treasured understanding of the "individual as unique — valued yet opaque and unknowable because (in the currently fashionable term) 'other'... is informed by hundreds of years of puzzlement over embodiment."

Nevertheless, the world Bynum so lovingly presents is, for the most part, lost to us. We cannot adopt patristic and medieval solutions as they stand. The contemporary inclination to do away with all differences in eternity in favour of egalitarian conceptions of external life (an outcome of 16th-century Protestant understandings of the spiritual body) has encouraged us to abandon serious reflection on the notion of bodily resurrection. Most important, we no longer view change as the ontological scandal. Change is now presumed to be good until proven otherwise. Stasis, tradition and the past now need defense.

Our paradigm of human change is not the decaying corpse but the vital, growing, beautiful, perfect televised body.

Yet in our most private recesses, and despite our culture's efforts to deny it, we know that decay, death and putrefaction await our bodies and the bodies of all those we love. The benefits of change cannot obscure this elementary fact. Thus, the question of resurrection has not disappeared entirely. Films such as Ghost and Dead Again are efforts to remove the sting from even the most violent terminations of the body, assuring us that we shall be again what we once were. Like medieval representations, these images are materialistic, literalistic promises of perfection. In both films, moreover, evil's fate is exactly what it was in medieval art — dismemberment of the body.

The themes that Bynum identifies continue to shape not only the conceptions of resurrection but our own broader religious and cultural life. Bynum points to at least two continuing difficulties in our culture. First, we have dissociated our earthly lives from our final destinies. The close marriage of heaven and earth that Bynum describes meant that religion was as much a matter of earthly life as heavenly joy. For good or ill, what one did and experienced would be preserved in the resurrected body. We, however, often view religion as helpful only in answering (often quite arbitrarily) questions of how we can reach eternal blessedness, not how we might live better while we are here. What the patristic and medieval worlds joined, we have torn asunder.

On the other hand, we unite what they did not. Difference is significant to us as it was for earlier Christians; but unlike them, we try to yoke difference with egalitarian conceptions of heaven and earth. It is worth asking whether our contemporary social egalitarianism is derived from the Protestant denial of differences in the intensity of the eternal vision of God. In any event, we have departed from medievals, but only partway. This half-leave has put us in a peculiar position; in our political and social life we seem to swing wildly between desires for full egalitarianism and rigidly hierarchical authority. Moreover, we tend to spiritualize both hierarchy and egalitarianism. We fail to connect these concepts to bodies wounded by hierarchy, or to the material differences between people regarded formally as equals. Whether our quandary is soluble remains to be seen. For their part, the patristics and medievals, justly and unjustly, and despite their juggling of other contradictions, resolutely refused to detach questions of difference, hierarchy, destiny and change from the body. They got the problem, right.

Resurrection of the Body is a jewel among current intellectual endeavours. Bynum takes the histories of thought and society (and their relation) seriously and on their own terms. In addition, she asks us if we have the courage to face this strangest of all Christian doctrines. We have hardly begun to make sense of it. To begin, we will have to think seriously about the value of change, the nature of the body and the significance of difference.

Bynum has provided indispensable aid to any investigation of bodily resurrection, whether historical or theological. She has made the task both easier and more difficult. If the luminaries of the past are not sufficient for us, if they too are internally inconsistent and perplexed, we must still use their lights to make our way. At the same time, Bynum has opened our ears to tones of beauty long unheard, opened our eyes to a more expansive and lovely vision of the body, and opened our hearts to the desire for body and the hope that the body — despite decay and death-might remain integral to the beauty of the person.

Sophisticated Primitives Then, Primitive Sophisticates Now

Primordium: It's time to get used to the term. Next to it one might mentally store such words as "primitivism" and "restorationism," terms that will come in handy for interpreting America's past. Paradoxically, though they refer to various sorts of pasts, they are also convenient tools for understanding how many Americans are interpreting the present and envisioning the future—though they may not know they are primitives or restorationists or that they believe in and measure life from a primordium.

Among these are members of the Churches of Christ and the Church of Jesus Christ of Latter-day Saints (Mormons), two of the fastest growing bodies in the U.S. and wherever they send missionaries.

"Primordium" is the most obscure and thus the easiest to define of the three words. University of Iowa professor Theodore Dwight Bozeman in his sound and exciting new book *To Live Ancient Lives: The Primitivist Dimension of Puritanism* relates it to Mircea.

Eliade's concepts. Eliade spoke of an "originative, repeatable primordium, "a sacred, mythic "Great Time," which invited mortals to a consoling "nostalgia for the perfection of beginnings" and which helped them explain the world, even as it became "the exemplary model for all significant human activities." But for Eliade as for Bozeman and other historians, the Puritan primordium, differed from others in that the Great Time occurred not in prehistory but within human history.

Specifically, the Puritan and Christian American

primordium — not the only primordium available on the current market — refers to a sort of mythic time. In essence this was "the primal (or "primitive" or "first") time in which Christianity was given and unfolded in fullness. "The time of Jesus, the apostles and the earliest Christian community was "the normative time to which men and women of the present must, in imagination, 'return' for saving guidance and empowerment."

There were some early warning signals that the community of scholars and citizens would some day have to attend to this subject. Bozeman connects the restoration of primordial concepts to *Primitivism and Related Ideas in Antiquity*, which Arthur 0. Lovejoy and George Boas published in 1935. Eliade's concepts were translated in 1960 and 1963.

Those of us who sat at the feet of Sidney E. Mead, as I did at the University of Chicago and as Bozeman, Hughes and Allen did at Iowa, heard him saying what he wrote in 1956 about "the tendency chronic in Christendom, but perhaps more acute among Englishmen, to support every contemporary innovation by an appeal to 'primitive Christianity.'"On the frontier, leaders insisted "that there was really nothing new but only the repristination of the apostolic and hence normative ways. "In 1968 I signed off as adviser on a thesis by Marvin S. Hill, "The Role of Christian Primitivism in the Origin and Development of the Mormon Kingdom, 1830-44. "So those who studied Great Times with Eliade or who had great times with Mead were long being pushed to clarify the concept.

With the publication of *The American Quest for the Primitive Church*, edited by Richard T. Hughes, and *Illusions of Innocence: Protestant Primitivism in America, 1630-1875,* by Hughes and C. Leonard Allen, primitivism is becoming a key interpretive category the way "millennium" once did. Of course, the "millennium" had always been a theme in doctrinal works (with which American Catholics, Lutherans, secularists and others did not much bother). But it was inert until books like Ernest Lee Tuveson's *Redeemer Nation: The Idea of America's Millennial Role* (1968) appeared. Today knowing the difference between pre-and postmillennialism is important for interpreting the interpreters of both Middle East and domestic politics When former President Ronald Reagan told a group that he had been reading "'your" theologians, he was referring to Armageddonned millennial tracts.

The new category is "primitivism." Historians will argue endlessly, but not fruitlessly, about definitions of the term, but their colleagues and the public will not wait for a neat definition. The book that Hughes edited contains an exchange between a Churches of Christ scholar, Thomas Olbricht, and evangelical Mark Noll. Noll is puzzled: how can Olbricht include as primitive the impulse of New Englanders to collect European books, to write 6,000 pages of manuscript as Cotton Mather did, to study German as Moses Stuart did, or to undertake perilous voyages to the Old World to hear complex lectures on early Christianity?

"All of these seem like traditionalism instead of primitivism," Noll observes. Precisely. But, imprecisely, Noll will lose his effort to narrow definitions. Paradoxically, Olbricht and Noll agree that the sophisticated early Unitarians were the true biblical primitives of early America, since they "rested their case with the primitive Christian documents. "Again: precisely.

Which suggests that it always took sophistication, even on the frontier where books were few, to work one's way across history, to forget what today we call hermeneutics and to claim to be replicating, restoring, repristinating, the pure norms of early Christianity. Some of the pioneers called themselves Disciples of Christ or members of the Churches of Christ, and others called themselves Latter-day Saints. Methodists and Baptists also found complex ways to say that they were following simple, unsophisticated ways. But Alexander Campbell and Joseph Smith, the grand gurus of Great Time thought and action, were anything but intellectually primitive.

Let me illustrate how primitivism surfaces. I recall visiting the World's Fair in New York in the mid-'60s. A religious pavilion featured a large display by the Churches of Christ. The showpiece was a primitive but to us, then, awesome computer, surrounded by beautiful young women and dashing young men as acolytes. The banner of the display said something to the effect that here were first-century answers for 21st-century life. Passersby could ask the computer any of 300 questions. The prepacked answer, a kind of Chinese-fortune-cookie type message, came inside a capsule. In each case, the answer was simply a Bible verse. I tried out the question about the proper age, mode and purpose of baptizing and got back a very non-Catholic/Anglican/Lutheran/Orthodox answer. We were back to the beginnings, as the boothkeepers saw them.

The incident seems trivial, but I suggest that the popularity of that crowded display at the fair points to a deep need among moderns. It was satisfying to know that in the midst of technology and pluralism one could rely on the simple message of early Christianity. All through American history, especially Protestant history, the winners of disputes seem to be those who have best made the case that they represent the authority and purity of the simple Bible and the primitive Christian generation.

Letters to the editor in Baptist, Methodist and many other kinds of denominational magazines reveal how simple and primitive the concept of a primordium, a Golden Age of beginnings, remains. The writers want all arguments settled on the basis of the simple gospel of the first generation of the church. Intervening history not only does not matter; it corrupts.

Simplicity is hard to come by. Think of how complex it is to live with wood-burning stoves, to find or grow organic food, or to replicate the little white church and little red schoolhouse world in metropolitan and pluralistic America. One recalls the observation made years ago when, to compete, Detroit automakers built economy cars with expensive gadgets: "This proves that Americans want economy, and they will pay any price to get it." Americans want simplicity, purity, beginnings, and they will go through tortured, compromising and historically "fallen" routes to convince themselves that they have found them.

While the heirs of the sophisticated primitives live on, the land is full of primitive sophisticates. The Puritans and Campbell and their kinds, and even Smith in his own way, had to retrace all Christian history and doctrine to posit or find the restorable early Christian primordium. Today one finds everywhere analogues to that primordium. The market is full of products gobbled up by hungry consumers who are unaware of how much work it takes to be simple. Consumers confront on every corner someone who reduces complexity to a single key, be it New Age, macrobiotics, holistic health care, the latest variation on Zen or "the simple Jesus." But the impulse that unites sophisticated primitives and primitive sophisticates is the search for purity, simplicity and wholeness.

The drive toward primitivism has four aspects. Psychologically, modernity fragments life and lives. It generates what Peter Gay called a "hunger for wholeness, "which William James claimed impels a *restitutio ad integrum*. The term is an analogue to our subject: there is to be a restitution to wholeness, integrity, a presumed earlier condition of simplicity and health.

Ideologically, there is a strong drive to follow the simplifiers. Gay, writing of the hunger for wholeness in the Weimar Republic, sees that drive leading to an acceptance of Nazism's totalitarian simplicities. In America the search for the simple, whether at Walden Pond for Henry David Thoreau, Yosemite Falls for John Muir, or in the pure gospel for the millions, usually comes down to the notion that with a few clear absolutes in mind, life will hold together and we can outargue other sects and outlast the ayatollahs.

Politically, there is constant appeal to the purity of the founders, beginning with George Washington and the Constitutionalists. One does not go far in politics without, as the media say today, "dumbing it down" or following the injunction KISS, "keep it simple, stupid." "Simple" does not just mean linguistically or conceptually so, but also substantially. Politicians and economists like to suggest that we as a nation "fell," first into the clutches of robber barons or, later, into the hands of Keynesians and socialists and bureaucrats. Purity calls us to reduce and simplify government and restore primitive individualism of the sort our grandparents exemplified. Frederick Jackson Turner's influential frontier thesis in historical studies was but one evidence of this drive. David Noble in *Historians Against History* anticipated the current interest in primitivism by showing how the semisecular historical tradition uttered constant jeremiads against an America falling into complexity.

Ecclesiastically, in a nation in which churches have

mattered much, everyone from fundamentalists through ecumenists argues for the "one" church that he or she represents. The liberal ecumenists spoke of the "reunion" of Christendom, even though most scholars say earliest Christianity was itself divided and complex, an intricate web whose essences and outlines cannot be retrieved.

The past in "simple" Christian history is not Eden but early Christianity; in the Republican version, not current times but antiquity or the age of the national founders. One cannot test whether advocates of such purity are right in contending for their particular versions of it against myriad competitors. The past is irretrievable; one can argue only about the traces, which look simple to primitivists and complex to others.

The primitive cannot be clearly assessed in the present, either. All who advocate simplicity, whether they are the Milton Friedmans in economics, the "Small Is Beautiful" E. F. Schumachers or the holistic therapists, make the rules of the game too tough for verification. When the economy goes wrong, the environment gets polluted, or the cancerous cells multiply, we are told that it was not the simple prescriptions that were at fault, but that the public simply did not trust these enough.

And, of course, one cannot accurately predict the future of a primitivist movement. Historians do not have to be cynics but only historians, however, to show that all past envisionings of millennium, utopia, or primordium-projected-forward have been complex and have failed. Campbell produced a scheme for a single, pure, primitive church, and he was opposed to denominationalism and even the term denomination (and Churches of Christ still resist the inevitable designation). But he succeeded only in adding one more denomination--no, many more, for there were schisms — to the *Yearbook of American*

Churches. When the future becomes present, the simplicity disappears. This means that one takes the future on faith — which in no way diminishes simplicity's imaginative and summoning power.

Primitivism and restoration are always under threat. In psychology, schizophrenia at worst and distraction at least complicate efforts at *restitutio ad integrum*. In philosophy, relativists are always at hand to threaten absolutist simplicities. In politics, there is always the danger of anarchy and the confusions of the other party. In church life, schismatics and dissenters haunt the structure. Meanwhile, scholars jumble things by pointing to the falleness of even the pure in history, the diversities and divisions of earliest Christianity and the difficulties of remaining historyless while moving through history.

Once one puts on restorationist spectacles, it gets ever easier to see the primitivist impulse in American history. What Tuveson accomplished with a few colonial millennialists, extending their vision into the whole mission of America, all kinds of Americans are doing with the primordium.

Catholics have not used the language of primordiurn much because they see biblical history within the tradition and the tradition within history, but the conservatives are often primitive in their views about origins of episcopacy and papacy, and contemporary moderates often try to settle things by going back to biblical accounts of early ministry and communal life. Hans Kung and Edward Schillebeeckx both have acquired American followings for arguing thus.

As for the Puritans, Bozeman has elaborated on their sophisticated primitivism in detail and with stunning impact. If he is right, they were much more primordial than they were progressivist millennial thinkers. If he is but slightly right, one would still be ill-advised to talk about Puritanism without at least accounting for his evidence. As for the extension of Puritanism to the frontier, where Disciples of Christ, Mormons and Churches of Christ made and lived the case, Hughes and Allen and their companions are making that case forcefully. And utopian communities, Shakers, Oneidans, Owenites and all the rest, also sophisticatedly worked for primitive restoration.

One should not close the book on these signals by restricting them to formal religion from Native American through present-day Churches of Christ. From at least Daniel Boorstin and Sidney E. Mead on, scholars have seen the leaders of the American Enlightenment—the religion of the republic that animates present-day civil or public religion--as being advocates of some sort of primitivism. Hughes and Allen devote only five pages to this subject, since it falls beyond their "Protestant" scope, but they are clear: "the quest for the primordium persisted; the rationalists simply substituted one book—the book of Nature—for another and exchanged the primordium of the early church for the primordium of Eden. The basic theological question continued to be What is truth?"

The authors cite Thomas Paine and Thomas Jefferson as what I call sophisticated primitives. In a deliciously perverse last chapter they see the attraction of elites to Allan Bloom's absolutist simplicities in *The Closing of the American Mind* as an example of what I am calling primitive sophistication. That is, the Thomases knew what they were doing and argued strenuously; Bloom, in their reading, does not seem to know what he is doing, and is apodictic rather than argumentative in his historyless presuppositions and statements. Bloom's book was "fundamentally a restorationist treatise, tapping deeply into the bountiful wellspring of American restorationist ideology."

So the primitive sophisticates live on, advocating a return to a Native America that never was, an Enlightenment that never could be simple, a Socratean set of absolutes, an Africa untainted by Western corruption, the timeless, historyless religion of the East. The back-to-the-basics Christian fundamentalists, the Nature Religionists and the New Agers complexly live their dream of remembered and mythic simplicity, recalled from the primordium. Where such a pursuit is part of a worldview and not just the latest marketed fashion, it is impossible to argue someone out of it.

Hughes and Allen and Bozeman and their colleagues serve the primitivist tradition well, if ambiguously. They cherish its impulses and artifacts, they devour its documents, mostly they adhere to its heritage. But they pick up enemies by showing that historylessness has a history, absolutists get relativized by everyone else, purist dreams become inevitably compromised, and one should never simply trust the advertisements of the simplifiers. They recognize the power in myth and the mythic power of this set of "illusions of innocence." People acting on illusions can produce realities of power, as Americans have proved in politics these past eight years.

Through it all one sees ironies. That is what the realization of "illusions" is all about. Because all historical intentions turn out somewhat differently than intended, it would be easy for condescending and cynical historians to say simply, "What fools these mortals are," or "Hindsight tells us how stupid our ancestors were," or "It does not pay to try anything." But to do so would be a failure of Christian and other humane ironic visions, which intend only to bring perspective. They remind us that humans are not God, that God is beyond human intention and aspiration and advertisement and yet that God holds humans responsible and encourages and, yes, expects and blesses action. So the ancestors were not, or at least not simply, foolish; no more foolish than we are. They were wise and ambitious in their own ways.

Some of the tests one can put to them are pragmatic. If their outlook produces better relations between whites and Native Americans, leads people to care more for the environment, promotes good health or encourages political reform and Christian unity, it is hard to wish away the primitivist impulse even while relativizing it with historical perspectives.

Maybe the impulse one needs in the face of the lures of primitivism, restoration and the search for a primordium is best stated in Alfred North Whitehead's words to natural scientists: "Seek simplicity and distrust it."

The Anachronism of Jonathan Edwards

A highly popular, widespread impression of Jonathan Edwards is the one expressed in verse by Phyllis McGinley: "Whenever Mr. Edwards spake/In church about Damnation,/The very benches used to quake/For awful agitation." A somewhat less impressionistic portrait, though drawn also from folk memory more than from life, was offered by Vernon Louis Parrington in his Main Currents in American Thought. In that history of the liberal mind Jonathan Edwards is described as the great "anachronism."

He was an anachronism to Parrington because in him the conflict of ancient dogma with the new liberalism was re-enacted and resolved in favour of the old. The brilliant idealist metaphysician warred in him with the traditional theologian; and the theologian won. The Emersonian mystic "consciousness of the divine life flowing through and around him, making him one with the Godhead," fought in him with the Calvinistic theocrat; and Calvin won; the new churchman, opening the doors of the sanctuary to all seekers after peace, contradicted in him the loyalist to ancient discipline, for whom the company of the faithful was the selected band, the trained shock troops of the kingdom of God in a rebellious planetary province.

Parrington concludes his account in these words:

> *"Cut off from fruitful intercourse with other thinkers, drawn away from the stimulating field of philosophy into the arid realm of theology, it was his fate to devote his noble gifts to the thankless task of reimprisoning the mind of New England within a system from which his nature and his powers summoned him to unshackle it. He was called to be a transcendental emancipator, but he remained a Calvinist."*

Later writers, notably Professor Perry Miller, have corrected this account in certain respects. College students, introduced to Edwards via other routes than the sermon on "Sinners in the hands of an angry God," can set Phyllis McGinley right. But in the main the judgment stands in America, in American Protestantism, in literary and academic, even in most theological circles: Jonathan Edwards was a great man, but he was wrong on almost every issue for which he contended — the gloriousness of inscrutable, almighty, universal, majestic, wrathful God; the depravity and corruptness of the human heart; the need for the reconstitution of the church not as catholic and all-inclusive but as the selected group of the convinced; the determinism, the unfreedom of human existence; the glory of God as the chief and only end of being, which in reconciliation man serves willingly as a "cosmic patriot," but will serve in his unwillingness by his destruction, as Hitler's patriots in their catastrophic ending may be said to glorify the rule of justice.

Since the judgment stands, and is no doubt explicitly represented in the thoughts of many of us as it is implicitly represented in the value standards of the great dominant majority of Americans, of American Christians and of American intellectuals, we must ask by what right, with what rightness can we honour Jonathan Edwards today?

By what right do we join the funeral procession, stand beside the grave, intrude ourselves into the company of those who mourn him? When we think of his exile from Northampton and his more inclusive exile from the company of all right-thinking modern men, we must apply to ourselves on this occasion the indictment that Jesus made of "hypocrites" who "build the tombs of the prophets and adorn the monuments of the righteous, saying, 'If we had lived in the days of our fathers, we would not have taken part with them in shedding the blood of the prophets'" (Matt. 23:29-30). We are quite sure we would have been less gentle with him than our neighbours or forebears.

When we read the story of his dismissal from the Northampton church and then think of the temper in other New England towns two centuries ago, we cannot honestly say that he would have fared better elsewhere. The Cambridge and New Haven that offered him no alternative to life at Stockbridge would probably not have suffered him as long as Northampton did, had he been pastor there. If smallpox had not removed him quickly from Princeton, how long would he have remained an honoured head of the college in New Jersey? When we move from the 18th century down to our present time we cannot really convince ourselves that if Edwards now lived among us he would be more respected than he was in the 1750s.

The issues on which he was then tried and found wanting seem to have been so universally decided against him by the court of American and Christian opinion that they scarcely remain issues today. What hearing could he gain if he stood in this pulpit today, or in any pulpit in America, and spoke to us now about our depravity and corruption, about our unfreedom and the determination of our lives, about the ineffable gloriousness of God, and about the awfulness of his wrath? About the necessity of reconstituting ourselves a holy community?

By what right do we, who seem to disagree with him more strongly than his contemporaries did, now honour him? Can this commemoration of his death be an honest gesture of respect or does it merely express the desire to be in the company of the great, for the sake of sharing in a superficial and reflected glory? This question a speaker at such an occasion as this must ask himself even more than his fellow celebrants.

Let us raise in another way the question of our right to honour Edwards. If we met in his spirit today, if we wanted to honour him in a way that would be acceptable not to his human vanity, for which he would need to do bitter penance, but to his central purpose and will, how would we go about it? His own conduct at the time of David Brainerd's death—his son-in-law, missionary to the Indians—gives us a clue. We cannot honour him at all except we do so in the context of honouring what he stood for, of honouring the cause to which he wanted above all else to be loyal. Have we any right to honour him otherwise?

To exalt him as a great thinker, as though he could

take delight in being praised for having honed his mental tools very sharp, no matter what they cut; to speak admiringly of him as an excellent orator, as though adeptness in the use of images were an enviable thing, no matter what they imaged; to do him reverence as a great student who learned from Newton and Locke and the Platonists, from nature itself, no matter what he learned—to honour him thus is to do him no honour that he could accept—or which, accepting, he would not thereafter bitterly rue.

So to honour him would be as though we commemorated Nietzsche as a great Christian, or praised George the Third as a great American. It would not only be irrelevant, it would be contradictory to the intention, the understanding, the spirit of the man. To Edwards the desire of man to be great in himself, and to be honoured for his eminence, to stand out in comparison with his fellows, to be more loved than his companions — even by God — this is man's pettiness, his perversity, his pustulant sickness, as he might have said.

There is no really honest and consistent way of honouring Edwards except in the context of honouring, of acknowledging and renewing our dedication to his cause. That cause was nothing less than the glory of God. I do not know whether this is the audience which can hear the summons to think in the terms of that theme, to lift up mind and heart into regions of thought and imagination so majestic, to dedicate itself to a cause so tremendous. I only know that your preacher is not adequate to preach upon the text that Edwards himself would have chosen for this occasion:

> *"Now unto the King eternal, immortal, invisible, to the only wise God be honour and glory, forever and ever. Amen." (1 Tim. 1:17)*

Since it lies beyond the scope of my mind and spirit to direct your meditations so to honour Edwards in the only context in which he can honestly be honoured, we may venture to try to do him less adequate justice by letting him, or rather our imagined reincarnation of his spirit, speak today to his detractors.

The first charge against me, he might say, is this, that I have demeaned man in order to glorify God. "You charge me with having said that our experience teaches us the truth of the scriptural saying, 'There is none righteous, no not one' (Rom. 3: 10). 'They are filled with all manner of wickedness, evil, covetousness, malice. Full of envy, murder, strife, deceit, malignity; they are gossips, slanderers, haters of God, insolent, haughty, boastful, inventors of evil, disobedient to parents, foolish, faithless, heartless, ruthless.' You charge me also with saying, again pleading the support of the scriptures, that though we humans have many kindly affections, love of children, love between men and women, love of country, all these too are corrupted and defiled; and that though we have very agile minds, able to penetrate into the mysteries of nature, we put this gift and attainment to ignoble uses."

Some, Edwards could say, have dismissed my indictments as wholly false. Particularly from the men of the generation that succeeded his, he could have heard much praise of men. Using Shakespeare instead of the scriptures as the source for their text, but without reading the passage to the end, they said with Hamlet:

> *"What a piece of work is a man! how noble in reason! how infinite in faculties! in form, and in moving, how express and admirable! in action how like an angel! in apprehension how like a god! the beauty of the world! the paragon of animals!"*

But a strange thing has happened. A later generation has revised the judgment of the romantics. Its experience of the extent to which human brutality can go, of the fury that can be unleashed when the human animal is attacked, its acceptance in wry cynicism of the venality of great and small; its acceptance, too, of a psychological analysis that tends to show how slight the power of reason, how great the strength of obscure passions; how corrupting of children the possible love of mothers and the wrath of fathers; its portrayal of men and mankind in bitterly disillusioned novels and in shuddering chronicles of man's inhumanity to man—in all this the 20th century has perhaps gone beyond anything that Edwards said in dispraise of men, individually and in the collective. But though on the surface this generation seems to accept something that is like the Edwardsean estimate, it still rejects Edwards no less than the Emersonians did, though for other reasons.

How would Edwards speak to this situation? He might answer something like this: "'With what measure you mete you shall be measured.' You resented my measuring man by the standard of his position before God; you resented that I said: as a loathsome insect is to man, so man is to the Holy One that inhabits eternity. You applied the standard of man's position before other men; or before himself, and having begun by saying: man to himself is like a god, you are now tending to say, he is like a devil to himself; he will destroy himself."

Now who demeans humanity? The one whose standard for man is small or the one whose standard is very great? The one who judges him as a domestic lover or as a citizen of a universal commonwealth? The one who looks on him as faithful or unfaithful administrator of lawns and stores, of stocks and bonds, or the one who sees in him the steward of eternal riches? What is greater, a neatly painted, well constructed five-or eight-room house or the ruins of the Forum or the Parthenon?

What Edwards knew, what he believed in his heart and with his mind, was that man was made to stand in the presence of eternal, unending absolute glory, to participate in the celebration of cosmic deliverance from everything putrid, destructive, defiling, to rejoice in the service of the stupendous artist who flung universes of stars on his canvas, sculptured the forms of angelic powers, etched with loving care miniature worlds within worlds. In the light of that destiny, in view of that origin, because of the greatness of that calling, it depressed him, angered him that men should throw away their heritage and be content with the mediocrity of an existence without greater hope than the hope for comfort and for recognition by transient fellow men. Man who had been made to be great in the service of greatness, had made himself small by refusing the loving service of the only Great One; and in his smallness he had become very wicked, covetous of the pleasures that would soon be taken from him. But in the end, man could not make himself small, Edwards knew, for the way of man is not in himself.

That leads us to the second charge against Edwards, namely that his understanding of the sovereignty of God left no room for human freedom. This charge, like the previous one, is frequently so understood by unbelievers who cannot follow the logic of belief that they equate theocracy with priestliness. They think that Edwards, believing in government by God, must have derived from that premise the conclusion that therefore preachers were his lieutenants on earth and should be recognized as gods. This is about as illogical a deduction as one can imagine.

The consequence of the premise that God rules is, for the believer, "therefore I must obey," not "therefore I must rule." Because his will is to be done, therefore my will is to be denied. I believe that any reading of Edwards's life, including the story of the sad controversy in Northampton, will make quite clear that he was no self-willed man talking the name of God in vain to fortify his wishes. But this is the minor point of the charge. The major complaint was that in Edwards's world of determinism no room was left for human freedom.

How would he reply today to this charge? I think it is quite possible that, zealous student of philosophy as he was, he might admit that the way he argued his position was somewhat overly indebted to the mechanical thinking of his time and of the Reformers. But his main point would stand; and as in the case of the charge about demeaning man, time has reversed the opinion of his antagonists, though it has not reversed men's opinions about Edwards.

You were concerned, Edwards might say, about the freedom of the will, to choose its goods, to choose good or evil, God or the devil. You were concerned to say that man was somehow the master of his fate, so that without his will God himself was unable to save him from disaster.

Look now, he might go on to point out, how you have conceded my point that man is determined by his strongest motive and that his strongest motive is so much the love of self, self-interest, that there is no way of moving him to anything at all save by touching this spring of his action. Regard your society, the free-enterprise system, the operation of the hidden persuaders and of the open ones. Who is free? Man is free to follow his self-interest. But is he ever free from his self-interest? Is he free to follow any road but that of self-interest?

Or consider your international politics. Do you not recognize that national self-interest is a law the nations obey with such invariableness that you must base all your calculations on how to maintain your own nation on the assumption of that law? Or consider your freedom of religion; is it not the freedom to be religious or irreligious, to worship or not to worship, in accordance with your self-interest, whether you think it is good for you or not? Your free religion of self-interested men has made God into an idol. How are you free to love God, since you are bound to love yourselves, even in religion?

The will is as its strongest motive is and its strongest motive is self-interest, and so man is determined and cannot by any new freedom at his disposal change his determination by self-interest.

After 200 years there are very, very many who agree with Edwards on the proposition about our freedom and our bondage. Many who accept this determinism still think, however, that self-interest will continue to ensure for us the enjoyment of our civil liberties. We have seen other nations, to be sure, in which self-interest has made itself felt as an invincible motive for the giving up of what we call such freedoms. And when we think of this we begin to wonder whether civil and religious liberty can indeed be based on the position of Edwards's opponents or only on the kind of foundations he provided not in but in connection with his determinism.

Edwards on human unfreedom is not so anachronistic as he was. Yet for some reason we do not dare to follow his logic even when we accept some of his premises, such as this one of our determination by our strongest motive.

A third count of the constant indictment against Edwards has also lost something of the persuasiveness it once had. The threat of destruction, of hell, which

Edwards used to stir his people toward, that revolution of thought and conscience which could be the occasion for the entrance of new freedom has always called forth strong reaction. Preaching about hell is always resented by men of so-called liberal mind. How could the infliction of torment be rhymed with the rule of a merciful God? What human wickedness deserved such a consequence?

Yet on this point also in some ways Edwards seems less anachronistic than he did. If you will read again "Sinners in the hands of an angry God" you will note that the emphasis lies not on hell but on the terrible uncertainty of life. "Thou hast set their foot in slippery places"—that was the text. There is no guarantee anywhere, he points out, that this comfortable life of ours will go on and on and on. What awaits us is death, and it may come at any moment—and death is not nothing. It is the beginning of another state of being.

Now we find it difficult to accept the mythology of Edwards, though we may need to accept again something like it, when we come to the full acceptance of the realization that as we did not and cannot elect ourselves into existence, so neither can we elect ourselves out of it, if the inscrutable power that cast us into being wills to keep us in being after our biological death. But aside from that, we have a mythology of our own. We see before us in social if not in personal terms the real possibility of a future hell. Of a state of existence in which surviving souls, condemned to live, crawl about scrofulously among the radiations of insidious poison, among emanations of noxious gases, on a planet unfit for habitation which they must nevertheless inhabit. Or we envisage the possibility of that anarchy in which every man's hand is raised against his neighbour—where there is no truth but only deception and lies. Or the hell we envision is that of

Huxley's Brave New World or Orwell's 1984, or the culmination of the life of Organization Man.

The mythology has changed. The possibility that Edwards saw before man is now our possibility, though in a different setting. Those critics of his who saw no other alternative before man than progress toward perfection and heaven on earth have become rather quiet. They are not even greatly stirred by the prospect that we shall export our wars with our machines to other planets and re-enact on a larger scale the kind of history with which we have become too familiar.

We tend to agree more with him also on the tenuousness of the hold we have on ordered life. Our feet, we know, are set in slippery places. A single trigger-happy or nervous bomber, flying now with a load of destruction in the vitals of his plane, can inaugurate at any moment the beginning of our end. A missile gone astray by the failure of a tiny and fragile device may shoot us into the inferno. Or a statesman's unthinking remark may begin the debate that will end not in death for us but in an unforeseeably long process of destruction.

Edwards is not so anachronistic on this point as he was, not so anachronistic as his 19th-century critics now seem.

But at the central point he remains alien to us as to them, more alien than he was in the 18th century with its Benjamin Franklins. And because he is alien at that point the sorts of agreement we may be able to achieve with him on other ideas seem superficial and unreal.

We will concede perhaps that man is as wicked as Edwards said. What we do not know—or do not yet know—is that God is as holy as Edwards knew him to be. We have in our wisdom substituted for the holy God a kind

Heavenly Father. A holy God will not suffer his plans for a vast, stupendously intricate, marvellous creation and the men designed to be his sons to be flouted and destroyed by self-willed and proud little delinquents, aged 60 as often as 16, called nations or civilizations as often as persons.

Or we have substituted for the holy God, the sovereign source and determiner of being, Being simply considered, the Constitution of the universe, a wildly running chance. Our feet are standing in slippery places, to be sure, but we are not being held this side of destruction by holy power and determined will; it is chance that keeps us from slipping. There is no wrath in heaven directed against us, because there is no holiness, no will for wholeness, for integrity and for glory. And since there is no holiness there is no hope for us except the hope that we'll get by a little longer with our compromises and our superior animal cunning.

Edwards used to say that the trouble with men was not that they had no ideas of God, but that they had little ideas of God. We might add that they are ideas about little Gods. The anachronism of our Edwards celebration is not so much that we try to honour him in a time of atheism, when men do not believe in God, but that we seek to know and respect a servant of the Almighty, of the Lord, the Source of Being itself, of Power beyond all powers, in a time when our God is someone we try to keep alive by religious devotions, to use for solving our personal problems, for assuring us that we are beloved.

He is without wrath, because we have made this image wrathless; his love is not holy love because we have painted the icon without holiness.

If Edwards's God is not with us, what meaning is

there in our agreement with his propositions about human wickedness, human determinism, about the threat of destruction? Our sense of wickedness is without repentance, our sorrow over it is not a godly sorrow leading to life, but cynical and accepting, leading to death. Our knowledge of our determinism is without struggle, because we know of no power that can set us free to be free indeed; our visions of possible life amidst destruction are unaccompanied by visions of possible life in the presence of glory and everlasting joy.

But now a possibility presents itself to us as we remember Edwards and remember man's remembrance of him. We have changed our minds about the truth of many things he said. Or rather, our minds have been changed by what has happened to us in our history. We have seen evil somewhat as he saw it, not because we desired to see it, but because it thrust itself upon us.

If that has happened, why shall we not hope—and fear — that what has not yet happened will also occur. That once more, by no sudden event it may be but by the same kind of accumulative experience that has made us aware of the evil emptiness that surrounds us, we shall be lifted to see and know—in our time—the Holy One that inhabits eternity and yet is near to the humble and contrite in heart. Then we shall be able to meet in the presence of Edwards, saying

"Now unto the King eternal, immortal, invisible,

to the only wise God—

be honour and glory, forever and ever. Amen."

The Man who Belongs to the World

The following article is excerpted from the concluding chapter of historian Jaroslav Pelikan's book titled Jesus

Through the Centuries: His Place in the History of Culture, scheduled for October publication by Yale University Press. The book examines the impact of Jesus on the cultural, political, social and economic history of the past two millennia. Studying the images of Jesus cherished by successive ages — from rabbi in the first century to universal man in the Renaissance to liberator in the 19th and 20th centuries — Pelikan suggests that the way a particular age depicted Jesus is an essential key to understanding that age.

Nazareth was what is known in colloquial English as a hick town, an insignificant village. It almost sounds like a proverbial saying when in the Gospel of John, Nathanael asks (John 1:46), "Can anything good come out of Nazareth?" Thus Jesus of Nazareth was a villager and a provincial.

Whatever may be the historical status of the story of his flight to Egypt as an infant with his parents, he never as an adult travelled beyond the borders of the Levant. As far as we can tell, he did not command either of the world languages of his time, Latin and Greek, although both are said by the Gospel of John to have appeared in the inscription on his cross (John 19:20).

The only reference to his having written anything in any language, when he stooped to write with his finger on the ground, comes in a passage of dubious textual authenticity, which most manuscripts include somewhere in the Gospel of John (John 8:6, 8). He spoke of how "the rulers of the gentiles lord it over them, and their great men exercise authority over them" (Matt. 20:25), but as of a phenomenon belonging to a world far removed from his own. And even when, in an appearance after the resurrection, he is represented by the author of the Acts of the Apostles as having referred to the outside world, it was as a provincial might, dividing the world into the immediate environs and everything that was elsewhere: "Ye shall be witnesses unto me both in Jerusalem, and in all Judaea, and in Samaria—and unto the uttermost part of the earth" (Acts 1:8).

Therefore his cosmopolitan detractors in the Roman Empire were able to sneer that he had put in his appearance "in some small corner of the earth somewhere," and not (to borrow a modern phrase that seems appropriate) out here in the real world.

Jesus of Nazareth may have been a provincial, but Jesus Christ is the Man Who Belongs to the World. By a geographical expansion shattering anything that either his cosmopolitan detractors within paganism or, for that matter, the author of the Book of Acts within Christianity could have imagined, his name has moved out far from that "small corner of the earth somewhere" and has come to be known "unto the uttermost part of the earth." In the words of the paraphrase of Psalm 72 by Isaac Watts.

Jesus shall reign where'er the sun
Does his successive journeys run,
His kingdom stretch from shore to shore
Till moons shall wax and wane no more.
People and realms of every tongue
Dwell on his love with sweetest song.

When that hymn was published in 1719, the most dramatic growth in the extension of his influence ever known was just beginning. Because of that quantum increase, the best-known history of Christian expansion in English devoted three of its seven volumes to the 19th century alone, calling it *The Great Century* (Kenneth

Scott Latourette, *A History of the Expansion of Christianity* [Harper, 1939-45]). The sun never sets on the empire of Jesus the King, the Man Who Belongs to the World.

Not coincidentally, the great century of Christian missionary expansion was also in many ways the great century of European colonialism.

As in past centuries of Christian conversion, the missionary and military sometimes went hand in hand, each serving the purposes of the other, and not always in a manner or a spirit consonant with the spirit of Christ. The medieval method of carrying on Christian missions was often to conquer the tribe in warfare and then to subject the entire enemy army to baptism at the nearest river.

That pattern continued to appear in modern missions, despite the many differences between their methods. Consequently, although Jesus himself had lived in the Near East, it was as a religion of Europe that his message came to the nations of the world and the islands of the sea — a religion of Europe both in the sense of a religion from Europe and, often, a religion *about* Europe as well. Indeed, at the end of the "great century," and on the eve of the First World War, the provocative aphorism was coined, apparently by Hilaire Belloc: "The Faith is Europe and Europe is the Faith" (*Europe and the Faith* [Paulist 1921], p. viii).

The identification of Europe and "the faith" implied, on the one hand, that those who accepted European economic, political and military domination and who adopted European civilization thereby came under pressure to undergo conversion to the European faith in Jesus Christ. It likewise implied, however, that faith in Jesus Christ must be on European terms, take them or leave them, and that the forms it took — organizational, ethical, doctrinal, liturgical — must be, with as much adaptation as necessary but as little adaptation as possible, the ones it had acquired in its European configuration.

Although it has become part of the conventional wisdom in much of contemporary anti-colonialist literature, both Eastern and Western, it is an oversimplification to dismiss the missions as nothing more than a cloak for white imperialism.

Such an oversimplification ignores the biographical, religious and political realities running through the history of Christian missions during the "great century" and long before, as missionaries have, in the name of Jesus, striven to understand and learned to respect the particularities of the cultures to which they have come. It should be noted, in addition, that there was historically a sharp difference on this count between the missionary methods of the Eastern and the Western churches. When Constantine-Cyril and Methodius came as Christian missionaries to the Slavs in the ninth century, they translated not only the Bible but the Eastern Orthodox liturgy into Slavonic.

By contrast, when Augustine had come to the English in 597, he had brought with him not only the message of the gospel and the authority of the See of Rome but the liturgy of the Latin mass, and he had made the acceptance of this a condition of conversion to faith in Christ.

While Greek-speaking missionaries like Cyril and Methodius did not teach their Slavic disciples to read Greek, Western missionaries had to provide the nations they converted with the rudiments of Latin and the means of learning it. In the Carolingian period, "the use of Latin was everywhere and irrevocably narrowed down to liturgy and the written word," and Latin became a "purely artificial language." Nevertheless, it was also the "sole medium of intellectual life" and could become again, incidentally to the process and quite unintentionally, a way of access to the heritage of pre-Christian Roman culture and classical Latin literature (Erich Auerbach, *Literary Language and Its Public in Late Latin Antiquity and in the Middle Ages* [Pantheon. 1965], pp. 120-21).

The most celebrated instance of the Christian understanding and respect for a native culture, however, was in the work of a Roman Catholic rather than of an Eastern Orthodox missionary, the Jesuit Matteo Ricci, in China. He has been called by a modern English historian of Chinese culture "one of the most remarkable and brilliant men in history" (Joseph Needham, in *Science and Civilization in China,* 2 vols. [Cambridge University Press, 1961], 1:148).

The first generation of Jesuits, under the leadership and inspiration of Francis Xavier, made the mission to China a major item on their agenda. But in carrying out the mission, the Jesuits had followed the medieval pattern of the Western church, introducing the Roman Catholic liturgy of the mass, forbidding any of the Chinese vernaculars in worship, and enforcing tho use of Latin

With Ricci's arrival at Macau in 1582, that strategy underwent drastic revision. Ricci adopted the monastic habit of a Buddhist monk, then the garb of a Confucian scholar, and became a renowned authority both in the natural sciences and in the history and literature of China.

This erudition enabled him to present the person and message of Jesus as the fulfilment of the historic aspirations of Chinese culture, in much the way that

Jesus had been presented by the early fathers as the culmination of the Greco-Roman faith in the Logos and by the New Testament as the fulfilment of the Jewish hope for the Messiah.

The Chinese, Ricci maintained, "could certainly become Christians, since the essence of their doctrine contains nothing contrary to the essence of the Catholic faith, nor would the Catholic faith hinder them in any way, but would indeed aid in that attainment of the quiet and peace of the republic which their books claim as their goal" (quoted in Jonathan D. Spence, *The Memory Palace of Matteo Ricci* [Viking. 1984]. p. 210).

Already in his lifetime and even more in the years of the "rites controversy" over the legitimacy of "accommodationism" that followed his death in 1610, Ricci was accused of having compromised the uniqueness of the person of Christ.

But the upsurge of interest in his work has made it clear, on the basis of such theological works in Chinese as *The True Meaning of the Lord of Heaven* of 1603, that Ricci was and remained an orthodox Catholic believer, whose very orthodoxy it was that impelled him to take seriously the integrity of Chinese traditions. Although with a less dramatic involvement in native thought and culture than Ricci's, both Roman Catholic and Protestant missionaries in the 19th century often managed to combine a commitment to evangelization in the name of Jesus with a deep (and ever deepening) respect for the native culture and indigenous traditions of the nations to which they had been sent.

As in the past, Christian missions in the 19th and 20th centuries have involved many social changes as well as changes in religious affiliation. Perhaps the most important of these changes for the future cultural development of the nations was the close association between the missions and the campaign for world literacy. A monument to the importance of that achievement for the history of the Slavs is the very alphabet in which most Slavs write, which is called Cyrillic, in honour of Saint Cyril, the ninth-century "apostle to the Slavs," who, with his brother Methodius, is traditionally given credit for having invented it...

Not only among the Slavs in the ninth century, but also among the other so-called heathen in the 19th century, the two fundamental elements of missionary culture for more than a millennium have therefore been the translation of the Bible, especially of the New Testament, and education in the missionary schools.

In one after another of the nations of Africa and of the South Seas, Christian missionaries found, upon arriving, that none of the native languages had been committed to writing, and that therefore it was necessary, for the sake of the translation of the word of God, to reduce one or more of those languages to written form. In many cases, therefore, the first efforts ever at a scientific understanding of the language, by native or foreigner, came from Christian missionaries. They compiled the first dictionaries, wrote the first grammars, developed the first alphabets.

Thus it came about that the first important proper name to have been written in many of these languages must have been the name of Jesus, with its pronunciation adapted to their distinctive phonic structure, just as it had been in all the languages of Europe. The Protestant missionary Bible societies, especially the British and Foreign Bible Society and the American Bible Society, owed their origins to Christian missions in the 19th century. During the 19th and 20th centuries, they have put at least the Gospels, and sometimes the rest of the New Testament and of the entire Bible, into more than a thousand additional languages, which averages out to more than five new languages per year.

In the memoirs of Asian and African leaders who were graduates from these schools it has become almost obligatory, as part of an attack upon white Christian colonialism, to express bitterness and recrimination about the loss of native roots that came as a by-product of missionary education and of imperialist schools both in the mission field and in the home country.

Jawaharlal Nehru, for example, was educated at Harrow and Cambridge, becoming, in his own eloquent English phrase, "a queer mixture of the East and West, out of place everywhere, at home nowhere' and sensing a profound alienation between himself and the religion of the common people of India—an alienation from which he never quite recovered (*Toward Freedom: Autobiography* [Beacon, 1958], pp. 236-50). Nehru could have been speaking for several generations in many nations, some of them committed Christians and others merely deracinated Asians or Africans, who were "out of place everywhere, at home nowhere."

Thus it was with a grim literalness that there was fulfilled, in the life of entire cultures and not only of individual families, the alienation described by the saying of Jesus in the Gospels: "I have come to set a man against his father, and a daughter against her mother, and a daughter-in-law against her mother-in-law; and a man's foes will be those of his own household" (Matt.10:35-36).

Significantly, Jesus was seen as a Western figure, and in the early religious art of the "younger churches" he often continued to be represented as he had been in the evangelical and pietist literature of the missionary movements in Europe, England and America. Beginning already with Ricci and even earlier, however, Christian art in the mission field recognized the need to present the figure of Jesus in a form that was congenial to his new audience.

Yet evangelicals and pietists, too, early recognized, sometimes far more explicitly in the mission field than at home, that it was not enough to bring pictures of Jesus, even pictures of Jesus with native features, or words about Jesus, even words about Jesus in the native vernaculars, to the non-Christian world.

It had not been enough in the days of Jesus, either, and so he had come as a healer and not only as a teacher. Similarly, the mission of his followers in the second and third centuries had been one of help and healing, not of evangelization alone. For the word "salvation" — *soteria* in Greek, *salus* in Latin and its derivative languages, *Heil* in German and its cognate languages—meant "health."

In an age in which the healing of the nations from the ravages of hunger, disease and war has become the dominant moral imperative, Jesus the Healer has come to assume a central place.

It was an emblem of the central place of Jesus when, under the terms of the Geneva Convention of 1864 for the Amelioration of the Condition of the Wounded and Sick of Armies in the Field, the international organization created to carry out that moral imperative took the name "Red Cross Society"; its symbol, based on a reversal of the colours of the Swiss flag, is a red cross on a white background.

Yet the connection between evangelization in the name of Jesus and the mission of help and healing has also been an issue for debate, especially in the 20th century. This debate, too, comes as a commentary on the literal meaning of a word in the Gospels: "Whosoever shall give you a cup of water to drink in my name, because ye belong to Christ, verily I say unto you, he shall not lose his reward" (Mark 9:41).

It has almost seemed that in every epoch there were some who were primarily interested in naming the name of Christ, clarifying its doctrinal and theological meaning, and defending that meaning against its enemies — but who named the name without giving the cup of water. Yet it has seemed possible for others to give the cup of water, to provide the healing, and to improve the social lot of the disadvantaged — but to do so without explicitly naming the name of Christ.

Does that saying of Jesus mean that each of these ways of responding to his summons is only a partial obedience to this dual command? In the answer to this question, much of the debate over the primary responsibility of Christ's disciples in the modern world has concentrated on the disjunction between the two components of the imperative.

A growing feature of the debate has been the stress on cooperation rather than competition between the disciples of Jesus and those who follow other ancient Teachers of the Way. Those followers of Jesus who advocate such cooperation insist that they are not less committed to the universality of his person and message than are the advocates of the traditional methods of conquest through evangelization.

But the universality of Jesus, they have urged, does

not establish itself in the world through the obliteration of whatever elements of light and truth have already been granted to the nations of the world. For whatever the proximate and historical sources of that truth may have been, its ultimate source is God, the same God whom Jesus called Father; else the confession of the oneness of God is empty.

Criticism of many of the elements of historic Christianity, especially of its dogmatism and cultural imperialism, led to the suggestion that it had much to learn, as well as much to teach, in its encounter with other faiths. Jesus was indeed the Man Who Belongs to the World, but he was this because he made it possible to appreciate more profoundly the full scope of the revelation of God wherever it had appeared in the history of the world, in the light of which, in turn, his own meaning and message acquired more profound significance.

In the paradoxical formula of Archbishop Nathan Soderblom's Gifford Lectures of 1931, "the uniqueness of Christ as the historical revealer, as the Word made flesh, and the mystery of Calvary," which are an "essentially unique character of Christianity," compel the affirmation that "God reveals himself in history; outside the Church as well as in it" (*The Living God* [Beacon, 1962], pp. 349, 379). The most complete statement of that position was the thought-provoking and massive report, *Re-thinking Missions: A Layman's Inquiry after One Hundred Years,* published in 1932 by a Commission of Appraisal representing seven American Protestant denominations.

Having carried out an extensive survey of world missions, particularly in Asia and in Africa, the authors of this "laymen's inquiry" reviewed, in seven volumes of data, the state of evangelization and Christian world service, recommending far-reaching revisions not only of specific strategy but of underlying philosophy. They concluded that the stress upon the particularity of Jesus and the absoluteness of his message had been, though perhaps necessary, a temporary element in the programme of the missions. As one historian of missions has summarized the position of *Re-thinking Missions,*

The task of the missionary today, it was maintained, is to see the best in other religions, to help the adherents of those religions to discover, or to rediscover, all that is best in their own traditions, to cooperate with the most active and vigorous elements in the other traditions in social reform and in the purification of religious expression.

The aim should not be conversion—the drawing of members of one religious faith over into another or an attempt to establish a Christian monopoly. Cooperation is to replace aggression. The ultimate aim, so far as any can be descried, is the emergence of the various religions out of their isolation into a world fellowship in which each will find its appropriate place [Stephen Neill, *A History of Christian Missions* (Penguin, 1964), p. 456].

So drastic a revision of the traditional Christian understanding that "there is salvation in no one else than [Jesus]. for there is no other name under heaven [than the name of Jesus] given among men by which we must be saved' (Acts 4:12) would inevitably evoke vigorous discussion and extensive controversy, especially coming as it did just when the theology of Karl Barth was emphasizing again the uniqueness of Jesus and the centrality of his claims.

In connection with the World's Columbian Exposition held at Chicago in 1893 to commemorate the 400th anniversary of Columbus's discovery of the New World, there was held a world parliament of religions, whose purpose it was to draw the religious implications of the discovery that the human race was not exclusively European and therefore not exclusively Christian, but global and universal.

Despite the phenomenal successes of Christian missions during the 19th and 20th centuries, it seems incontestable that the percentage of Christians in the total world population is continually declining and therefore it seems inconceivable that the Christian church and the Christian message will ever conquer the population of the world and replace the other religions of the human race.

If Jesus is to be the Man Who Belongs to the World, it will have to be by some other way. Perhaps the most remarkable document to come out of this deepening sense of a new universalism was not *Re-thinking Missions* of 1932, but a decree published a third of a century later, on 28 October 1965, the Declaration on the Relationship of the Church to Non-Christian Religions, *Nostra aetate*, of the Second Vatican Council.

In a series of succinct but striking paragraphs, the decree described the religious quest and the spiritual values at work in primitive religion, in Hinduism, in Buddhism and in Islam; and in a historic affirmation the council declared:

> *The Catholic Church rejects nothing which is true and holy in those religions. She looks with sincere respect upon those ways of conduct and of life, those rules and teachings which, though differing in many particulars from what she holds and sets forth, nevertheless often reflect a ray of that Truth which enlightens all men (John 1:9).*

> *Indeed, she proclaims and must ever proclaim Christ, "the way, the truth, and the life" (John 14:6), in whom men find the fullness of religious life, and in whom God has reconciled all things to Himself.*

The two passages from the Gospel According to John quoted in the decree clearly identify the issue. For it is in that Gospel that Jesus speaks of himself as "the way, the truth, and the life" and says that no one comes to the Father except through him. And yet that same Gospel provided the epigraph for the universalism of the Enlightenment's portrait of Jesus; for the Gospel of John declares in its prologue that the Logos-Word of God, incarnate in Jesus, enlightens everyone who comes into the world. By citing the authority of both passages, the Second Vatican Council sought to affirm universality and particularity simultaneously and to ground both of them in the figure of Jesus.

A special issue at the Second Vatican Council and throughout Christianity, especially since World War II, was the relation between Christianity and its parent faith, Judaism. The Holocaust took place in what had been nominally Christian territory; moreover, the record of the churches in opposing it was not the noblest page in Christian history. Among both Roman Catholics and Protestants in Germany there were those who, as the New Testament says about the apostle Paul's involvement in the martyrdom of Stephen, were "consenting to the death" of the Jews (Acts 8:1), and many more who were (as it seems now, by hindsight) blindly insensitive to the situation.

The Second Vatican Council "deplores," it declared, "the hatred, persecutions, and displays of anti-Semitism directed against the Jews at any time and from any source," which would appear to include the official sources of the church's past. And it condemned any attempt to blame the death of Jesus "upon all the Jews then living, without distinction, or upon the Jews today," insisting that "the Jews should not be presented as repudiated or cursed by God."

It was in 1933, the beginning of the Nazi era in Germany, that there appeared, also in Germany, the first volume of one of the most influential biblical reference works of the 20th century, the multivolume *Theological Dictionary of the New Testament,* edited by Gerhard Kittel.

Probably the most important scholarly and theological generalization to be drawn from the hundreds of articles in the Kittel *Dictionary* has been that the teaching and language of the New Testament, including the teaching and language of Jesus himself, cannot be understood apart from their setting in the context of Judaism.

It was once again in the Gospel of John, despite the hostility of some of its language about Jews, that Jesus, speaking as a Jew to a non-Jew, was described as saying: "We [Jews] worship what we know, for salvation is from the Jews" (John 4:22). Directly he went on to say, in the very next verse: "But the hour is coming, and now is, when the true worshippers [which, obviously, refers to both Jews and gentiles] will worship the Father in spirit and truth." Once again the theme is universality-with-particularity, as both of these are grounded in the figure of Jesus the Jew.

By a curious blend of these currents of religious faith and scholarship with the no less powerful influences of skepticism and religious relativism, the universality-with-particularity of Jesus has thus become an issue not only for Christians in the 20th century, but for humanity.

As respect for the organized church has declined, reverence for Jesus has grown. For the unity and variety of the portraits of "Jesus through the centuries" has demonstrated that there is more in him than is dreamt of in the philosophy and Christology of the theologians. Within the church, but also far beyond its walls, his person and message are, in the phrase of Augustine, a "beauty ever ancient, ever new," and now he belongs to the world.

Bibliography

- Bernard McGinn: *Classics of Western Spirituality*, Paulist Press, New York, 1978.
- Brown, Raymond E.: *Introduction to the New Testament*. New York: Anchor Bible, 1997.
- Burton Mack: *A Myth of Innocence: Mark and Christian Origins*. Augsburg Fortress Publishers, 1988.
- Byron R. McCane. *Roll Back the Stone: Death and Burial in the World of Jesus*, Trinity Press Int'l, 2003.
- Dickson, John. *Jesus: A Short Life*, Lion Hudson plc, 2008.
- Dormeyer, Detlev: *The New Testament among the Writings of Antiquity*, Sheffield, 1998.
- Fornberg, Tord: *An Early Church in a Pluralistic Society: A Study of 2 Peter*. Coniectanea biblica, New Testament Series 9; Lund: Gleerup, 1977.
- Gamble, Harry Y.: *The New Testament Canon: Its Making and Meaning*. Guides to Biblical Scholarship; Philadelphia: Fortress, 1985.
- Gary R. Habermas: *The historical Jesus*, College Press, 1996 .
- Guenther, Herbert. V.: *Gampopa's Jewel Ornament of Liberation*, Rider and Co., London, 1970.

- Harris, Stephen L., *Understanding the Bible*. Palo Alto: Mayfield. 1985.
- John P. Meier: *A Marginal Jew: Rethinking the Historical Jesus: The Roots of the Problem and the Person,* Doubleday 1991.
- Kottackal, Jacob: *Religion and Ethics in Advaita*, C.M.S. Press, Kottayam, 1982.
- Mack, Burton: *The Christian Myth: Origins, Logic, and Legacy*. New York: Continuum International Publishing Group, 2001.
- Metzger, Bruce M.: *The Early Versions of the New Testament*. Oxford: Clarendon Press, 1977.
- Sanders, E.P.: *Jesus and Judaism*. Augsburg Fortress Publishers: 1987.
- Schwartz, H.: *Reimaging the Bible: The Storytelling of the Rabbis,* Oxford University Press, New York, 1998.
- Sushil, K.: *The Ethics of the Hindus*, Calcutta University Press, Calcutta, 1952.

Index

□□□